Right-Wing Culture in Contemporary Capitalism

Critical Theory and the Critique of Society Series

In a time marked by crises and the rise of right-wing authoritarian populism, **Critical Theory and the Critique of Society** intends to renew the critical theory of capitalist society exemplified by the Frankfurt School and critical Marxism's critiques of social domination, authoritarianism, and social regression by expounding the development of such a notion of critical theory, from its founding thinkers, through its subterranean and parallel strands of development, to its contemporary formulations.

Series editors: **Werner Bonefeld**, University of York, UK and **Chris O'Kane**, John Jay College of Criminal Justice, City University of New York, USA

Editorial Board:
Bev Best, Sociology, Concordia University
John Abromeit, History, SUNY, Buffalo State, USA
Samir Gandesha, Humanities, Simon Fraser University
Christian Lotz, Philosophy, Michigan State University
Patrick Murray, Philosophy, Creighton University
José Antonio Zamora Zaragoza, Philosophy, Spain
Dirk Braunstein, Institute of Social Research, Frankfurt
Matthias Rothe, German, University of Minnesota
Marina Vishmidt, Cultural Studies, Goldsmiths University
Verena Erlenbusch, Philosophy, University of Memphis
Elena Louisa Lange, Japanese Studies/Philology and Philosophy, University of Zurich
Marcel Stoetzler, Sociology, University of Bangor
Moishe Postone†, History, University of Chicago
Mathias Nilges, Literature, St Francis Xavier University

Forthcoming in the Series
Adorno and Neoliberalism: The Social Logic and the Critique of Value, Charles Prusik

Right-Wing Culture in Contemporary Capitalism

Regression and Hope in a Time Without Future

Mathias Nilges

BLOOMSBURY ACADEMIC
LONDON • NEW YORK • OXFORD • NEW DELHI • SYDNEY

BLOOMSBURY ACADEMIC
Bloomsbury Publishing Plc
50 Bedford Square, London, WC1B 3DP, UK
1385 Broadway, New York, NY 10018, USA
29 Earlsfort Terrace, Dublin 2, Ireland

BLOOMSBURY, BLOOMSBURY ACADEMIC and the Diana logo are trademarks of
Bloomsbury Publishing Plc

First published in Great Britain 2020
This paperback edition published in 2021

Copyright © Mathias Nilges, 2020

Mathias Nilges has asserted his right under the Copyright, Designs and Patents Act, 1988,
to be identified as Author of this work.

For legal purposes the Acknowledgments on p. ix constitute an extension
of this copyright page.

Cover design by Ben Anslow

All rights reserved. No part of this publication may be reproduced or transmitted
in any form or by any means, electronic or mechanical, including photocopying,
recording, or any information storage or retrieval system, without
prior permission in writing from the publishers.

Bloomsbury Publishing Plc does not have any control over, or responsibility for,
any third-party websites referred to or in this book. All internet addresses given
in this book were correct at the time of going to press. The author and publisher
regret any inconvenience caused if addresses have changed or sites have
ceased to exist, but can accept no responsibility for any such changes.

A catalogue record for this book is available from the British Library.

A catalog record for this book is available from the Library of Congress.

ISBN: HB: 978-1-3500-7406-4
        PB: 978-1-3502-5130-4
        ePDF: 978-1-3500-7407-1
        eBook: 978-1-3500-7408-8

Series: Critical Theory and the Critique of Society Series

Typeset by Integra Software Services Pvt. Ltd.

To find out more about our authors and books visit www.bloomsbury.com
and sign up for our newsletters.

for my mother, Susanne Bill, with unending gratitude and admiration

Acknowledgments

The core of this book is sincerely and unapologetically committed to the value of "dreams of a better life," the phrase which Ernst Bloch had originally selected as the title for his magnum opus *The Principle of Hope*. Dreaming of a better life, Bloch shows us, is ultimately not a solitary act, but it emerges out of and is at every point aimed at a common project. And just like we need help to dream of a better life, this book would not have been possible without the help, encouragement, and the intellectual and collegial generosity of a group of people whom I would like to acknowledge and thank here. Most importantly, I owe more gratitude than I am able to express in mere words to Maïca Murphy, my wife, my best friend, my most attentive and toughest reader, my partner in dreaming. Together, we shall carpet the bathrooms of our adversaries.

This book would also not exist without the encouragement, the advice, and the commentary that I have received from Madhu Dubey and Nicholas Brown over the years. In particular, Madhu has never tired of reading my work (at least officially), which baffles me greatly, for I cannot say the same of my own relation to my writing. Together, Madhu and Nick have taught me how academics ought to treat their work, their students, and each other, and their intellectual rigor and generosity continues to serve as my model for the kind of writer, teacher, and colleague I aim to be. Whenever I am lucky enough to spend some time with them, which is far too rarely these days, Emilio Sauri and Daniel Stout make me laugh and think with an ease that reminds me of the things that truly matter about what we do. I am humbled by their friendship and their intellectual generosity. Eugenio Di Stefano, a lovely though cranky old man, has sage advice and an understanding of time that makes the world a better place. Talk to him. But bring food. Over the years, Sarah Brouillette has made me smarter, more fearless, and more and more impressed by Sarah Brouillette. Such ferocity, such love, such a brilliant mind. Thankfully, she sent me a chocolate cookbook that was bad for my waistline, which means that there is indeed one thing that I can criticize about what she has done in this world. I also consider myself very fortunate to have had the support of a group of wonderful group of colleagues and friends at StFX. Maureen Moynagh and Rod Bantjes, our local partners in shenaniganing, have made Nova Scotia feel like home for us. Every completed project is somewhat bittersweet, since it is also a measure of the time that we were not able to spend together. I wish to thank Cory Rushton, Jason Potts, and Michael D'Arcy sincerely for their comradery and their steadfast support.

I would like to thank the following people for their advice, their intellectual and professional guidance, and their continued friendship: Imre Szeman, Walter Benn Michaels, Jennifer Ashton, Helen Jun, Alice Haisman, Tim Dayton and Jamie Owen Daniel (who fostered my love for Bloch), Kevin Floyd, Neil Larsen, Phil Wegner, Susan Hegeman, Carolyn Lesjak, Cristie Ellis, Peter Hitchcock, Stephen Shapiro, Sharae Deckard, Lee Medovoi, Michele Janette, Don Hedrick, Karin Westman, Greg Eiselein, Mitchum Huehls, Rachel Greenwald Smith, Anna Kornbluh, Mark Canuel, Bev Best, Kristin Bergen, Rich Daniels, Jeff Williams, Jen Hedler-Phillis, Davis Smith-Brecheisen, Vincent Adiutori, Joe Ramsey, Barbara Foley, Leigh Claire La Berge, Rei Terada, Eyal Amiran, Lauren Berlant, Kristy Ullibari, Pete Franks, Ericka Beckman, Paul Stasi, Bret Benjamin, Mitch Murray, Jeff Diamanti, Brent Bellamy, Ken Warren, Justin A. Joyce, Ryan Brooks, Maryanne Lyons, Lisa Freeman, Joe Tabbi, Linda Brigham, Richard Nemesvari, and Marie Gillis.

I consider myself immensely fortunate to be able to rely on the love, encouragement, and support of my family, a group of people who teach me every day anew how important it is to keep hope alive by taking a stand against those forces that would see us return to the darkest days of human history. Thank you for your hearts, your passion, your ideas, and thank you for the help and warmth without which I would not be where I am today. Thank you to my parents, Susanne and Jörg Bill, and Sylvie Poirier and Ron Murphy; thank you to my grandmother, Gisela Märker, to my brother Christoph Nilges, my sister-in-law Elisabeth Nilges, and my lovely niece Tilda Nilges. Thank you, too, to Angelika and Jürgen Märker, Ute, Roland, and Catrin Ploss, Melissa, Tomas, and Caitlin Murphy. This book is also dedicated to the memory of two dearly beloved members of our family whose passing left big holes in the world and in our hearts: Richard Märker and Mathew Charles Roy.

I also would like to recognize my wonderful students at StFX and, in particular, the students of my Cultural Theory course of 2017/18. Over the course of this year, we explored many of the ideas that ultimately fed into the analyses that make up this book. Being able to research this book while discussing some of its ideas with my students made the writing process even more rewarding. It did, however, also make me feel much older. Thanks for that. I would like to highlight the great work that my wonderful assistants and co-conspirators Emma Hofland-Burry, Keegan Currie, Renée Proctor, and Alejandra Torres have done over the course of the past two years. Their assistance was invaluable to my ability to complete this book. Finally, I would like to thank Chris O'Kane and Werner Bonefeld sincerely for believing in this project, Frankie Mace for helping me find where its handle is, and Liza Thompson for bringing it to completion. I am deeply honored to have been able to work with you.

1

Introduction: All We Have Is Now

A group of people, comprising engineers, designers, artists, and ultra-wealthy businessmen, is putting a big clock inside a mountain in the west of Texas. "It is a huge Clock," the group says in its description of the clock on the companion website for its project, "hundreds of feet tall, designed to tick for 10,000 years."[1] The clock also has a name. Two, in fact. It is The 10,000 Year Clock, to which the group also refers as The Clock of the Long Now. Its designers think of The 10,000 Year Clock as a millennial clock, as the first of several similar clocks that they wish to build and install in a variety of places around the world. The site for a second clock, they announce, is already being prepared in a mountain in eastern Nevada that the group has purchased. The clock's name indicates its underlying purpose and the reason why a group of people would build a big clock and put it deep inside a mountain. A highly ambitious and immensely intricate and complex design, The Clock of the Long Now is engineered to keep ticking for ten millennia, its chimes sounding across a long stretch of time in order to draw our attention to a different way of understanding both time and our relation to it. Ordinarily, and especially in our moment in history, the group argues, our conception of time is aimed at the short term. That is, we relate to time largely through the temporality of the everyday, the here and now, and we aim our actions or policies at spans of time usually no longer than a few years (strategic plans, election cycles, and so on). As a result, we struggle to consider our actions in relation to the long term.

However, the clock's makers ask, what if we adopted a long-term view of time and of our existence? Since "ten thousand years is about the age of civilization," they reason, "a 10K-year Clock would measure out a future of civilization equal to its past." This in turn assumes, they continue, that "we are in the middle of whatever journey we are on," and this, they conclude, is "an implicit statement of optimism." The optimism of the project lies for the group in the fact that the long-term view of time that the Clock seeks to foster stands opposed to the short-termism of contemporary life and thought. If we aimed our actions in the present at the continued life of civilization, at those who come several thousand years after us, how might our understanding of, say, our relation to nature and the environment change? In a present that is so often marked by the threat of endings and moments of exhaustion, the big clock in the mountain seems to offer us a different way to tell time, a different way to evaluate the temporality of our existence and the stakes of our actions. "If you have a Clock ticking for 10,000 years," the group asks, "what kinds of generational-scale questions and projects will it suggest? If a Clock can keep going for ten millennia, shouldn't we make sure our civilization does as well?" In a moment in history that, as this book shows in some detail, is centrally defined by an erosion of trust in the long term and by our apparent inability to imagine profound, substantive, positive change and alternatives to our present, it seems at first blush that The 10,000 Year Clock provides us with a direly needed attempt at reenergizing utopian thought. But does this clock truly tell the time of a better future and of a different understanding of temporality and of the time of our lives?

The first step in the group's project was the construction of an 8-foot-tall prototype of the clock, which was completed in time to ring in the new millennium. The clock sounded twice to announce the year 2000, its makers explain, "in front of a small crowd at its temporary home in the Presidio, San Francisco." This prototype of the Clock is now on display at the London Science Museum, and more recent prototypes can be visited at The Long Now Museum & Store at Fort Mason Center in San Francisco. The idea of the Clock and the plans for a nonprofit foundation that would support its development were conceived by Danny Hills, whom the website of The Long Now Foundation describes as "a polymath inventor, computer engineer, and designer, inventor and prime genius of the Clock," and by Stewart Brand, "a cultural pioneer and trained biologist." A substantial portion of the project has been bankrolled by Jeff Bezos, founder and CEO of Amazon, who also owns the land and the mountain in which the clock will be installed. Musician Brian Eno joined the effort and developed the title "The Long Now" in order to "indicate the expanded sense of time the Clock provokes." The group subsequently adopted this title as the name of their foundation, as it describes the work in which they seek to engage: "to stretch out what people consider as now."

Everyone with at least cursory knowledge of the standard tropes and plot points of popular culture knows that it is worth taking a closer look at any project that involves ultra-wealthy individuals building large things inside of mountains. But James Bond-esque storylines aside, there is something about the logic of the project and of the idea of a long now as a way to facilitate long-term thinking that must strike us as decidedly strange. What exactly is this time that the project brought to us by Jeff Bezos and his partners wishes to usher in? What time does the Clock actually tell? If the project is aimed at fostering long-term thinking, then, one might wonder, why is the long term understood as a long version of the now and not in the way we might more readily expect, namely as the future? Why is the Clock bound up with an idea of time that seeks to stretch out the present as opposed to a view of the present that is formulated with an eye on the future? The standardized version of the relation between present and future, reiterated ad nauseam by marketers and advertisers, is that the future is the time for whose arrival we excitedly long. Advertisers love to dress up their latest products in a costume of precisely this temporal desire whenever they tell us that the commodity that we should excitedly embrace (finally!) marks the arrival of the future and thus tells the time for which we have all hoped. The regularity and predictability of the future's arrival thus conceived is an idea of time that is created through and that in turn helps maintain the temporal logic of commodification and innovation. The time of capitalism, a time told by each exciting commodity whose logic reveals the structural core of a system that does not reach for the future as much as it constructs alternate presents dressed in futuristic garb, is now. The idea of a long now, the seemingly paradoxical notion of a form of time that brings about the future by stretching out the present, therefore lays bare the inherent contradictions of the temporal imagination that underlies and that stabilizes capitalism. But if this is so, what are the social and political consequences of confining our imagination of time and of the future to the idea of a long now? And why, some will surely ask, especially in a moment when we are confronted with a number of pressing social, political, and environmental issues that demand solutions, should we be interested in a topic as seemingly ephemeral as time and futurity?

Pulitzer Prize-winning American author Michael Chabon writes in an essay on The 10,000 Year Clock that "the point of the Clock is to revive and restore the whole idea of the Future, to get us thinking about the Future again, to the degree if not in quite the way same way that we used to do."[2] This project, he argues, is particularly pressing, since "the Sex Pistols strictly speaking, were right: there is no future, for you or for me." But Chabon's point is not simply an expression of the well-known problem that the future does not really seem to exist, since it is "always just an idea, a proposal, a scenario." More strikingly, Chabon argues that the future is a story that used to be central to our lives but without which we have been living for a while now. The latter suggestion is important here, and it echoes, as the pages that follow show, one of the standard narratives about our moment in history: we live in a time without future. This, in turn, means that it is not just the intended diachronic function of the clock (the long-term time it seeks to tell) that matters. Rather, and possibly even more significantly, we must consider its synchronic function, its place and significance in our own moment in history that seems to be defined by a crisis of futurity, by our seeming inability to imagine the future as difference and as the time of substantive alternatives to our present. The latter tension also finds expression in the title of Chabon's essay, which expresses the peculiar relation between the idea of a long now and the future: "The Future Will Have to Wait." The tone of Chabon's essay is often mournful. Certainly, Chabon is genuinely enthusiastic about the ideas that the Clock raises, and he strongly agrees with value of trying to imagining a time far in the future and to "extend the horizon of [our] expectations for our world" beyond "the lifetime of [our] own children." To Chabon, the Clock expresses an optimistic belief in the survival of human civilization. Throughout his essay, Chabon returns time and again to the same problem: it is important to be able to develop optimistic, long-term imaginaries of our world—and yet we seem unable to do just that. For Chabon, the ideas that underwrite the Clock's project indicate a tragic form of optimism and a sense of loss, for the Clock tells a time that is unimaginable in our present.

For Chabon, the Clock indicates what he understands to be the very paradox that "lies at the heart of our loss of belief or interest in the Future," of "a collective cultural failure to imagine ... any Future beyond the time of a couple of centuries." Reflecting on the way in which his own son relates to the world that surrounds him and how he imagines the future fills Chabon with great sorrow. "If you ask my eight-year-old about the Future," Chabon explains,

> he pretty much thinks the world is going to end, and that's it. Most likely global warming, he says—floods, storms, desertification—but the possibility of viral pandemic, meteor impact, or some kind of nuclear exchange is not alien to his view of the days to come. Maybe not tomorrow, or a year from now.

To be sure, he notes, his child's life is not devoid of optimism. But growing up in our historical moment has restricted his optimism to the short term only. "The kid is more than capable of generating a full head of optimistic steam about next week, next vacation, his tenth birthday," Chabon notes. And yet, "the world a hundred years on … leaves his hopes a blank." The blankness of his son's hopes for the future stands tragically opposed to an imagination that is preoccupied with loss or destruction, since, Chabon notes, his son "seems to take the end of everything, of all human endeavor and creation, for granted." And it is in this aspect of its logical design that Chabon locates the tragic function of the Clock. The Clock seeks to restore our gaze on the long term and asks us to consider the future. It asks us, therefore, to do the very thing that, Chabon notes, seems to be impossible for us and for our children. By presenting us with the idea of a long now, the Clock ultimately further compounds the very problem that fills Chabon with great sorrow when reflecting on the fact that his son understands himself as existing in a long now, in a present that we can at best prolong but beyond which there is no tomorrow: "he sees himself as living on the last page, if not in the last paragraph, of a long, strange and bewildering book."

The time of the new millennium that the Clock announced is thus a profoundly troubled one. The tension between present and future and the disruption of our ability to imagine positive change that gives rise to the strange, conflicting temporality of the idea of the long now that Chabon's essay expresses are also reflected in engagements with the category of change itself. At the same time that Chabon composed and published his essay, an exhibition called "Massive Change" was hosted at museums and galleries across North America, including the Vancouver Art Gallery and the Museum of Contemporary Art in Chicago. Massive Change is a collaborative effort of Bruce Mau, Bruce Mau Design, and the Institute Without Boundaries, which showcases recent achievements in "global design" that draw upon fields including urban planning, architecture, technology, and politics in order to address some of the most pressing problems of our time—and to imagine the massive change that is possible in the world in which we live, which, Massive Change argues, is a "designed world." In the companion book to the exhibit with the same title, coauthors Bruce Mau and Jennifer Leonard describe the project of the Institute Without Boundaries as aimed at the production of "a new breed of designer who is, in the words of R. Buckminster Fuller, a 'synthesis of artist, inventor, mechanic, objective economist, and evolutionary strategist.'"[3] Massive Change features multimedia installations addressing eleven categories: urban, information, transportation, energy, images, markets, materials, manufacturing, military, health, wealth, and politics. The exhibition blends technological inventions, photography, and sets of catchphrases and statistics that advertise a global politico-philosophical and economic revolution. It shows us what change looks like. One of the most interesting characteristics of the exhibition, however, is its strange temporality. Massive Change markets a revolution, yet it is neither a revolution that will take place in the future nor one that requires our participation in order to be actualized. As it turns out, the revolutionary change that the exhibition showcases is not a matter of future possibility. Rather, it has already happened—and we somehow missed it. Massive Change strives to educate us on our present, and, as a result, it leaves us with the peculiar impression that, somehow, we are not very contemporary subjects. We seem to be lagging behind our own now. But how is this possible? After all, is living in the moment, in the now, not one of the easiest things to do? Ordinarily, living in the now is the signal phrase for an absolution from excessive thought, from worrying about the future. It denotes a comfortable sense of presence that we experience whenever we permit ourselves to drift effortlessly in time. But even this previously effortless nontask of living in the now appears to become much more complicated when, as in Massive Change, the future is indeed now.

Massive Change is the project of a vanguard group that does not intend to lead us into the future but into the present. The exhibit's argument is not that we can radically change the world but that a change has already taken place. Grammatically and ideologically, the "present perfect" tense dominates the narrative pieces of the companion book that outlines to us the kind of subjects we should be (or should have become by now). One example of the kind of subjectivity that would constitute an adequate and timely way of relating to the present is the "Prosumer." "With the proliferation of digital networks the world over," the authors explain, "the electronic marketplace has gone from empowering the consumer to supporting a global civic society. Power to the people."[4] The project of Massive Change is appealing in its simplicity. We do not have to do a lot apart from getting on board with the way the world already is—which means to participate in the electronic marketplace. As a result, the slogan "power to the people" is emptied of the exhausting component of agency that made it so inconvenient throughout history. In the past, the slogan implied that "the people" had to seize power through revolutionary means. Luckily, or so the reconstruction of the slogan in the context of Massive Change implies, in the present context we already possess the power that we have been trying to obtain for such a long time. We simply have to get better at exercising it through consumption and other forms of participation in the possibilities that the changed present contains. Massive Change urges us to embrace new technologies and forms of communication, the possibilities offered by globalized free markets, and what the exhibition understands as the possibilities for the empowerment of the people inherent in mass participation in knowledge production. The future is the present, Massive Change argues, and the present is the time of a long now of free markets and of technological innovation, of a designed world that already contains all of the answers that we need to solve the world's problems and that is ready to empower us. In such a time, we do not need to look ahead. We just need to catch up. After all, who needs a future when all the change we need is already contained in the now?

What we begin to see here, in other words, is that the long now is the time of capitalism extended infinitely, containing all possible futures within itself. The horizon for change in the long now is the limit of capitalism. Thus, for all of its grand and often well-intentioned aspirations, the project of The Long Now Foundation not surprisingly also contains offshoots that reveal the connection to market thinking to which the idea of the long now remains connected and as a result of which its conception of the long term remains limited to the long now of capital. One of the other main projects of The Long Now Foundation, paralleling its work on The 10,000 Year Clock, is called "Long Bets." Long Bets seeks to "improve long term thinking" by making "enjoyably competitive predictions ... with philanthropic money at stake."[5] Featuring bets on the outcome of large-scale, long-term developments in our economy, society, technology, and politics, Long Bets transforms both history and the future into a playground for the wealthy. Substantial problems and questions regarding the future of humanity are reduced to bets, to a game whose callous cynicism is only thinly veiled by its claim to be a philanthropic project—all proceeds will go to good causes. And, of course, if future change is restricted to a choice between two options, such as that between Warren Buffet and Protégé Partners, LLC (who are engaged in a bet worth two million dollars), then it is no wonder that the idea of the future is contracted into a long now of capitalism. In keeping with this logic, The Long Now Foundation offers its version of long-term thinking also as "guidelines for a long-lived, long-valuable institution." To create such an institution, the site argues, it is necessary to "leverage longevity." This corporate-speak version of the idea of long-term thinking contains one of the crucial logical components of the long now. In spite of its initially declared goals, the idea of a long now is not a matter of addressing the possibilities of a radically different, distant future. It is instead about extending the now of capitalism into the future, defending the logic of capitalism by leveraging longevity, which is to say by turning the long term into a capitalist asset.

The logic of the long now, the absorption of all forms of futurity into capitalist presentism, the chapters that follow show, has become one of the defining aspects of our moment. In addition to shaping academic and popular dialogue, this problem is also mediated by recent art and culture. Novels like Nathaniel Rich's *Odds Against Tomorrow* (2013) to which I shall return in some detail in Chapter 4, for instance, grapple with the effects of the crash of the future into a long capitalist present. *Odds* is a novel about a brilliant, young mathematician and budding futurist who offers risk-assessment services to large corporations and soon begins to realize the true work of futurists: futurists are "asked to keep the future from happening."[6] The novel's protagonist struggles with a world in which the future collapses into the present and with his ensuing confusion about the time of our now and the long term. Either "the long term was now upon them,"[7] he reasons, or "the short term was all that mattered," in which case "there would be no long term."⁸ The choice between a short now and a long now, the novel argues, leaves us with a single conclusion, namely that the present is a time without future and possibly without time itself. In late 2014 and early 2015, The Museum of Modern Art in New York City hosted an exhibition titled "The Forever Now: Contemporary Painting in an Atemporal World." The unifying concept of the exhibition is that of a-temporality, which it borrows from novelist William Gibson. The Forever Now presents the work of artists whose work, the curators explain, "reflect a singular approach that characterizes our cultural moment at the beginning of this new millennium: a-temporality, or timelessness." The present of the new millennium, the exhibition proposes, is a never-ending now in which "contemporaneity as an indicator of new form is nowhere to be found."⁹

Right-Wing Culture in Contemporary Capitalism interrogates the consequences of the problem of the timelessness of our long now for culture, society, and politics. Peter Thompson argues that we may understand the crisis of our present with Alain Badiou as a "crisis of negation," as a moment when "many of the apparent certainties about the way in which the breakdown of social order almost automatically leads to new social alternatives have become severely dislocated."¹⁰ The core aspect of this crisis of negation is the "apparent loss of hope for change or improvement."¹¹ Strikingly, the minds behind the idea of the Clock, including Steward Brand, share Thompson's analysis. In his book *The Clock of the Long Now: Time and Responsibility* (2000), Brand anticipates some of the central arguments that have come to shape discussions about the crisis of futurity and imagination that appears to plague us. Time seems to be speeding up, Brand argues,¹² which causes the expansion of the present and our increasing inability to imagine a different future. Brand echoes an argument that underwrites the basic logic of the ways in which The Long Now Foundation describes its project. We live in an "accelerating culture," they write, and the fact that "civilization is revving itself into a pathologically short attention span" makes long-term thinking difficult if not impossible.¹³ Brand and his colleagues also trace this acceleration back to clear sources, including "the short-horizon perspective of market-driven economics." What is needed, they conclude, is "some sort of balancing corrective" to the "short-sightedness" that results from the material conditions of the current era—and they hope that the Clock and the idea of the long now may serve as this corrective. The example of the Clock and of The Long Now Foundation is illuminating, for it arises from a critique of the present that, as we shall see, also characterizes contemporary academic and mainstream analyses of our struggle to keep up with our times. And yet, in spite of the fact that the group understands that the crisis is clearly connected to the structures of contemporary capitalism, and in spite of their desire to foster a new way to think about time that is aimed at taking responsibility for the future, the Long Now project ultimately collapses back into the very logic of capitalism and economic presentism from which it seeks to depart. The time that The 10,000 Year Clock tells, therefore, is the seemingly inescapable time and the totalizing force of the long now.

In order to think about the future, Brand argues, we need to take time. And in order to make plans for the future, we need stability, predictability, and reliability. But if we live in a present that is widely associated with instability and volatility, and if our now is defined by a loss of hope in the change and improvement that the future may bring, then where are we to turn if we seek to find answers to the problems of our present? *Right-Wing Culture* shows that the crisis of futurity and temporal thought that is said to define our era is deeply involved in the rise of some of the most dangerous, dark, and reactionary tendencies in our time. As the future no longer seems to offer viable solutions to the problems of our present, we begin to witness not only a widespread cultural and social crisis of futurity but also a forceful turn toward the past. Right-wing agitators understand the value of fostering the notion that our present is a time of chaos and instability, a narrative that they use to their advantage. In a chaotic present without future, the past seems to offer us models for the forms of stability and order that we lack in our present— the way forward, the Right argues, lies in a return to the past. The seeming inescapability of the long now is deeply involved in the rise of a widespread nostalgia for idealized forms of certainty and stability that are said to have been lost, for simulacra of a world and of possible futures that as such never existed and that are retroactively created as the image of an abandoned, better past to which we shall return. *Right-Wing Culture* traces the sources of the current crisis of futurity in recent developments in capitalism that create not only a crisis of imagination but also a growing cultural and sociopolitical backlash against the time of our present. This backlash, this book shows, provides fertile soil for right-wing agitation and gives rise to new forms of old problems: xenophobia, racism, and misogyny. The long now is a time in which reactionary thought and culture flourishes. The long now is a time of danger.

Analyses of the present increasingly frequently involve critiques of capitalism or even strongly anti-capitalist thought and sentiments while also indicating the same problem that The Clock of the Long Now exemplifies: our efforts at imagining substantive change and the future are ultimately limited by and thus collapse back into the logic of a seemingly inescapable capitalist present. But while the suggestion that it seems to be easier for us to imagine the complete destruction of civilization or of our world than to imagine even a modest change to our capitalist present is one of the most frequently cited diagnoses of our time,[14] what requires closer analysis is the fact that this crisis of imagination is directly bound up with the emergence of a new right-wing push in culture and politics. This book shows that critiques of our present that originate in a backlash against the totalizing nature of the capitalist present not only run the risk of further reifying the very problem they set out to critique, but that this anti-capitalist energy is also seized by the Right in the context of which it ultimately comes to function as a form of capitalist crisis management. Seemingly paradoxically, anti-capitalist critiques of the present constitute a crucial aspect of the development of new right-wing thought and culture, and yet also serve as one of the most significant protective mechanisms of capitalism today. *Right-Wing Culture* shows that right-wing opportunists benefit greatly from the widespread assumption that we live in a wasteland of history, in a time without time, in a present without future. One of the most successful strategies of the contemporary Right capitalizes on the crisis of temporality by touting nostalgically idealized forms of the past as solutions to the fears and worries to which the long now gives rise. Constructing the present as a time of chaos and fragmentation, and leveraging the impression of the collapse of the future into an inescapable present, the image of past unity, order, and stability is the snake oil that right-wing opportunists and charlatans peddle. But, like all snake oil peddlers, the solutions that they offer are less aimed at solving problems than at personal enrichment and empowerment, safeguarding the very structures that they purport to attack and perpetuating the system that exploits and disenfranchises those on whom they prey for support. Much like "Rattlesnake King" Clarke Stanley's snake oil did not in fact contain actual snake oil, right-wing anti-capitalism does not contain actual anti-capitalism.

In a moment when it is once again of crucial importance to trace the relationship between the contradictions of capitalism and the complex social, cultural, and political responses with which this relationship is bound up, critical theory offers us an important set of methodological tools perfectly suited for this task. Even mainstream commentary has begun to recognize the value of the work of the Frankfurt School and its affiliated thinkers in our time. Sean Illing writes in *Vox* that the age of Trump is "a great time to dust off" what he describes as a "forgotten school of criticism," the "motley collection of philosophers, cultural critics, and sociologists" who are associated with the Frankfurt School. The time is right to revisit critical theory, Illing believes, foregrounding the fact that a wide readership, not just academics, sees the value in the analytical approach that critical theory offers in our time. After all, Illing reminds us, *The New Yorker*'s Alex Ross even penned a piece last year arguing that the Frankfurt School "knew Trump was coming."[15] The work of Ernst Bloch in particular allows us to address not only the danger of a new right-wing turn but also the crises in our temporal imaginary to which current forms of reactionary thought are connected.

This book attempts to bridge mainstream, popular commentary and analysis on one hand and academic work on the other. The recently reinvigorated interest in Frankfurt School critical theory and in the work of Bloch presents an opportunity to reintroduce this work to a wider audience and to make the often highly abstract and complex models of thought and analysis with which critical theory provides us more accessible for a general readership. After all, much of the work of Bloch and indeed much of the history of the Frankfurt School is determined by a passionate and urgent opposition to the rise of right-wing sentiments and politics and to the threat of fascism. And while critical theory affords us some of the most sophisticated models for the analysis of art and literature, it also emphasizes the importance of analyzing mass culture in order to trace dangerous desires and political tendencies as well as possible sources of hope and progressive transformation. *Right-Wing Culture* therefore attempts to strike a balance between accessibility for a wider readership and more detailed engagements with the complexities of theoretical models that are aimed at an academic readership. Of course, such a balance requires compromises. This means, for instance, that this book seeks to find a balance between exploring the details and stakes of a given theoretical position without alienating or boring the nonspecialist. In the same vein, the book strives to outline larger social, political, and philosophical problems in an accessible manner through analyses of mainstream culture and commentary that will also be useful to those who are mainly interested in the specific engagements with critical theory and the work of Bloch. Similarly, specialists in novel studies might have wished me to linger more on some of the literary critical facets of this book. What I wish to provide here, however, is a snapshot of the specificity and indeed of the importance of the novel for the kinds of political and philosophical discussions in which this book engages. Those who are interested in this book's discussions of literature may find more detailed analyses of the contemporary novel in my literary critical work. Ultimately, I hope, by frequently switching between registers in order to vary the book's stylistic and analytical rhythm, and by attempting to balance overall accessibility and occasional theoretical deep dives, this book will offer something of value to both a wider readership and specialists.

Those with a keen understanding of critical theory and of the work of Bloch know well that Bloch is not usually counted among the key members of the Frankfurt School. In fact, the history of Bloch's relation to the Frankfurt School is as importantly characterized by the substantial differences between the ideas of Bloch and the Frankfurt School's key thinkers as it is by their commonalities. And while this book is not able to engage with such important aspects of intellectual history in detail, we will see, however, that Bloch's work and thought exerted an important influence on individual members of the Frankfurt School like Theodor W. Adorno as well as on the development of critical theory in general that remains important for the theoretical models that, as this book shows, provides us with important analytical lenses for our present. For those with only a cursory knowledge of the work of Bloch, it is important to know that although he influenced the Frankfurt School directly, and although he maintained long, intensive relationships with Adorno, Walter Benjamin, and Georg Lukacs, Bloch remains in the Anglophone academy to this day the least frequently discussed critic in the Frankfurt School's orbit. Much of his work still remains to be translated into English, and the relationship between Bloch's thought and the development of critical theory is rarely explored. By committing itself primarily to an examination of the present through a Blochian lens, *Right-Wing Culture* also seeks to add to our understanding and appreciation of the significance of Bloch's work. After all, if critical theory is a "forgotten" tradition of thought that should be remembered today, then, I hope to have shown persuasively by the end of this book, Bloch's work makes a particularly strong case for the renewed value of critical theory in our time. After all, Bloch's work allows us striking insights into the power of the forgotten, into the potential that the past holds for both new moments of danger and the formulation of new forms of utopian thought that our era urgently needs.

Chapter 2 of this book traces the prevalence of the crisis of futurity in our moment and forwards an analysis of its sources in a historical transition in capitalism. It illustrates why crises and transitions in capitalism register particularly strongly on the level of time, and it shows why time, so seemingly ephemeral and nebulous a category, is centrally involved in some of the most pressing social and cultural struggles of the present. Through an exploration of the work of Ernst Bloch and of Frankfurt School critical theory more widely conceived, the chapter argues the centrality of art and culture in our ability to examine and indeed to respond to and potentially move beyond the crises of our imagination that result from the transition into the current stage of capitalism, which we may describe as "real time capitalism." Of particular importance in our moment, this chapter shows, is literature in general and the novel in particular. By outlining the significance of the novel as a form of thought and as a form of critique in the context of the problems with which this book deals, the chapter anticipates the central role that the novel plays in *Right-Wing Culture* and anticipates the theoretical account of the novel as a form of thought and of Blochian utopian thought that Chapter 5 forwards. Finally, Chapter 2 introduces a set of methodological propositions and key operative concepts, including that of "nonsynchronism," that will guide the examinations of the subsequent chapters.

After having laid out the basic terms and methodological framework for this book's analysis, Chapters 3 and 4 examine some of the most significant aspects of contemporary right-wing culture and thought and traces the relationship between the rise of new right-wing agitation and contemporary capitalism. Chapter 3 focuses in particular on the rise of a new form of right-wing paternalism that bills itself as a defense against a chaotic, fragmented present. Positioning itself logically incoherently, albeit in ways that are historically as well as politically telling, against concepts such as "postmodernism" and "cultural Marxism," the contemporary Right sells nostalgically idealized forms of masculinity, fatherhood, and paternalistic order as remedies for the ills of our present. Rejecting the now and finding no answers in the future, the temporal populism of the Right today advocates for a return to the past. And while mainstream commentary has only recently turned to this phenomenon, this chapter shows that, beginning as early as the 1980s, novelists have been warning us about the potential for a new turn to the Right or to fascism that our moment may harbor. Strikingly, these novels together also indicate the sources of this new turn to the Right: a transition in capitalism that gives rise to key aspects of right-wing thought such as the association of the present stage of capitalism with a crisis of masculinity. By examining the ways in which novelists trace the danger of new forms of right-wing extremism over the decades through the work of Bloch, this chapter reveals the relationship between contemporary capitalism and current forms of nonsynchronism of which the rise of new forms of right-wing thought and culture is the most nefarious.

Chapter 4 examines the ways in which the right-wing turn to an idealized past and the embrace of new forms of racism and ideas of racial, national, and identitarian purity serve to veil the contradictions of capitalism from which the current crisis emerges. What begins with anti-capitalist rhetoric, the chapter shows, displaces economic critique onto the level of identity, race, and nation, thereby mystifying the actual sources of present structures of inequality and exploitation. The new Right and new forms of racism and xenophobia, this chapter argues, are strategically deployed to veil the contradictions of capitalism and to provide safeguards for capitalism. The chapter traces the emergence of right-wing strategies for mystifying the present's substantial socioeconomic problems, a strategy that further compounds the current crisis of temporality and futurity, since it distracts us from addressing the pressing structural problems of our time in a way that could produce actual, substantive future change. Right-wing rebellion without actual rebellion, pseudo anti-capitalism that serves to protect capitalism, and touting opportunistic, populist solutions to complex problems (such as getting back in touch with nature and masculinity to solve the problems of an increasingly abstract world and form of capitalism), these are some of the key strategies of the new Right.

The crucial contribution of a Blochian analysis to such an analysis is not only that it offers us a model for examining the sources of a turn to the Right or to fascism in times of capitalist crisis. Bloch also foregrounds that, insofar as fascism to no small degree finds its origins in the contradictions of capitalism, right-wing thought ought not simply be ridiculed for its apparent irrationalism. Rather, Bloch's work allows us to see, by tracing the origins of the turn toward the Right today in capitalism, we can see how the contradictions of capital can under specific conditions give rise to a new wave of progressive politics or decline into its dark other. Even in the Right's turn to the past that arises from an abandoned form of capitalist critique, we are able to trace a glimmer of hope as long as we work to return current forms of resentment to their origins and direct them back at those contradictions in capitalism out of which they emerged.

Chapter 5 suggests that a Blochian analysis of the contemporary Right and of the function of the past in our time may offer us ways to wrest hope and utopian thought from the grip of the long now. Instead of merely ridiculing right-wing sentiments, Bloch shows us, it is possible to foreground how closely related a reactionary turn to the past and a utopian relation to the past may in fact be. Instead of turning to the past in the hope to restore lost forms of order, we may understand the past as an archive of unheard appeals, unfulfilled hopes and dreams, of silenced demands for liberation and freedom—and such a relation to the past in turn shows us what is missing in the present and what cries out for completion. Understood in this manner, the past models for us not mythical unity and purity but the history of systemic injustice, oppression, and exploitation, which in turn means that the past contains the energy that leads the way into the future. The past is not just what was. It is that which was never allowed to be, that which never could be, and it therefore indicates and demands that which may yet be. Blochian thought lays out for us a relation to the past that stands opposed to reactionary desires that seek to restore the past's mythical lost greatness. The utopian imagination, on the other hand, examines the past as an archive of appeals for liberation and wishes for a better life, of projects and ideas that went unheard, that were repressed or abandoned but that reach into our present and anticipate a future through their continuous demand for realization. Such a relation to the past that sets in motion a radical refusal of the limits of the present, this chapter shows, is particularly powerfully modeled for us in contemporary Indigenous literature.

It is ultimately this understanding of the relation between past, present, and future for which this book argues, an understanding that is of crucial importance not just in the context of the long now but also with regard to the danger of a new turn to right-wing extremism and fascism that the temporal crises of our moment harbor. Taking thought and politics beyond a future that is colonized by capitalism and a past that becomes the mystical playground for the new Right, this book seeks to foreground the great value of a different conception of both past and future in our time. Through a Blochian understanding of temporality, *Right-Wing Culture* traces the remnants of hope and utopia in our present. The political power and the possibility of utopian thought, the kind of thought that stands steadfastly opposed to capitalist presentism and right-wing reaction, this book shows, lies not in what was or in what may never be but in that which was never allowed to be … in that which may yet come to pass.

2

Looking Backward: Nonsynchronism in the Long Now of Capitalism

In 2017, *Slate* declared "Flying Cars in the Future" the "perfect meme for this dumb year."[16] The meme proposes that "at some point in the past we imagined the future would bring us flying cars," Jacob Brogan explains. "But here in 2017 … things are a little different." The meme suggests that we live, as Brogan puts it, "in fallen times" and takes aim at our understanding of our present as defined by a "debased state of innovation." With fellow *Slate* author Henry Grabar, Brogan argues that flying cars are "the quintessential undelivered promise of future"—and even if we are by now closer to making them a reality, Brogan concludes, "we're no better off for it." The future, it seems, is no longer what it was. In fact, as we began to see in the previous chapter, we are not just confronted with a situation in which our present reality does not quite measure up to the grand dreams of the future that we were promised. The future has not only failed us. More problematically, it seems to have disappeared. In the same year that according to *Slate* was poignantly summed up by the "Flying Cars" meme, Canadian author and artist Douglas Coupland, most well known for his 1991 bestseller *Generation X*, published an essay in which he asks: "what if there's no next big thing?" Looking at our present, Coupland wonders if we are confronted with a historical endpoint of sorts. Could it be that true change and innovation, along with art, have died?[17]

Even science fiction, which we often associate very closely with or even consider to be one of the go-to cultural forms if we look for the future, has been experiencing a crisis of futurity in recent years. In fact, David M. Higgins illustrates, this problem has become ubiquitous and is in fact by now one of the definitive traits of contemporary science fiction. Surveying recent studies of the genre, Higgins finds that "science fiction has increasingly shifted away from utopian imaginings, now either dwelling on the wonders and terrors of the technofuturistic present or forecasting inevitable apocalyptic collapse."[18] Entire special issues of academic journals have been dedicated to this problem, including an issue of *Paradoxa* titled "SF Now," coedited by Mark Bould and Rhys Williams, which "examines science fiction's engagement with what Mark Fisher calls 'capitalist realism'—the breakdown in our ability to imagine viable alternatives to capitalism since the end of the Cold War."[19] Other publications, Higgins shows, such as another special issue of *Paradoxa*, edited by Sherryl Vint, that is dedicated to "The Futures Industry," confirm the impression that the future has become "a time of crisis"—both in the sense that "real devastation looms on the horizon (as a consequence of climate change and economic instability)," Higgins notes, "and also in the sense that we seem to have collectively lost the ability to imagine futures that offer plausible alternatives to the seemingly unstoppable trajectory of the apocalyptic present."[20]

Even the gurus of venture capital like Peter Thiel and the Founders Fund, a venture capital firm that Thiel cofounded, grapple with the same problem. In a lengthy publication on the firm's website, "What happened to the future?," Bruce Gibney, writing for the Founders Fund, argues that "from the 1960s to the 1990s, venture capital was an excellent way" to support technological development and earn returns.[21] But from 1999 to the present, the Founders Fund's studies show, "the industry has posted negative mean and median returns." Describing the present as a "long nightmare" for venture capital, the document that Gibney has authored on behalf of Founder's Fund expresses that it is of the utmost importance for venture capitalists to engage with this problem and to seek answers to one crucial question: "what happened?" To answer this question, Gibney knows, it is important to examine how we imagine the future, and the document does so by asking how we "approach the future through the lens of VC." The Founders Fund's inquiry into the problems finds that the present world lacks the sense of "radical transformation and advancement" that seemed to define the 1960s, 1970s, and 1980s. As a result, one of the main mechanisms that used to "drive the performance of venture capital and venture portfolios" has disappeared. Venture capitalists, Gibney explains, are confronted with a problem. Until recently, they continued to expect "rapid progress and advances." "And we," Gibney adds, "continued to invest in their anticipation." However, he concludes, transformational change, along with the future, seem to have disappeared. Venture capital itself, he finds, functions differently today, for it "has ceased to be the funder of the future and instead has become a funder of features, widgets, irrelevances." The answers that the document proposes in order to save venture capitalism are striking. Venture capitalists, Gibney argues, must try to foster radical change and join him in the call for experimentation, for embracing the unknown, and for maintaining a belief in hope and the future. These suggestions are striking, since they echo the language and logic of examinations of the current crisis of futurity that we find in cultural theory, philosophy, political theory, as well as in culture and art. But while the latter tend to trace the sources of the crisis of futurity back to capitalism itself, the Founders Fund's account of the crisis of futurity is aimed at a defense of capitalism. As a result, by cynically seeking to defend that which is fundamentally involved in the creation of the crisis in the first place—namely the contradictions of capitalism—Gibney's analysis of the crisis of futurity reveals possibly nothing as poignantly as the consequences of accepting the limits of capitalism as the limits of our (temporal) imagination.

What we see in documents like "What Happened to the Future?" is a clear sign that the present problem is not merely a crisis in art and culture but rather a structural one, a crisis that illustrates the connection between crises in capitalism and crises of our imagination, which are in turn bound up with distinct social and cultural problems. This chapter traces the relation between the current crisis of futurity as a large-scale crisis in thought that brings with it a range of pressing social, cultural, and political problems. It is important for us to understand the relation between these different dimensions and to take seriously the crisis of futurity as indicative of a substantive problem that is definitive of our moment in history. For understanding the nature of these relations, this chapter shows, allows us to trace one of the main root causes of the recent emergence of right-wing culture and politics. In this way, we are able to develop a better understanding of the emergence of right-wing thought and culture works today, and we can gain insights into those cultural narratives about our time that fuel current forms of right-wing agitation. This chapter shows that the current crisis of futurity and temporality is a symptom of contemporary capitalism's struggle to manage some of its defining contradictions. These contradictions are in turn bound up with an erosion of established social structures and give rise to what Ernst Bloch describes as forms of "nonsynchronism": narratives and desires that are centrally involved in the rise of a new wave of right-wing extremism in our time. This chapter also serves as an introduction to the key methodological propositions and concepts of Blochian thought that the chapters that follow will deploy in order to gain a better understanding of right-wing thought in our time and in order to propose alternatives to it.

The long now, a crisis of capitalist temporality

Critical accounts of the current crisis of temporality and futurity tend to traces its sources back to the end of the Cold War. Harry Harootunian, for instance, describes our moment in history as defined by "the installation of a new time marked by a boundless present," by the rise of "a new temporal architecture" that defines our "new reality" as a "perennial present."[22] The future, he continues, "has been emptied of its promise of progress,"[23] and it has been "both severed from its historical past and indefinitely deprived of a future from which it once derived expectation."[24] In Harootunian's estimation, "if any axial event marked the turn in time it was undoubtedly the collapse of the Berlin Wall and the subsequent end of the cold war."[25] But while Harootunian's account of the origins of this crisis map convincingly onto well-worn accounts of the fall of the Berlin Wall as a marker of the end of history, the disappearance of a socialist or communist alternative to capitalism alone cannot fully account for the complexities of the crisis in our imagination with which we are confronted. Peter Thompson's passionate argument for the value of a return to Bloch's work today indicates why this is the case. Concepts like hope, utopia, liberation, fulfillment, and transcendence, he writes, those ideas that contribute to what Thompson following Bloch describes as the "warm stream" of human history, have become "subsumed under the 'cold stream' of economic reductionism"[26]—an argument poignantly supported by the Founders' Fund's strategy for saving the future. In a society whose motto has become "living for the day," Thompson argues, "any sense that we were involved in any kind of process or dynamic that would lead to something different, something new, something better ha[s] all but disappeared."[27] But while Francis Fukuyama "proclaimed the end of history in 1989," and while "despite our objections to it on various grounds, usually ideological, everyone largely accepted that he was right," Thompson suggests, "that particular end of history itself ended in 2008."

What Thompson's argument indicates, in other words, is that the 2008 crash fundamentally disrupts the notion that, after the effective fall of communism and socialism, capitalism presents the only functioning world system. The crash laid bare the internal contradictions and the structures of massive inequality and exploitation of capitalism even for those whose view of capitalism had been largely positive. Thus, while the crisis of imagination and of temporal and utopian thought was no doubt exacerbated by historical events like the fall of the Berlin Wall and the attacks of 9/11 that Harootunian invokes in his analysis, it must also be understood in direct relation to capitalism itself—specifically, in relation to the historical, immanent limits and contradictions of capitalism. Thompson consequently understands our moment in time as "a Gramscian interregnum," as a moment when "the old world of the absolute hegemony of capitalism and its ideology is dying, but a new world, or even the semblance of a new world, has not yet emerged to replace it."[28] Finding a new way to imagine alternatives to the long now of capitalism must therefore involve an analysis of capitalism's crises. But what exactly is the nature of the relation between the current crisis of our temporal imagination and a transition or crisis in the history of capitalism that such an analysis would seem to indicate? What particular development in capitalism is able to cause a large-scale disruption of our temporal imagination and of our understanding of our relation to both our present and the future? And how is it possible for a development in capitalism to create such profound problems for our temporal imagination that even capitalism itself, as we have seen with regard to venture capitalism, struggles to manage and contain?

In order to answer these questions we must return to the category of time itself and examine how we understand it that aspect of time that we often disregard: time's relation to material reality. Omnipresent yet ephemeral, seemingly natural yet also often utterly abstract, time is a concept about which we may not think directly all too frequently in spite of the fact that virtually all aspects of our existence are structured or even dictated by time. Time seems to be everywhere and nowhere at once. It defines the rhythm of our lives, and yet, if we seek to pinpoint or define it, it tends to escape our attempts at grasping it. Not surprisingly, time is one of the most widely discussed and examined philosophical concepts, After all, time is deeply involved in how we imagine our place in and relation to the world—it is one of the most foundational forms of narrative and thought through which we make sense of the world and through which we know ourselves and our time in history. Telling time is always also a way of telling stories about ourselves, about our relation to the world that we inhabit, and it is a way of knowing ourselves and this world. Time is a narrative that is as much a way to describe the world as it is a matter of world making. And yet, while we are rather familiar with the infamous tension between natural time (the time of seasons and natural rhythms) and the human experience of time (which seems to be subject to a myriad of forms of distorting, bending, and stretching time), what we often forget is that time itself has a history—and a material one to boot. While the time of nature itself seems to be virtually timeless or eternal (a point that reveals itself whenever we declare that something is "as old as time itself"), and while the human experience of time also presents us with seemingly timeless problems (such as the infamous problem of the vanishing present, the time that escapes us as soon as we seek to indicate it), time as a form of human knowledge does itself exist in time. Time, in other words, has a history. Our imagination of time changes and develops, and if we study these changes, then we are able to reveal the fascinating, complex history of time. We have not always imagined time in the same way. Different moments in human history gave rise to and were deeply influenced by specific temporal imaginaries and by specific conceptions of time. But time begins to appear natural to us as soon as a given conception of time becomes so deeply ingrained into our daily lives and into the rhythm of our existence that we no longer notice it as a new human creation. If we do, however, study the history of time itself, which means nothing other than studying the different conceptions of time and different forms of temporal thoughts that attend specific moments in history and particular social, cultural, and material structures, then we are able to see two important things: (1) ideas of time rise and fall throughout history, they have their uses and functions, and they lose their utility as history moves on; but precisely because specific conceptions of time ingrain themselves necessarily so deeply into our imagination and into our ways of making sense of the world and mapping our own existence, the exhaustion of established temporal imaginaries always bring with them severe moments of crisis, of disorientation, and of fear and anxiety. (2) Given that time has a time and history, and given that ideas of time tend to reach their limits of utility, it is important to understand periodically occurring crises in our temporal imagination not as the categorical exhaustion of time itself but rather as indices of a larger historical transformation. In other words, if we seek to understand our current inability to maintain established notions of futurity, of present, and of time itself, then we should not simply suggest that we are living in the end time or in an age marked by the end of time itself, but we should try to ask which underlying historical transformation has caused the exhaustion of our established temporal imagination. This, in turn, is the first step into the direction of confronting the impression that we have reached the end of time and the end of our imagination as a known problem: as an interregnum, as a point in time when we must develop new ways of telling the time of our lives that allow us to make sense of the changed material world in which we live.

No doubt, this still rather abstract point will benefit from more concrete clarification. Scholars like Amy Elias stress the great value of analyzing the "relation between historiographical traditions and particular chronometric practices" in order to gain insights into the relation between time and the cultural and sociopolitical structures to which our imagination of time is connected. Building on the work of Reinhart Koselleck, Elias emphasizes the importance of tracing the relation between our conception of history (our efforts at writing, narrating, and understanding history) and what we may simply call the practices of timekeeping that subtend a particular historical period.[29] The rise of capitalism brought with it specific forms of timekeeping and a particular understanding of time and history, and these forms of thought and narratives, these modes of telling time are of particular significance for our understanding of the current crisis of temporality. For the rise of capitalism not only brought with it but indeed depended upon and would not have been possible without the establishment of a new way of understanding time. David Harvey argues, for example, that the rise of the money form is inseparable from a very specific understanding of spatiotemporality. "Money," he writes, "is perpetually internalizing effects of the spatiotemporal world which its circulation creates and in which its valuations are occurring."[30] Barbara Adam, in turn, foregrounds the ways in which clock time, a form of time that we have come to treat as virtually natural in our lives, is a particular (and indeed quite recently developed) form of imagining time that emerges in relation to capitalism in the context of which it carries out a necessary supporting function. "Time is grounded in the material conditions of historically constituted modes and relations of production," she argues, adding that "clock time, the imposed time to human design" is "internalized in socioeconomic relations."[31] Bliss Cua Lim reminds us of the centrality of historical and material analyses of time in critiques of capitalism: "in his classic treatment of labor and time-discipline, E.P. Thompson writes, '"Time is the employer's money'; Jean Baudrillard conceptualizes the commodity as crystallized time; and in different ways, they, like Theodor Adorno, trace the subjugation or growing impossibility of 'free' or leisure time."[32] And precisely because the rise of capitalism marks an important event in the history of our temporal imagination, bringing with it new forms of thinking time that gave us new ways of navigating our way through material life, capitalism, Lim stresses, cannot be fully understood without grasping the crucially important role that time plays in its structure. Marxist analysis, too, is fundamentally connected to a historical and material analysis of time. After all, Lim emphasizes, Marxist analysis reveals "the alienation of the worker from the possibility of an autonomous control of time … as a characteristic feature of capitalism."[33] Lim stresses the particular importance of temporal analysis for Marxist analysis by reminding us of an important line in Karl Marx's work that expresses the significance of the relation between time, capitalism, and the reification and alienation of work and worker: in capitalism, Marx writes, "time is everything, man is nothing; he is at most an incarnation of time."[34]

One of the key characteristics of capitalist time is the rise to dominance of a form of abstract temporality that can serve as a form of standardization and as a measure and equivalent of value and labor. In fact, Norbert Trenkle shows, the rise of capitalism would not have been possible without the dialectically connected abstraction of labor and time: "abstraction in the realm of labor also reigns in the form of a highly specific rule of time that is both abstract-linear and homogeneous."[35] The linearity of time, therefore, which we have come to understand as an almost self-evident feature of temporality today (which in turn lends a-linear cultural narratives their particular subversive appeal and function), must be understood in relation to capitalism in the context of which time's linearity was standardized as an important aspect of capitalism's basic architecture. Similarly, Trenkle stresses, time had to be homogenized, and human activity itself was categorized in and widely reduced to homogeneous units of time, which presupposes and is possible only through "the existence of an abstract measure of time."[36] And because linear, abstract, and homogeneous time secures capitalism's logic and function and must therefore be standardized in nearly all aspects of work and life, it is particularly deeply ingrained in our imagination. After all, capitalist standardization requires the replacement of competing ideas and conceptions of temporality with that of capitalist time, with abstract, linear, homogeneous clock time in which our work, lives, and value can be measured. And while previous moments in world history were still defined by a plurality of temporal narratives and imaginaries, the global spread of capitalism has led to a reduction of temporal imaginaries and to a previously unseen degree of temporal standardization. No wonder, then, that any crisis of capitalist time creates large shocks and registers as a crisis of time itself. When capitalism standardizes its form of time across the globe, fissures in the time of capital are perceived as signs of the end of time. And since, as Massimiliano Tomba argues, "the modern image of the indefinite and unlimited character of progress" is directly bound up with capitalist temporality, thus with a form of "homogeneous and empty time,"[37] it is no surprise that a disruption of capitalism and its sense of temporality creates a large-scale crisis of futurity.

But what happened in the recent history of capitalism that caused this crisis? One important aspect of contemporary capitalism that changes its relation to time is the increasing financialization of the economy. To be sure, Cédric Durant argues, finance itself has a long history and reaches as far back as fourteenth-century Florence. Recently, however, financialization has risen to the dominant logic of capitalism, and this new dominant logic introduces a range of new problems, including capitalism's reliance on what Durand describes as finance's appropriation of our future.[38] In his 2010 book *The Futurism of the Instant*, Paul Virilio suggests that finance capital's commitment to instantaneity and speed in the context of trade and communication requires a logic of time that surpasses traditional notions of clock time that underwrote previous stages in capitalism. The result of this new form of time is the rise to dominance of what Virilio describes throughout the book as the sense of an "omnipresent instant" that defines our era. In fact, Virilio suggests, such a situation may also force us to rethink the very definition of progress:

> In the nineteenth century, Progress meant the *Great Commotion* of the railways. In the twentieth century, it still meant more the *Great Speed* of the bullet train and the supersonic jet. In the twenty-first century, it means the *Instantaneity* of the interactive telecommunications of cybernetics.[39]

It is this process of acceleration and the speed of capitalism that aims toward instantaneity and immediacy that exhausts narratives of progress and thus also results in what Virilio understands as a "sudden loss of memory" that carries with it a loss of imagination, which parallels the exhaustion of our "great progressive illusions."[40] "When time is money," Adam writes, "speed becomes an absolute and unassailable imperative for business."[41] Moreover, she elaborates, "when speed is equated with efficiency, then time compression and intensification of processes seem inevitable."[42] The problem of the long now and of our inability to imagine alternatives or outsides to the capitalist present can thus be understood in relation to what we may call "real time capitalism." The transition into the real-time era, Mark McGurl argues, creates severe problems for thought and critique, for any form of real-time data "closes the gap between the occurrence of an event and its subjective or machinic apprehension as information."[43] The immediacy and instantaneity of real-time transactions or data leave no room for thought, for critical analysis, for evaluation, or inquiry. Consequently, McGurl suggests, "reality and representation crowd together in the urgent space of a perpetually self-renewing now."[44] Not only does the advent of real-time capitalism mean that capitalism operates on a fully abstracted logic of time that relies upon a speed that is no longer thinkable in established terms (when its units approach immediacy, time becomes less and less real), but the instantaneity at which the system is aimed operates on a logic of time that exhausts established conceptions of temporality and duration, thus collapsing all time into an omnipresent, long now.

Similarly, Bernard Stiegler shows in great detail in his 2010 book *For a New Critique of Political Economy* that contemporary capitalism requires a constitutive commitment to what he calls a "systemic short-termism."[45] Economic relations that we had become used to understanding as a matter of cycles, flows, and spatial connections are contracted into points of immediacy. Everything happens at once. Even the management of large-scale crises in capitalism, Stiegler notes, is aimed at the short term only. Stimulating investments, for instance, express a hope for the restoration of "entrepreneurial dynamism itself founded upon consumerism and its counterpart, market-driven productivism," Stiegler argues, yet these investments are made without being able to offer a concrete long-term view. For Stiegler, this contraction of the future into an all-consuming present constitutes one of the main contradictions of contemporary capitalism. In fact, Stiegler suggests, what we see is the development of *"systemic stupidity that structurally prevents the reconstitution of a long-term horizon."*[46] In recent years, we have seen a variety of studies that arrive at the same conclusions, including the work of philosophers like Franco "Bifo" Berardi, who has published several books on this topic, including *After the Future* (2011), *And: Phenomenology of the End* (2015), and *Futurability: The Age of Impotence and the Horizon of Possibility* (2017). Capitalism's drive toward immediacy and instantaneity, critics agree, appears to be bound up not only with a crisis of thought that makes it more difficult for all of us to imagine the future outside of a perpetually expanding capitalist present, but it is also connected to a gradual erosion of capitalism's own foundations. Indeed, it seems that we are confronted with a temporal, epistemological, and an economic singularity, a moment when the temporal logic of our existence, capitalist real time, exceeds the limits of human cognition and calls into question the stability of the system itself. And this is not surprising. After all, as Jared Gardner shows in his examination of the topic, simultaneity is much harder to think than seriality and linearity.[47] And yet, it is crucial to remember that the end with which we are confronted and the moment of exhaustion that we are sensing is not in fact the end of time, of the future, or of history. The disruption of our temporal imagination signals nothing other than a crisis in capitalism resulting from capitalism's systemic struggle to transition into a logic of capital that exhausts its established temporal foundation, into a capitalist long now that presents as many problems for our imagination as for capitalism itself. If we are truly seeing an end, therefore, it is important to understand it not as the end of the future but as the end of the time of capitalism.

The temporal demos undone

When popular dialogue and mainstream publications try to grapple with the topic of time today, one frequently encounters references to the work of Italian physicist Carlo Rovelli, one of the most widely discussed public intellectuals in recent years who has at times been hailed the intellectual heir to Stephen Hawking. In particular Rovelli's 2018 bestselling book *The Order of Time* has received a lot of attention, in part because it strikes a laudable balance between scientific rigor on one hand and the ability to communicate complex ideas to a broad audience on the other. Based on the success of his book, Rovelli has been interviewed countless times, and publications including *The Guardian* and journals of ideas like *Nautilus* have featured essays in which Rovelli discusses facets of his work.[48] In addition to wielding the phrase "The End of Time" in order to show us that time, especially linear time, as we traditionally understand does not in fact exist in the fundamental physics of the universe, Rovelli also loves to point out that there is no such thing as common time. And while he is, of course, correct to make this point from the standpoint of his particular background in physics, one must wonder what work such a suggestion does in the general context of our historical moment. Is celebrating the idea of the end of time not somewhat tone-deaf in a situation in which some of the most pressing social, political, and philosophical problems are connected to just this impression that we have reached the end of time and the horizon of possibility? And do we really need physics to demonstrate to us that, strictly speaking, there is no such thing as a common, natural, shared sense of time when, as we will see, everyday life in capitalism makes this point much more directly? After all, if we understand time not as a universally shared, trans-historically stable idea or as a constant in the fabric of our universe but instead historicize our understanding of time itself, then we see that the idea of time and its particular manifestations such as linearity or its standardization emerge under and are inseparable from specific historical and material conditions in the context of which they assume their meaning and carry out a specific function. To suggest, therefore, that there is no such thing as common time in one important sense misses the mark insofar as time does not come to us as philosophical idea or aspect of nature or the universe that exists in stable form across all of time but rather as a capitalist imperative.

What we understand as common time is indeed a creation of capitalism—it is by no means a natural form of universal time. But capitalism also works neither without a common form of time nor without standardized forms of abstract labor, production, industry norms, and so on, which is why capitalism is built around a central temporal imperative: we must live and work according to capitalist common time. And yet, while common time constitutes one of the foundations of capitalism, contemporary capitalism in another sense also wishes to encourage us to agree with Rovelli. Instead of common time, we are encouraged to focus on its seeming opposite: me-time.

As philosophers like Christian Marazzi suggest, contemporary capitalism productively integrates and valorizes activities and aspects of our lives that were not previously understood as aspects of economic production.[49] Intellectual, creative, and emotional activity, Marazzi argues, and the general intellect that had previously been conceived of as merely a matter of fixed capital, have become crucial parts of contemporary capitalism. In the present economic system, Berardi likewise suggests, even our soul is at work.[50] As a result, we witness a gradual blurring of the distinction between work and leisure time. In addition to capitalism's move toward immediacy and instantaneity, real time capitalism is also characterized by the fact that it gradually absorbs all forms of time into labor time. But we are not only confronted with the rise of what we have come to know as cognitive capitalism, creative capitalism, the knowledge economy, or affective capitalism. Contemporary capitalism assigns creative or critical thought a productive function. However, it also advertises the need for certain kinds of mental activity and forms of spending our time that can increase productivity and value precisely by seemingly standing opposed to work time.

A recent article published in *The Cut* excitedly announces that new research has confirmed the immense value of letting our minds wander.[51] But what may initially sound like good news for daydreamers, artists, or anyone who enjoys the brief moments of pause that offer a momentary reprieve from the rhythm of capitalist common time is ultimately only good news for capitalism itself. Work in creative or cognitive capitalism is not easy. To be sure, it may not involve a lot of heavy lifting, but it does require us to constantly come up with new ideas and to solve problems or manage projects creatively. This constant demand for ideas and the threat of potentially running out of them makes anxiety a constant condition of work in the new economy. But, as Kristin Wong suggests in her article, research shows that the answer to our problems is easier than we may have expected. "You're in the shower, or you're brushing your teeth, or you're blow-drying your hair," she writes, and "suddenly, brilliance strikes: You come up with the perfect idea to present to your boss at a meeting later that morning." As it turns out, one of the fundamental dimensions of time under capitalism—the rhythm of work and routine—is not good for the kind of work that the new economy demands. "It's not your morning routine that's responsible for your creative brilliance," Wong writes, "but something called the *default mode network*, a constellation of different areas in your brain that work together and increase in activity when your mind wanders." The solution to the constant pressure to come up with new ideas, therefore, is putting our brains on autopilot, taking a step out of the rhythm of the capitalist quotidian and letting our minds wander. And, good news for us and for capitalism, research shows that our brain "works just as hard when [we're] relaxed as it does when [we're] focused on a task."

Letting the mind wander and momentarily breaking or disrupting our normal rhythm, as *Scientific American* reports, allows our minds to "roam free, imagine new possibilities, and silence the inner critic." Any kind of activity that takes us outside of work time, Wong stresses, including showering but also "chopping vegetables and running," offers a perfect way to explore new ways for our minds to generate ideas. All remnants of our lives, all aspects of time, and all activities that were not previously included in the rhythm of capital therefore become part of it precisely by seemingly being external to capitalist production. Letting the mind wander, occasional acts that we previously understood as private refusals of the time of productivity and as minirebellions against the incessant flow of common work time, as moments, that is, when we reclaim small moments in time from capitalism for our own dreams, ideas, and hopes, as it turns out, has become a crucial aspect of work in the new economy. All that is left for us to do is become even better at letting our minds wander. Of course, we must not let our minds wander excessively. Out little mental strolls must be taken within the confines and under the conditions of capitalism, and we must avoid straying too far. The brain on autopilot should wander just far enough to explore valuable ideas beyond the rhythm of the everyday, yet not too far, so that the limit of capitalism and work time itself does not come under question. This example of utopia undone, of the productive integration of all aspects of thought and time in the circuits of capitalism, exemplifies the ways in which even "me-time" ultimately feeds back into the common time of capitalism, revealing the new forms of exploitation and alienation on which capitalism rests and illustrating the difficulty of conceiving of a time and life outside of a seemingly all-encompassing system of valorization.

Paulo Virno argues that the relation between the individual and the social is transformed under contemporary capitalism. "Social time, in today's world, seems to have come unhinged," he writes, "because there is no longer anything which distinguishes labor form the rest of human activities. Therefore, since work ceases to constitute a special and separate praxis ... completely different from those criteria and procedures which regulate non-labor time, there is not a clean, well-defined threshold separating labor time from non-labor time."[52] And since the life of the mind "is included fully within the time-space of production," he concludes, "an essential homogeneity prevails."[53] In such a situation, we frequently encounter the call for more me-time, which furthers the fragmentation of social and common time at the same moment when capitalism absorbs all time into its own structures. The impulse to demand more me-time is understandable. And yet, me-time is not the opposite of work time. It is an extension of it. Social time, on the other hand, is not only an integral part of the emergence of modern sociability, but it is also the time of common political and social projects, projects that might be aimed at different futures, at better worlds. At the same time that capitalism absorbs all aspects of time into its structure—even forms of time that were previously considered "unproductive" such as daydreaming—it also encourages the fragmentation of social time into me-time. The time of contemporary capitalism is the time of the temporal demos undone.

In recent years, there has been much talk about unstructured time. Websites like *The Fullest*, a "contemporary culture publication that fiercely believes in the intelligence of its readers" and that creates "content that is both timely and timeless," have featured segments on unstructured time. As part of a segment titled "Being vs. Doing," Dr. Julie Von, a frequent contributor to *The Fullest*, advertises the benefits and importance of unstructured time, "the new wellness trend."[54] Invoking images of a happy, carefree childhood, Von asks us to remember the last time we "experienced a day, or even an hour, which was not filled" with "task-oriented achievements," with work. Childhood, on the other hand, she writes, was filled with emptiness—with unstructured time that had not been claimed by work and that allowed our imagination to roam free. But today, "when we over-determine our schedule and experiences," Von argues, "we disconnect from the part of our being that dreams and creates." The radical refusal of such a life, she proposes, lies in a return to childhood emptiness—leaving holes in our schedules for unstructured time. Like a wide range of other current, corporatized wellness trends such as mindfulness, unstructured time begins with what claims to be a softcore, largely gestural critique of capitalism's tendency to take hold of all parts of our existence, of all of our time. But instead of continuing down this road and aiming for a systemic critique of the conditions under which we live and work (and under which the former increasingly becomes a matter of the latter), wellness and the idea of unstructured time depart from what is ultimately a social and structural matter and turns it into a matter of individual responsibility and strategy.

Whether it is mindfulness or unstructured time, capitalism's universal hold on our existence is maintained by offering small, personalized spaces and times of what Von calls "individual fulfillment," small tokens of individual gratification that distract us from the fact that the larger social solidarities that may provide us with ways to think about, critique, and systematically refuse and change the structure that we experience as oppressive and omnipresent are being dismantled with the help of the self-care industry. Instead of addressing the systemic sources of the new forms of alienation that are indeed creating increasingly widespread discontent and resentment, the wellness industry sells us me-time as the solution. We get fidget spinners to distract us from the structural source of our exploitation, weighted blankets to counteract the anxiety that work in contemporary capitalism produces, we are told to breathe deeply, reflect on ourselves, and think positively in order to let go of bad energy (that is our fault, not the fault of our working and living conditions), and we are told to reclaim bits of our lives through unstructured me-time. Me-time is marketed to us as a matter of our right to freedom, as in Von's article, and as a matter of reclaiming lost childlike innocence that allows us to momentarily forget a life that is not understood as a life of capitalist alienation and exploitation but simply as adult life (which is hard). But, of course, it is quite clear that unstructured time, much like instances of strategically letting our minds wander, is no more than an attempt at crisis management, at allowing the worker of contemporary capitalism to recharge. And, as we saw, it turns out that me-time, unstructured time, is also crucial for the creation of new ideas and new energy for work time. It is thus not surprising that we witness the rapid growth of the wellness field precisely in a moment when real-time capitalism claims the time of our lives and leaves us longing for brief moments of reprieve, for small steps outside of the system. The wellness trend is able to capitalize on even these seemingly trivial moments in time, encouraging small, strategic steps outside of work time in order to maximize the productivity of time itself. Instead of actually wresting time from the grip of capitalism, me-time allows us to recharge and provides us with new energy for work in real time capitalism. Free fuel for the fleet vehicle, hooray!

Contemporary capitalism fractures old solidarities and social and political projects by championing identity and individualism over those forms of understanding our present that may give rise to recognitions of commonality. Capitalism, that is, seeks to fragment contemporaneity, our shared sense of being in time, into empty, isolated instances of me-time, compounding the impression that we live in a long now, in a present that expands infinitely and to which we cannot imagine an outside or a future alternative. Collective or social futures are disappearing, and what is left of the future, it seems, has been claimed by the superrich. The future is a time for the few, brought to us by futurists like Elon Musk, Richard Branson, and Jeff Bezos, as, in the words of a recent *The New York Times* article, "the rich are planning to leave this wretched planet."[55] The future is no longer the time of common aspirations or of dreams of a better world. It is the time for the few, the privileged, the powerful. Understood in this way, it is true: there is no common time.

The dialectic of aesthetic form and anticipatory consciousness

Where might we turn, then, in order to recover the remnants of the utopian imagination? Where might we find the kind of time and thought that does not simply feed back into the long now of capitalism and that may afford us a different sense of time and of futurity? One way to address this question, as the remainder of this book will illustrate, is by returning to the work of Ernst Bloch. As Chapters 3 and 4 show in some detail, Bloch's work is especially significant in our time since it allows us to make sense of the relation between a crisis in our temporal imagination and the forms of reactionary thought and the temporal backward orientation that characterizes right-wing culture and politics. However, Bloch's attention to the relation between our temporal imagination and political form also provides us with valuable analytical tools for addressing the crises of our time. Cat Moir reminds us that one of the fundamental assertions of Blochian thought is that "anticipatory consciousness" comes to us in "aesthetic form."[56] Art and culture, Bloch suggests, assume a crucial role in the continued life of the utopian imagination, since art engages thought in a critical project with regard to lived reality that stands directly opposed to the aims of, say, unstructured time. While unstructured time is designed to recharge us in order to allow us to function more effectively in work time, and while the capitalist version of letting our minds wander is aimed at creating valuable ideas for capitalism, art, by contrast, engages us in a fundamentally different relation to our environment. Art, Bloch suggests, is not a matter of escapism or of simply allowing our minds to take time off. Rather, art is about a critical examination of the present that, as we will see in great detail in the remainder of this book, is more concerned with what is missing from our lives than with that which is already present. In other words, art and culture contain demands for freedom, for liberation, for a better life, and, unlike wellness, art is not in the business of simply calming our minds when we recognize our present as lacking. Art fans the flames of critical thought and discontent, and it reminds us of the urgent need to contemplate and address the root causes of the problems that determine our now.

As Ruth Leys shows, Bloch was deeply interested in the critical, utopian function of music. On Bloch's account, one which Leys echoes and further develops in her own work, music illustrates art's utopian potential through its ability to create a "cultural surplus," a surplus that "overflow[s] its historical location and conditions of production and points toward that which is not yet."[57] Utopia, Leys argues, ought to be understood as a method, one aimed at what she calls "the imaginary reconstitution of society." The function of art and culture is central to this conception of utopia. Bloch's emphasis on the importance of art and culture, as Thompson reminds us, is wedded to the conviction that "even in its apparently reactionary forms at worst, and certainly in its progressive forms at best," art "contains elements generated by and borrowed from the surplus of utopian drive."[58] One of the most pressing projects of our time is the recovery of our social and critical imagination, and Bloch's work and the work of Frankfurt School critical theory more generally provide us with an invaluable basis for this project, a project that for critical theorists always centrally involved a commitment to the importance of the social, political, and epistemological work that art can do. In this book, I turn specifically to the work of novel, for the novel provides us with a striking form of critique in the time of the long now. I emphasize the role of the novel in our moment specifically because the novel is at its heart a form of art that, since its rise, has dedicated itself to the question of how we tell time. It is a well-worn argument that the rise of the novel is bound up with the rise of capitalism, but it is also important to remember that the novel from its beginning addressed itself to making sense of and critically examining the new sense of history and temporality that the rise of capitalism brought with it and in dialectical relation with which we must understand the work of the novel. The novel is a form of thought and critique that draws our attention to temporal thought in history. I only anticipate this argument here in abbreviated form to set the stage for the analysis that follows. In Chapter 5, however, after having shown the work that the novel does in our time, I will also forward a theoretical account of the novel as a form of utopian thought and politics in our time, one that can concretely model for us precisely the kind of Blochian thought and analysis that, as this book shows, is required in our moment. For the time being, suffice it to indicate that the novel assumes a particularly significant function as a form of aesthetic critique today because it addresses itself to some of the central problems that characterize the present crisis of temporality as well as right-wing thought today.

The rise of the novel, as Guido Mazzoni shows in his 2016 book *Theory of the Novel* in great detail, is also bound up with the tension between the social and the individual in the context of capitalism. For this reason, too, attention to the work of the novel is of great importance in the era of the long now, since the novel's history of critically examining individualism and the tension between capitalism and the social assumes renewed significance in our time. In fact, Mazzoni suggests that Western modernity and its increasing fragmentation and individualization that peaks in our historical moment presents a problem of thought that has direct consequences for the development of art in general and the novel in particular. "The consecration of individuals, the right to subjective freedom, and the growth of material wealth accompanying the development of middle-class society produced one of the fundamental turning points in human history," Mazzoni writes, illustrating that this historical development is a central coordinate of the novel's rise.[59] The novel centrally grapples with the fact that, as Mazzoni argues, "Western humanity lives in private little spheres that, for now, are quite protected," spheres within which "individuals seek personal happiness."[60] Through its attention to the rise of individualism and the private sphere that characterizes Western modernity, Mazzoni shows, the novel also continually draws our attention to the disintegration of "collective bonds that is inherent in modern, middle-class individualism." And this disintegration of established collective bonds, Mazzoni argues, is shown to us by the novel as creating a form of presentism in its own right. Ventriloquizing Toqueville, Mazzoni writes: "the thread of time is ever ruptured and the track of generations is blotted out ... those who have gone before are easily forgotten and those who will follow are still completely unknown. Only those nearest to us are of any concern to us."[61] Quoting Raymond Carver, Mazzoni puts the problem more bluntly with regard to our own times: "two things are certain: (1) people no longer care what happens to other people; (2) nothing makes any real difference any longer."[62]

In particular in the present moment, Mazzoni shows, we seem to face a significant contradiction. While on one hand the "importance of individual people increased and collective transcendences were pulverized," on the other hand we face an increase in large, complex systems of mutual dependence and interrelation. "The era in which the absolute value of each individual is affirmed," Mazzoni argues, "has been the same as the period in which there emerged, with absolute clarity, the power of large, impersonal forces—in planetary wars or global economic crises, in the mechanisms of capitalist markets, or in the changes of the *Zeitgeist*."[63] But what appears to us like a contradiction that further complicates the distinction between the individual and the collective, the private and the public, Mazzoni shows, is revealed to us by the novel as inseparable and as always necessarily dialectically connected. In this way, the novel affords us a critical, historical view of this relation. The novel never presents us with a simple choice or distinction between the individual and the collective. Rather, the dialectic of individual and collective, particular and universal, constitutes one of the bases of the novel form, and it illustrates that the novel itself provides us with a form of thought and of critique that is aimed at reading this dialectical tension temporally, historically. This tension, in other words, is a central aspect of the temporality and history of capitalist modernity, as the contradiction itself lends momentum to social, economic, and political relations that the novel seeks to understand. It is in this way, then, that we can begin to see what it means to suggest that the novel is the art form that tells the time of capitalist modernity.

Today, the importance of the novel and the novel's function as a form of thought and of critique can be understood as residing precisely in this aspect of its history. Since its rise, novel has been tracing the relation between the social and the individual. Over the course of the past few decades, it has turned its attention to the rapidly spreading fragmentation of the demos and to its consequences. And, as we will see in the chapters that follow, the novel has for a while now examined the relation between the crisis of temporality that defines our long now and its sociopolitical dimension, including importantly the rise of new forms of nostalgia, of narratives of loss and exhaustion, which play an important role in the development of new forms of social resentment of which the rise of a new extreme Right is the most troubling. We will see, for example, that we find in contemporary novels some of the most striking analyses of the standard rhetorical strategies of the Right today. This includes, for example, the claim that our present is a time of fragmentation that calls for the return to older, more stable, and "pure" notions of identity, which novelists reveal as being directly connected to the crisis of the social and the crisis of temporality that arises from contemporary capitalism. And while all too many of us claim to have been more or less surprised by the return of right-wing extremism in recent years, the next chapters show that novelists have been warning us about this very danger that our time harbors for roughly three decades now. We will see that the novel examines the relation between some of the most dangerous developments in our time, including right-wing extremism, new forms of paternalism and authoritarianism, and the threat of neofascist thought, in close relation to the temporal crisis of our time. Continuing the important work that it has done since its earliest days, the novel provides us with striking insights into the dangers but also the moments of hope that are contained in our long now. It also shows that that we must trace the crisis of futurity and of our imagination today and its associated contradictions like the fragmentation back to its source in capitalism itself. In a time marked by new forms of alienation, exploitation, and disenfranchisement, the novel shows, we must not demand to return to a lost past or to mythical notions of stable and pure identity. Instead, we must demand a better world, we must recover a sense of hope and utopia in the now that is aimed at the abolition of exploitation, alienation, violence, segregation, and the global wars of capital.

Nonsynchronism and the distribution of time

Time, Rita Felski stresses, "is not just a measurement but a metaphor, dense in cultural meanings."[64] As a result, competing conceptions and meanings of time are not just deeply embedded in but also contested on the terrain of culture. Culture, therefore, serves as one of the most important planes of analysis for our understanding of the current crisis of temporality, and it also constitutes a crucial arena for the reconstitution of temporal thought that in turn directly affects social and political debate and action. "Sociologists have long argued that the coordination of temporal rhythms is a particularly powerful technique of social cohesion," argues Caroline Levine.[65] Rhythms, she stresses, can be punishing, and they "can do powerful political work."[66] Rhythms "can produce communal solidarity and bodily pleasure," but they can also "operate as powerful means of control and subjugation."[67] It is for this reason that analyses of the relation between rhythm and time of capitalism and culture, society, and politics assume a particularly important and pressing function in the context of the long now. Judy Wajcman has recently emphasized that the fact that contemporary capitalism leaves us increasingly pressed for time means that this phenomenon should be understood as an "important dimension of social justice and of legitimate political concern."[68] What this means, she proposes, is that "we should be looking at the changing dynamics of the distribution of time."[69] What should be added to this project, I would argue, is an examination of the political consequences of this project. While the basic impulse of a critique of capitalist time may lead to a concern with social justice, it may also be absorbed back into the wellness industry and into other forms of containment and hyper-exploitation. Yet, and this is the topic to which the remainder of this book addresses itself, it can also give rise to what we may call right-wing temporal populism, opportunistic utilization of the temporal contradictions of real-time capitalism in order to strategically fan the flames of discontent while touting reactionary thought and an idealization of the past as a solution to the problems of the present.

Harootunian emphasizes the significance of the rise of archaic forces and ideas in the context of the presentism of our world. What he describes as the "potent mixture of modernity and archaisms" is in his estimation "inaugurated the removal of a conception of the future."[70] "What the current conjunctures disclose," he continues, "is a configuration Edmund Husserl once thought of as a '"thickened' present," a present filled with traces of different moments and temporalities, weighted with sediments."[71] Our present, he concludes, is a time that is "teeming with competing temporalities from the past recalls ... repetitions from other times and places."[72] But while Harootunian is in a sense quite correct to point toward the relation between the rise of archaisms in the present and the gradual erosion of futurity, I would suggest that we can gain a deeper understanding of the relation between archaic desires and forms of thought and the temporal crisis of the long now if we understand the rise in reactionary thought as a symptom of the contradictions of capitalism that create the crisis in our temporal imagination in the first place. That is, instead of counting archaisms among one of many causes for the erosion of the future, we should strive to understand the sources of archaic thought in more detail. This project reveals the double function of the archaic in our time, in particular in the context of right-wing culture and thought. While the reactionary turn to and idealization of the past emerges as a response to the contradictions of contemporary capitalism, it is precisely this most sinister symptom of these contradictions that ultimately serves as one of the strongest safeguards for capitalism today. The chapters that follow will show this in great detail. However, first it is necessary to establish the basic methodological framework and some of the fundamental assumptions of this project. One of the most valuable concepts at our disposal for the analysis of the relation between capitalist crises and reactionary thought is Bloch's notion of nonsynchronism.

Harootunian, too, recognizes the value of Bloch's concept in the context of his analysis. However, Harootunian's account of Bloch's thought is somewhat foreshortened. Harootunian associates Bloch's idea of nonsynchronism with "unevenness with fascism in the Germany of the early 1930s" in the context of which, Harootunian suggests, Bloch "observed, the coexistence of different times" that "reflected the disjuncture between the new and the traditional (city and countryside) and what he described as a subjective "muffled non-desire for the Now."[73] What interests Bloch is the temporal plurality of the present. The present, he argues, is always composed of a variety of competing temporalities. And, it is true, some of these times are related to instances of conflict or disjuncture between the old and the new. It is precisely because the logic of the present may seem alienating, particularly in periods of historical transition, that the rejection of the logic of the now presents itself as a temporal contradiction—Harootunian's "muffled non-desire for the Now." The latter expresses itself in the desire for unstructured time or for other instances of disrupting or temporarily escaping the time of capitalism that structures our lives. However, it can also lead to the perception of standing in a nonsynchronous relation to the now—we may feel as though we are lagging behind. And it is precisely in moments when this feeling of lagging behind, of not quite being able to keep up with the new rhythm of capitalism and with the speed of the present, that projects like that of Massive Change that we encountered in the previous chapter emerge. Massive Change is designed to bring those of us who may be somewhat slow up to speed and into the time of the capitalist present. However, nonsynchronism can also take a range of other forms, Bloch argues. One of these forms, for instance, involves the reactionary attachment to previous moments in history, either by way of nostalgic idealization or by turning toward remnants of prior social, economic, and political structures that continue to exist in the present. The latter form of nonsynchronism, Bloch stresses, contains a particular moment of danger, for it constitutes one of the fundamental aspects of right-wing and fascist thought and culture. We must therefore ask two related questions: in what ways may Bloch's account of nonsynchronism allow us to gain a better understanding of the relation between the rise of a new extreme Right and the temporal contradictions of contemporary capitalism? And how may we understand the role and renewed force of nonsynchronism in a moment that creates a range of problems for thought, culture, and politics precisely by appearing fully synchronous, entirely present, and temporally homogeneous to us?

We may begin this inquiry by reiterating the importance of locating the sources of the current crisis of temporality in capitalism itself. If we understand the problem in this way, then we can examine it as a historical phenomenon that has clearly identifiable sources, and that is but the latest instantiation of a range of large-scale crises in our temporal imagination that occur whenever moments of historical change call into question our established ways of telling and imagining time. Additionally, we are able to restore to the surface the kinds of temporality that stand in contradiction to the time of capital or that the dominant form of temporality seeks to overwrite. This form of temporality, in its simplest terms, is what Bloch has in mind when he tries to understand the now as plural time that, while defined by a dominant sense of temporality, always also contains within it a range of contradictory times—nonsynchronisms. "Not all people exist in the same Now," writes Bloch. "They do so only externally, by virtue of the fact that they may all be seen today," he explains, "but that does not mean that they are living at the same time with others."[74] The sense of feeling out of time in our now, that under certain conditions we do not see ourselves as fully synchronous with the time in which we live, is likely well known to all of us to varying degrees. After all, when can we say that we truly feel synchronous, that we are fully "of the now?" The more substantive versions of nonsynchronism, however, emerge in direct connection to the time of capitalism. "One has one's times according to where one stands corporeally, above all in terms of classes," Bloch writes. We need only look toward the ways in which economic status is temporally coded in our time to get a basic sense of what Bloch has in mind. While the superrich have claimed the future, the majority of the population struggles to keep up with the speed of the contemporary. And, of course, the idea of temporal lag or temporal underdevelopment is a well-established strategy for denying presence to the poor or the postcolonial and the racialized subject—instead of understanding their living conditions and the forms of exploitation and segregation from which they suffer as an integral part of the capitalist present, common dialogue and countless narratives instead code their existence as nonsynchronous, as removed from the present, as past.

Certainly, Bloch suggests, there are simple, personal reasons for the emergence of nonsynchronous relations to the now. "A person who is simply awkward," he writes, "and who for that reason is not up to the demands of his position, is only personally unable to keep up."[75] This form of nonsynchronism, an occasional personal conflict with the now and the connected sense of feeling out of time, is without doubt one of the most common manifestations of the phenomenon, one that expresses itself in a range of longings for previous moments in history that seem to stand opposed to our present as less alienated and more enjoyable. In fact, it is connected to one of the most ubiquitous aspects of contemporary culture, which engages in a frenzied attempt to service the nostalgia industry by producing countless TV programs and movies that showcase life and work in what is portrayed as the simpler, less complex good old times. But there is another sense of nonsynchronism to which Bloch draws our attention. "Times older than the present" continue to affect our now, and in such cases a form of nonsynchronism emerges precisely because "it is easy to return or dream one's way back to older times."[76] It is this sense of the term that contains the substantial value that Bloch's conception of nonsynchronism has for our ability to analyze the culture and politics of our long now. Frederic J. Schwartz in fact argues that Bloch's concept is crucial for our understanding of the value of critical theory and of Left political strategy. Nonsynchronism, Schwartz writes,

> [I]s the concept through which Bloch develops a Marxist theory of the nature of culture under twentieth-century modernity, a theory that allows him to cast considerable light on the reasons for fascism's popular success and socialism's failure in Germany at the same time as he begins to work out a strategy by which the Left might reclaim political ground by cultural means."[77]

Thus, while our analysis must point toward the ubiquity of common forms of nonsynchronism in contemporary culture and popular dialogue, there are also other, decidedly more dangerous forms of nonsynchronism that we must understand. In order to foreground this point, Bloch introduces different conceptions of nonsynchronism: objective and subjective nonsynchronism.

Personal refusal, what Bloch simply describes as a "not wanting of the Now," is a subjectively nonsynchronous relation to the present. However, any worker whose knowledge or skills have been rendered obsolete by a transition in capitalism or by computerization or automation also stands in a nonsynchronous relation to the time of capital—she has fallen behind, capitalism has moved on. In such a case, we are confronted with objective nonsynchronism. Insofar as the present is also characterized by the existence of "outdated" forms of work, of skills that have been rendered obsolete by capitalist innovation, and by forms of social and cultural existence whose value, quite materially and literally, has been canceled out by developments in capitalism, Bloch insists that we must also focus on those aspects of the present, those forms of objective nonsynchronism that are holdovers of previous historical moments or stages in capitalism. In the context of the anxious anticipation of a new wave of automation that threatens to render a wide range of skills, forms of knowledge, and kinds of work valueless, and in the context of the desperate struggle of an entire generation of young people to "future-proof" their skills and knowledge, this point rings particularly true in our historical moment. "The objectively nonsynchronous," Bloch explains, "is that which is far from and alien to the present."[78] It includes both declining remnants as well as aspects of an uncompleted past that have not yet been "sublated" by capitalism. But while the nonsynchronous also contains a particular kind of utopian potential, it also gives rise to dangerous reactionary tendencies. In Bloch's time, this duality of the nonsynchronous found expression in the German peasantry, for instance, who constituted an entire segment of society that saw its former central role in the state radically devalued by developments in capitalism. This group's "untimeliness," Bloch shows, played a crucial role in the rise of German fascism, which understood to take advantage of this form of nonsynchronism that contradicted, in Bloch's terms, "the Now in a very peculiar way … from the rear."[79] Bloch notes with great alarm the power of this form of untimeliness in his own era, and he is especially troubled by the ability of fascists to exploit it. By aiming their rhetoric at those who stand in what he describes as an objective nonsynchronous relation to the now, Bloch argues, fascists were able to exploit the discontent created by the capitalist new and ground their opposition to the present by promising grand returns to the old. "The strength of this untimely course has become evident," Bloch writes with grave concern as he witnesses the rise of German fascism. "It promised nothing less than new life, despite its looking to the old," he notes, observing that "even the masses flock to it since the unbearable Now at least seems different with Hitler, who paints good old things for everyone."[80] Bloch's words of warning with which he concludes this section in his analysis constitute an important warning for us today, and they should also draw our attention to the importance of analyses that examine the relation between capitalism and the rise of the Right on temporal grounds: "there is nothing more unexpected, nothing more dangerous than this power of being at once fiery and puny, contradicting and nonsynchronous."[81]

Subjective and objective nonsynchronisms also operate in unison and are often brought together in right-wing thought. Bloch writes:

> The subjectively nonsynchronous contradiction activates this objectively nonsynchronous one, so that both contradictions come together, the rebelliously distorted one of pent-up anger and the objectively alien one of left-over being and consciousness. Here are elements of the old society and its relative order and fulfillment in the present disorderly society, and the subjectively nonsynchronous contradiction revives these in a way both negatively and positively surprising.[82]

In our moment, the nostalgic appeal of previous social and economic arrangements and to forms of labor that have been or that are in the process of being rendered obsolete (or geographically displaced as part of outsourcing strategies) goes hand in hand with a longing for ideas of identity that are said to have been lost or dismantled in the present. What may begin as subjective nonsynchronism for those who, in Bloch's words, "have been for a long time merely embittered" binds itself to objective nonsynchronism and ultimately expresses itself as "pent-up anger."[83] The countless narratives of the good old times in contemporary culture, for instance, though seemingly benign, in fact fan the flames of the general anger and discontent that emerged out of the widespread, embittered rejection of our now. The problem is exacerbated when subjective nonsynchronism binds itself to objective nonsynchronism. And we do not have to look very hard in our own culture to find clear traces of this connection. For culture not only brings us romanticized images of the good old times and of better ways of life that culture locates in the past, but the better life, and the better way of being (of being a family, of being a man, and so on) is also directly bound up with objective nonsynchronism: with forms of labor that capitalism has left behind. And while our desire to watch the spectacle of old-timey labor on our screens may at its core involve a critique of the capitalist now, it is also easily leveraged by right-wing agitation. In this way, systemic critiques of the capitalist now easily disappear into a concern with identity and pave the way for turning the nonsynchronous contradiction into the past to dangerous longing for lost forms of a better life associated with the myth of national, cultural, or racial purity. Bloch foregrounds the complex interrelation of capitalism, time, culture, and politics in order to illustrate the danger that may lie in the sense of temporal lag, of temporal alienation, of not feeling at home in our time. Fusing subjective and objective nonsynchronism, and capitalizing on the anger and anxiety that the present may produce harbors great danger, Bloch stresses. In the case of German fascism, Bloch stresses, we see that its appeal to nonsynchronisms such as that bound up with the German peasant binds itself to identitarian logic, a connection that gives rise to the logic of "blood and soil." As we will see in detail, this is a strategy that we can once again recognize in right-wing rhetoric, thought, and culture in our time.

Chapters 3 and 4 will show in great detail that while contemporary forms of right-wing thought arise out of and bill themselves as critiques of capitalism, they ultimately function as a protective mechanism for capitalism and serve to veil the contradictions and crises of the now. We can begin to see why this is so through Bloch's analysis of nonsynchronism. Nonsynchronism is a contradiction, Bloch explains, but it is not an actual political, structural contradiction. To be sure, nonsynchronism is a symptom of capitalism, but it ultimately obfuscates the contradictions out of which it emerges. As indicated above, a clear example of this becomes evident in right-wing strategy, which utilizes anti-capitalist energy but then displaces it from a critique of capitalism onto a concern with race, gender, and nation. "The nonsynchronous contradiction is in this way the opposite of a driving, exploding contradiction," Bloch argues, since "it does not stand in the battlefield between proletariat and ... capital."[84] While the nonsynchronous contradiction and its content "broke loose only in the general vicinity of the capitalist antagonisms," it departs from its original source and therefore cannot lead to sustained critique or systemic change.[85] As such, the nonsynchronous contradiction is not aimed at a future politics and cannot lead to the systemic change at which it claims to be aimed. "The nonsynchronous contradiction, as that of merely declining pasts that themselves are not completed," Bloch reiterates, "cannot change into a new quality."[86] The radical claims of the new Right, as we will see, therefore best serve one single goal: the protection of the status quo of the capitalism.

As we saw above in the example of Harootunian's reference to nonsynchronism, engagements with Bloch's idea of nonsynchronism often restrict their account of the concept to its connection to reactionary thought. However, this leaves our understanding of Bloch's thought incomplete, and it also underutilizes his concept. Nonsynchronism, Bloch shows, is not only bound up with reactionary connections to the past—the nonsynchronous contradiction surprises us "both negatively and positively." Instead of reactionary attachments to the past, nonsynchronism can also give rise to very different, positive, and politically progressive results if it is understood differently, namely dialectically. Nonsynchronism, Bloch argues, contains both danger and possibility, and understanding the relation between both sides of this dialectical relation is crucial to our ability to understand some of the root causes of the rise of a new extreme Right today as well as of the challenges and opportunities of our time for utopian thought. Thus, nonsynchronism is not simply a matter of repetition, as Harootunian proposes. While nonsynchronism is connected to the dangers of fascism, it is also connected to a kind of thought that restores our attention to the latent possibilities that lie dormant in the now, and it affords us a different understanding of the past and of its relation to both present and future. Nonsynchronism, Bloch shows, may also provide us with an idea of the past that understands it not as the time of loss, as a time of completion sealed off from the present, but as a time of the incomplete, the foreshortened, and the unfulfilled. The nonsynchronous allows us to understand the past not as the time of what was, but also as the time that contains an archive of that which never was and that which was not allowed to be. The past, in other words, provides us with an archive of unfulfilled dreams and wishes, of unheard appeals, of silenced demands for liberation and for a better world. Understood in this way, the past exerts an important influence on the present, since the present becomes the time that registers that which is missing from our lives. The past provides us with energy for utopian thought, since the unfulfilled dreams of the past demand actualization and realization in the future. The unfulfilled past, which we may trace in what is missing in our present, pushes us toward and demands a better future. In this way, the past serves not just as a vehicle for nostalgia and for right-wing agitation, and it does not function as the untimely telos of reactionary desires that wish to return to the old. Rather, turning toward the past is not simply the sign of reactionary thought or latent fascist forces, but it is also an important way to recover hope and the utopian imagination in a present that seems to foreclose all paths of our imagination and block all paths that may lead to future change. The past, that is, must also be understood as an archive of unfulfilled futurity.

In *Heritage of Our Times*, Bloch argues that nonsynchronism ought not simply be understood as the problem of "a little man who deceives himself." "Besides daybreak produced by musty surroundings," he stresses, nonsynchronism is also bound up with "genuine daybreak."[87] Providing us with an important vocabulary for setting apart the different temporal contradictions of our time, Bloch argues that we should distinguish between our relations to the now that express a temporal relation to and account of the material conditions of the present. "The subjectively nonsynchronous contradiction is pent-up anger," Bloch explains, while "the objectively nonsynchronous one is unsettled past." Connected to this, we should understand the "subjectively synchronous" contradiction as "the proletariat's free revolutionary act," whereas the "objectively synchronous" contradiction should be understood as "the impeded future contained Now."[88] Thompson emphasizes this important aspect of Bloch's work on nonsynchronism that, he argues, models for us a more complex and in times of great danger necessary relation to the past. Thompson draws our attention to Bloch's interest in the German preacher and radical theologian Thomas Müntzer, one of the leaders of the German peasant and plebeian uprising of 1525. What matters for Bloch, and what the example of the peasant uprising illustrates, as Thompson emphasizes, is not its ultimate failure but its untimeliness: the time was not yet right for its success, but the ideas that underpinned the uprising returned and resulted in profound changes to German society at a later point. This example illustrates the dialectical other of the reactionary desires that may emerge from the nonsynchronous. It furthermore foregrounds the importance of the nonsynchronous as a time of possibility, as also pointing toward unfulfilled desires for liberation whose day has not yet arrived. "Rather than reject the failures of the past," Thompson therefore stresses, "we must build on them."[89] "Mankind is not yet finished," Bloch writes in his essay "Dialectics and Hope," and since mankind is not yet finished, "neither is its past."[90] "The past," Bloch insists, "continues to affect us under a different sign, in the drive of its questions, in the experiment of its answers."[91] In this way, the nonsynchronous also establishes a relation to the past that trace is the past the unfulfilled possibilities and demands for liberation that continue to affect the present in their absence. The now is therefore deeply influenced by what is missing, which bears the traces of the past and in this way indicates "the not yet present world." The nonsynchronous contradiction in the now, in other words, also contains within it a crucial aspect of utopian thought understood as "those properties of reality which bear the future."[92]

Bloch now: Tracing hope in a time of crisis

"Not all days sink below the horizon without a trace," writes Bloch in his essay "The Magic Flute and Contemporary Symbols."[93] Especially in times when revolution is in the air, he continues, "people have the unusual ability of wresting ceremonies and symbols from the clutches of obscurantists, and infusing them with revolutionary light."[94] Bloch develops this point through a comparison of the work of Wagner and Mozart. As opposed to the work of Wagner, Mozart's *The Magic Flute* remains significant, Bloch argues, because it deploys symbols "as mirrors of what has not yet come into existence, of that which strives to reach the light."[95] *The Magic Flute* and *Fidelio* continue to be relevant according to Bloch because of their "ongoing call to action, their posing of new problems" which will continue to be so "until the world desired by the revolution (the realm of freedom) comes to pass."[96] And yet, as Bloch's discussion of Wagner and Mozart shows, light and darkness lie closely together in this regard. While moments of upheaval, transition, or historical foreclosure may lead to returns to the past that re-energize projects whose time had not yet come and that endow symbols and ideas with new momentum and significance, these moments can also give way to the dark, dialectical other of this utopian impulse. The activation of past utopian possibility in the present emerges out of the same conditions and has some of the same points of origin as the desire to return to the past and to search for easier life narratives in idealized versions of the lost good old times, thus replacing a utopian anticipation of the future with a reactionary escape from the present. Bloch's thought is of great importance in our moment, therefore, since it is finely attuned to the fact that both possibility and utopian thought as well as the desires and the thought that underpins the rise of a new extreme Right emerge out of the same situation and the same set of impulses—a critique of our capitalist long now.

The first section of Bloch's *Literary Essays*, titled "Estrangements I," also bears a second title: "Janus Portraits." This second title invokes Janus, the god of beginnings, gates, transitions, and time, of passages and endings of ancient Roman myth, who is generally depicted as having two faces: one facing toward the future, one toward the past. Janus is also the god of change, and serves for Bloch as a reminder of the complexities of our engagement with the relation between past and future, of the "Janus-faced" responses that a moment in history may produce. Bloch wishes to foreground those elements of the now that may be understood as giving rise to Janus-faced responses insofar as they carry the potential of creating reaction and regression as well as progressive change and futurity. Bloch understands his own time in precisely such a manner and emphasizes the need to appreciate how closely utopia and fascism (which emerges, Bloch stressed, out of an impoverished utopian impulse in its own right) are related. And while Bloch can therefore provide us with an important analytical approach to the sources of the most recent wave of right-wing extremism, attention to the Janus-faced nature of the long now is also of central importance to our understanding of Left wing thought and politics. After all, it is precisely because the Right knows to use the widespread rejection of the long now to its advantage that it is able to successfully poach disillusioned voters, including potentially Left-leaning voters who demand a politics that addresses the contradictions of contemporary capitalism and who believe to have been politically abandoned. What we need today, in other words, is a thought and politics that not only renews its commitment to the many who suffer most from the contradictions of the long now but that also understands that the inability to provide a sense of futurity to those who are alienated and exploited by contemporary capitalism aids right-wing agitators who usurp the energy of critique and discontent by promising to leave behind the contradictions of the present through a return to the past. The Left today must heed Bloch's words of caution and address itself to the contradictions of the present and reclaim it as a time of critique. The gaze that has been diverted from the crises of capitalism to matters of identity and the lost greatness of a past that never was must be returned to the present and to its origins: a critique of the capitalist long now. In this way, we can also reclaim the past from the Right and foreground it as the time of utopian thought—instead of a lost past, we may understand it as what Bloch calls an "impeded future."[97] Such an understanding of the past, Bloch, proposes, is "the fruit of dialectical knowledge of synchronous contradiction."[98]

They key to this project, Bloch argues, lies in our ability to conceive of the now differently. "The concordances of the genuine now-time refer exclusively in form and content to the future in the past, that which has not become, which is in process," he writes, adding that this conception of now-time makes legible the present as a time defined by "the repressed, the interrupted, the indelible on which we can in one and the same act fall back upon while it reaches forward to us in order to develop in a better way."[99] In particular in a moment when the present is frequently understood as a totalizing time, as a perpetually expanding, uniform sense of temporality to which we are unable to imagine alternatives, an understanding of the present as the time that bears the traces of and that can activate the past is of particular significance. Such a view of the present also replaces the impression of a singular, universal now that results from the fall of communism with a conception of time that we find in the work of contemporary philosophers like Jacques Rancière, whose logic in this instance strikingly recalls that of Bloch. The time after the fall of communism, Rancière writes, "is not the morose, uniform time of those who no longer believe in anything. It is the time of pure, material events, against which belief will be measured for as long as life will sustain it."[100] And it is precisely through such a relation to the present, by addressing ourselves to the material contradictions of the now, that we are able to set apart utopian thought and its dark, stunted other that is associated with the rise of right-wing extremism and the threat of new forms of fascism. After all, fascism, too, proposes to address those aspects of our present that appear to be missing. But fascism does not seek to mobilize the traces of unfulfilled wishes as much as it professes to restore lost values and forms of identity back to life. It promises to return us to a better past to solve the problems of present crises, a present that, we hear so frequently in right-wing discourse, "has gone too far."

Much has been made of the fact that our present without future is also an era in which the zombie genre once again flourishes. But while there is no doubt something zombie-esque about the large-scale return of fascism and the extreme Right, forces that we hoped were dead and gone, contemporary fascism is not a matter of the return of a dead past as much as it pursues a strategy that is contained in all periods of capitalist crisis: it promises to revive something that never existed. In this sense, it is perhaps in the most outlandish cultural engagements with the history and presence of fascism that we find accurate engagements with the logic of fascism's own untimeliness and relation to our present. Timo Vuorensola's movies *Iron Sky* (2012) and *Iron Sky: The Coming Race* (scheduled for release in 2019), for instance, feature space Nazis who have settled on the dark side of the Moon and who have spent the years after the end of World War II preparing for an invasion of Earth in 2018. The movies' blend of history, science fiction, fantasy, and its general anti-realist mixture of historical events, and cartoonish characters and plot poignantly express a crucial aspect of the logical fabric of the new Right and of neofascism. The past is neither a genuine historical referent for the Right nor an object for serious inquiry and analysis. Instead, it serves as a fantasy space for nonsynchronous desires that the Right strategically steers and fuels. The Right promises to deliver a monstrously distorted future that requires the return of a dead past. All that the Right is able to deliver, however, and all that underlies its conception of the past, are empty caskets. The core of fascism's promises and its relation to the past are always empty. And yet, we know that the emptiness of the mythical, constructed past that the Right holds out as a lost version of a better life as well as the emptiness of the Right's promises with regard to addressing the systemic and structural contradictions of capitalism are precisely the point of the underlying strategy. Empty times and spaces are effective spaces for the creation of the fears, fantasies, and hopes that the Right seeks to create. Vague references to a better past ask the audience to fill in the gaps in content and logic with their own nonsynchronous projections, and a rhetoric of broad strokes and of vague slogans, provocations, and propositions replaces clearly articulated programs. The point is not precision or to communicate actual information but to create spaces in which fears and anxieties can play themselves out and which can amplify discontent rather than finding answers to it. The role of nonsynchronous culture is crucial in this context, since fascism must also be understood as a matter of the narrative construction of reality.

The Right promises to return us a past that never was. Capitalist futurists seek to skip over the problems of our present entirely, proposing to leave our planet and promising a fresh start in a different time and place—for those who can afford a future. What is required instead, in such a situation, is a third option, namely a conception of futurity that arises from genuine nowtime, one that emerges through a critical engagement with the present. For Bloch, Cat Moir explains, "the human being, as the form at the front of the material world process, is capable of grasping a tendency latent within matter itself toward the realization of a radically new, simultaneously emancipated and redeemed world."[101] As such, she concludes, "educated hope is the proper attitude toward a future which is potentially (utopically) immanent in the world."[102] But we must remember that hope or Bloch's notion of latency, possibility, and utopian thought is not a simple antidote to the threat of fascism. We must remember that hope is not confidence, Bloch stresses, but that "hope is critical and can be disappointed."[103] Hope, Bloch writes, emerges not in isolation from but out of the dialectical negation of moments of danger: hope "is surrounded by dangers, and it is the consciousness of danger."[104] A focus on the material contradictions of the now can safeguard hope. In this way, the relation between nonsynchronism and objective synchronism may transform into a source of utopian thought, for, as Moir argues, "material possibility ... is located not in an ontology of the being of that which has existed up to now but in the being of that which is not yet."[105] This account of hope and its relation to the material conditions of the present also affords us a better understanding of one of Bloch's most famous concepts: the "not yet." The "not yet," Thompson reminds us, "means not simply that whatever is is not yet present but that it is in becoming, not yet complete or even visible, but all the same present through its absence."[106] It is in this way that we may understand hope, for in hope is the *Vorschein*, the preillumination of a better world. It is formulated out of that which is lacking in the present, the absences and the residues of unfulfilled prior demands that create the hunger for liberation and for the improvement of our world that we call hope. Hope is generative. It is rooted in real conditions and in absences. It is not simply a flight of fancy. Instead, it is born out of our understanding of the world, of history, and of ourselves as unfinished, as in a constant state of becoming. Bloch's system of thought and concepts such as hope and the not yet therefore allow us to appreciate one of the most famous sentences in Honoré de Balzac's work: "hope is a memory that desires."[107]

Bloch's thought also provides us with a system of thought that can make a crucial contribution to current debates surrounding the temporal crises of our time. Blochian thought resides on a decidedly a-linear and multiple understanding of temporality. Time in Bloch is not simply sequential, but it is discontinuous, marked by stops and starts, incompletions, fissures, and by prior ideas and demands that return under new conditions. Understanding the relation between past, present, and future in Blochian terms asks us to trace those instances in which time folds back on itself, revises itself, and generates a present that always bears the traces of a plurality of times and temporal contradictions that in turn constitute the motor of futurity. In addition to providing us with a tool to grasp and address the moments of danger and hope that are contained in our now, Blochian thought constitutes an alternative to the linear, successive imagination of time, change, and progress that is currently experiencing a moment of severe crisis. In particular in the context of the long now, Blochian thought is particularly significant and indeed timely, since, as Thompson foregrounds, it is a system of thought that is directly aimed at the problems that arise from a "closed system," and time and structure "in which everything is always already present."[108] In the context of the long now, Blochian thought gives us a different understanding of our world, one that conceives of the present as an open system that is marked by the anticipation of "the new, the surplus ... that could exist outside the totality."[109] We need Bloch's not yet especially in a time when capitalism convinces us that everything already is. All innovation takes places within the confines of capitalism, capitalism itself is posited as the limit of thought, imagination, and possibility, and we all too frequently hear the same expression of resignation: capitalism may not be perfect, but it is the best system we can imagine. Blochian thought asks us to revisit the lines of possibility that we have abandoned, the attempts at creating better systems that were impossible or that were made impossible under the conditions of their original emergence but that contain possibility for completion in the future. It is often quipped that Marxism is first and foremost a theory of its own failures. In a Blochian sense, this observation is quite correct, for it is precisely through the engagement with failures that demand the rearticulation of thought and practice with an eye on the process of history, Bloch shows us, that better answers may emerge. As Bloch suggests in *Tendenz-Latenz-Utopie*: "the Real in and around us has in, as well as before it, the surplus of enormous possibility above and beyond the given ... This is a new transcendence, namely: into an Immanence which has not yet become."[110]

The untimeliness of Bloch: Utopian thought and critical theory

We are not hard pressed to find expressions of a belief in utopian thought that bear a stark resemblance to Blochian thought in Bloch's own time. Jean-Paul Sartre, for instance, in a brief essay on William Faulkner's novel *The Sound and the Fury* (1929), suggests that "Man is not the sum of what he has, but the totality of what he does not yet have, of what he could have."[111] Sartre concludes his examination of this account of futurity with a question that could serve in the era of the long now as a slogan that cuts through the purported omnipresence of the capitalist now that makes impossible any account of the future and that illustrates the importance of Blochian thought today: "if we are thus immersed in the future, is not the irrational brutality of the present diminished?"[112] And yet, the relationship between Bloch's work and the development of political philosophy in general and that of critical theory in particular remains notably underexplored. Max Blechman argues, for instance, that "the importance of Ernst Bloch's thought for Adorno has received very little attention in English criticism."[113] One small exception that indicates both the significance of Bloch's work for Adorno's thought and the absence of fully developed accounts of this relation is a brief mention in the Susan Buck-Morss's *The Origin of Negative Dialectics*: "reading the nonidentity of the particular as a promise of utopia was an idea that Adorno took from Ernst Bloch."[114] Adorno himself, however, assigns a crucially important role to Bloch's work for the development of his own thought. Bloch's *The Spirit of Utopia*, Adorno writes, a book which he understands as "bearing all his later work within it," exerted a particular strong influence on him.[115] "I do not believe I have ever written anything without reference to it, either implicit or explicit," Adorno concludes.[116]

S. D. Chrostowska argues that the Blochian utopian imagination is of crucial importance for the development of the work of both Adorno and Horkeimer. One of the most famous lines in their *Dialectic of Enlightenment* that describes the project of the book and of critical theory as Adorno and Horkheimer envision it indicates just this: "what is at stake is not the conservation of the past but the redemption of past hopes."¹¹⁷ What is necessary today is not the fight for the preservation of monuments to a past that was but the fight for the fulfillment of past hopes and of demands for liberation that history silenced but that demand to be realized. In a conversation with Bloch in 1964, Adorno argues that, "whatever utopia is, whatever can be imagined as utopia ... is the transformation of the totality."¹¹⁸ "It seems to me," he elaborates, "that what people have lost subjectively in regard to consciousness is very simply the capability to imagine the totality [of human relations as well as categories] as something that could be completely different."¹¹⁹ Adorno here follows the model of utopian thought that Bloch outlines for us, as we saw above, according central importance to the relation between past and present that focuses on what is missing. Adorno's account of the "awakening" of thought, Chrostowska shows, relies on remembrance, for thought in Adorno's work "is to be roused by a *Lücke* (gap) in memory, by something missing from it."¹²⁰ "Thought waits to be woken one day by the memory [*Erinnerung*] of what has been missed, and to be transformed into teaching," we read in *Minima Moralia*.¹²¹ Thought in Adorno's work "'waits', slumbering, devoid of the desire called utopia," Chrostowska writes, "and what it waits for is the past (that part of it since gone missing)."¹²² And like Bloch, Adorno does not search for "time regained" but for "time redeemed."¹²³ Moir argues that Bloch's reformulation of Hegel's concept of nonidentity is a direct influence on Adorno's work, which becomes visible in the reliance of Bloch's reformulation of Hegel and of Adorno's dialectical thought on the notion of lack or absence. Bloch, Moir argues, conceives of material reality as defined by a "radical openness and incompletion," by "that which is missing."¹²⁴ In fact, Moir shows, the "whole" can according to Bloch only be thought from the perspective of this "hole," which he describes as the "darkness of the lived moment."¹²⁵ What we see here once more, it should be added, is the great value of Blochian thought in the context of the temporal crisis of our present, since it illustrates to us a radical alternative to the idea of a foreclosed presence by illustrating the dialectical function of the darkness of the lived moment in utopian thought itself. Bloch's account of the "radical incompleteness and openness of the world toward an as yet indeterminate future," Moir stresses, constitutes also one of the fundamental aspects of Adorno's thought, in particular of negative dialectics, which is aimed at identifying "real contradictions in the world which are not yet dialectically resolved."[126]

There is, in other words, much more work to be done with regard to our understanding of the profound contribution to Bloch's work has made to the development of critical theory than I can do here. More generally, however, we must also foreground the dearth of engagements with Bloch's work in the North American academy and in the Anglophone academy. Bloch's work certainly did not experience a soft landing in North America. Zipes reminds us, for instance, that Bloch's *Principle of Hope* was greeted with harsh criticism. Before the backdrop of Stalinism, Bloch's embrace of hope and his argument for the importance of socialism as the political system that can make possible an understanding of the world that is aimed at resolving the present's contradictions and thus always conceiving of itself as a system of becoming was derided as "obscene."[127] Utopian thought, hope, and engagements with communism and socialism certainly do not have an easy time today either, in particular since the fall of communism is often understood as a sign of the historical illegitimacy and of the social, political, and economic failure of these alternatives to capitalism. But the fall of communism also further compounds the temporal exhaustion that accompanies the present, and thus hope faces a particularly notable crisis in our time. Hope today may not only seem obscene, it seems utterly impossible. To this day, in part due to the problematic original reception of his work in particular in North America, and in part due to the historical context in which Bloch's work was introduced, Zipes shows, "with few exceptions, Bloch has not been taken seriously by American philosophers."[128] He certainly has not received the serious treatment that the work of Adorno, Max Horkheimer, Herbert Marcuse, and Walter Benjamin have received in the North American academy, Zipes adds. The history of Bloch's reception, in particular understood in relation to Bloch's thought, Zipes suggests, leaves us to suspect that Bloch may have been a "nonsynchronous" philosopher in his own times.[129]

The lack of serious engagements with Bloch's work is a continued lament on part of those who have studied Bloch closely. Frederic J. Schwartz argues that *Heritage of Our Times*, to which I will return in some detail in the pages that follow, has to this day "not received the renown or reputation that it certainly merits."[130] This is particularly striking, Schwartz, argues, since "in contrast to the abundant attention paid to Walter Benjamin's relatively rare and occasionally oblique references to National Socialism and Siegfried Kracauer's approach to fascism through Weimar mass culture, scant notice has been taken of Bloch's ambitious work on the topic."[131] Schwartz's conclusion resonates with that of Jack Zipes: "the book appeared, we might think, too early to be part of a distanced debate over the problems of Nazism and culture; the time for reflection had not yet arrived."[132] Anson Rabinbach likewise considers *Heritage* an untimely book, arguing that the initial "raking over" that Bloch's book received by the American left is a testament to the Left's continued inability to come to term with fascism.[133] Bloch's work, he suspects, may be of better use in a different time.

In their introduction to their 2013 collection of essays that seeks to address this gap in scholarship and that aims to make a case for the value of Blochian thought in the context of analyses of contemporary capitalism, Thompson and Slavoj Žižek also find that the untimeliness of Bloch's reception is particularly striking. And yet, they argue, this may be an indication of the need to revisit Bloch. "Bloch is under-examined," they write, "and he seems non-synchronous insofar as he may be more applicable to our time than his."[134] Is this, then, a sign that the time, our time, is finally right for Blochian thought? I do not claim to be able to provide conclusive answers here or to be able to settle this debate, but, from the standpoint of the analysis that this book forwards, I very much believe that this is the case, that we are finding ourselves in a moment in time that benefits greatly from Blochian analysis and from an engagement with the past and the present that is focused on what is missing in order to provide answers to some of the most pressing social and political problems of our time. And, as it turns out, part of what is missing and what may be reactivated in the present in order to produce new forms of futurity is the work of Bloch. "We may disagree with many points made by Bloch," Thompson and Žižek conclude, "but," they add, "he is one of the rare figures of whom we can say: fundamentally, with regard to what really matters, he was right, he remains our contemporary, and maybe he belongs even more to our time than his own."[135] Ernst Bloch died in Tübingen, not far from my hometown, just a few days before I was born. And yet, as I read his work and examine my time through his ideas, his thought seems fresher and timelier than my own. In a very personal way, therefore, this book is my attempt to catch up with Bloch, to let him guide me into the future by helping me dream of a better world.

3

The New Paternalism: Anti-Capitalism and Right-Wing Nostalgia

Daddy is home. And he is mad about postmodernism. And about cultural Marxism. In recent years, Canadian psychology professor Jordan Peterson has found fame outside of academia, having become one of the most well-known and widely discussed right-wing YouTube personalities. *The New York Times* calls Peterson "the custodian of the patriarchy" and notes the ease and effectiveness with which he flatters the egos of angry young men, holding out the 1950s as the model for a better, more rational and reasonable time, a time in which women listened and behaved and in which there were only two genders.[136] "The messages he delivers," Nellie Bowles writes, "range from hoary self-help empowerment talk (clean your room, stand up straight) to the more retrograde and political (a society run as a patriarchy makes sense and stems mostly from men's competence; the notion of white privilege is a farce)." Bowles labels him both a "thought leader" and a "mystical father figure" who functions as "the stately looking, pedigreed voice for a group of culture warriors who are working diligently to undermine mainstream and liberal efforts to promote equality." Peterson's mystical appeal, Bowles senses, seems to lie in the particular way in which his ideas work. Peterson does not deal in new ideas. Rather, he reaches young men by helping them recover old, forgotten knowledge. "He is bringing them knowledge, yes," Bowles writes, "but it is knowledge that they already know and feel in their bones." Very much in keeping with his academic background, which involves a keen interest in C. G. Jung and myth, Peterson preaches what he casts as "ancient wisdom, delivered through religious allegories and fairy tales which contain truth, he says, that modern society has forgotten." Peterson bills himself as a paternal defender of young men, and stresses that his role is an important once because contemporary society is characterized by a backlash against masculinity.

As *BBC News* finds in a profile on Peterson, one of his standard arguments bemoans the damaging effect of the, on his account, widespread assumption that "there is something toxic about masculinity."[137] Simplifying and falsifying the critique of toxic masculinity in order to represent it as a general vilification of masculinity tout court, Peterson understands to foster a self-understanding of his attentive audience that revolves around the notion that white young men are the victims of our moment in history. Strategies such as this one underscore his role as the protective father of a generation of men under attack, a father who seeks to reintroduce rational rules and social norms that may once again guide young men into an easily understandable future. The chaos of contemporary society, Peterson claims, robs young men of a future to which they have a right, a future that can once again be guaranteed by the return to the past and by reviving a better time for men. On this journey toward the past, young men must be led by father figures like Peterson. And while Peterson markets himself as the last bastion of rational thought and common sense in a time and world that "has gone too far," the mysticism and the myth-heavy logic of the image and the narratives that surround him are bound up with some of the most dangerous aspects of the new forms of right-wing thought that emerge in the context of the long now. After all, Bloch argues, the expression "once upon a time" is a troubling, a treacherous one, for "no fairytale begins with this, only a myth."[138]

Bloch provides us with an important analytical basis for such reactionary responses to the present that aim to return to paternalistic narratives. Such forms of backward orientation, Bloch shows, emerge in the context of a troubled present that is understood as volatile and chaotic, and they are a clear expression of what Bloch describes as nonsynchronism. "Youth which is not in step with the barren Now," Bloch writes in *Heritage of Our Times*, "more easily goes back than passes through the today in order to reach the tomorrow."[139] The desire to look toward the past for easy answers, to project onto the past images of an idealized society that was built on now lost forms of order and easily attainable life narratives, images of the good, old simple life, Bloch stresses, is bound up with a dangerous longing for leadership and paternalism. "If boys recover bow and arrow, young lads easily join movements, and thereby seek friends and above all a father, who was often not their natural one," Bloch writes.[140] Of course, what Bloch has in mind here is the lure of paternalism and of the past that he identifies as a key characteristic of the rise of German fascism. However, Bloch's analysis of the conditions that enabled the rise of fascism in Germany provide us with lessons for our present, since we can identify similar preconditions for the rise of a new extreme Right to which Bloch's work alerts us in our moment, and we can also see that the contemporary Right relies on strategies that are well-established aspects of fascism's logical and rhetorical repertoire. The rise of fascism, Bloch shows, is intimately connected to romanticized narratives of paternalism and paternalistic authority, which flourish in a present that is perceived as chaotic and unstable. And, as we have seen in the previous chapters, this situation is in our moment exacerbated by the perceived foreclosure of the now, by the purported lack of futurity that the Right enlists in its effort to convince young men that the only way forward lies in a return to the past. We can also see here one central example of the proximity of light and darkness in moments of historical danger like ours, a moment when the inescapability of the long now calls for the engagement with unfulfilled desires for liberation in the past that harbor the utopian impulse that points the way to the future while also containing the risk for reactionary idealizations of the past. "The foundation of the nonsynchronous contradiction," Bloch writes, "is the unfulfilled fairytale of the good old times, the unsolved myth of dark ancient being or of nature."[141] And in particular when those figures who bill themselves as the new fathers of a generation in need of leaders represent themselves as the defenders of rational thought and of traditional values and morals, we must, Bloch argues, be especially weary of the "quiet book," of those parts of culture that praise the "moral discipline of our fathers."[142] For such culture, Bloch stresses, was in his own time followed by the "goose-step parades of Potsdam."[143]

Bloch teaches us that it is of crucial importance to understand the origins of right-wing thought and of the desires that underlie it. For these desires, he suggests, may contain something that is worth rescuing. Precisely because fascism emerges from the same material contradictions that under different conditions may give rise to utopian thought and progressive movements, Bloch maintains a sense of hope in the possibility to return to this origin and explore a different path. Such a project begins by trying to get a better sense of the historical causes of the forms of resentment that make young white men an easy target for right-wing populist rhetoric and agitation. How, for instance, may we understand the underlying logic of the resurrection of terms like postmodernism by the contemporary extreme Right?

Why anti-postmodernism now? Angry young men and the desire for fathers

Until recently, no one really seemed to care very much about postmodernism any more. If critics and philosophers discussed postmodernism over the past decade or two, it was largely in the context of trying to determine how we should describe its aftermath.[144] After all, already in the 1990s, critics, writers, and philosophers began to declare postmodernism's death.[145] Peaking in the 1960s and 1970s, the decades usually associated with high postmodernism, the term itself was never truly available to us as a precise, stable concept. Although there exist a variety of widely influential accounts of the term itself and of postmodernism as a historical period,[146] and while there certainly exist some common ground and generally accepted definitions of key aspects of the term, postmodernism functioned conceptually in a way that could possibly best be described as a *Kampfbegriff*, as a term or concept of struggle that was enlisted in and wielded in the context of a variety of cultural, philosophical, and political battles without allowing for a single, unified definition. And yet, those who wielded the term did so based on rigorously developed accounts of what postmodernism was and did. Since the term is first and foremost a periodizing term, that is, a term that articulates a historical transition and seeks to identify a new historical moment; it was deployed in the context of historical analysis. Certainly, since the arrival of the term and of the cultural and philosophical projects that it identified, there have also been those who could not be bothered to explore its fascinatingly rich tradition and valences in the realms of art, thought, and politics. Rather than developing rigorous critiques of postmodernism, such as the ones that in fact gave us some of the central definitions of the term itself (such as the work of Fredric Jameson), there has been a well-known knee-jerk rejection of the term, which by and large sought to reduce its complexity in order to discredit it. The wide variety of serious engagements with the term stood from the beginning opposed to accounts that reduced postmodernism to a stereotype or cliché: postmodernism was understood as mere relativism, experimental weirdness for the sake of being weird, a simplistic rejection of truth and reality, and so on. But these battles over different accounts of and responses to postmodernism as well as the battles between those who took the term seriously and those who simply wished that it, along with its associated art, politics, and thought, would quickly disappear, were fought several decades ago. In recent years, by contrast, it has been difficult enough to arouse even a modicum of academic and historical interest in the concept among students who encounter it in survey classes on twentieth- and twenty-first-century art and thought. It is a term and a period that must be covered in such surveys, but no student will recognize postmodern novels of the 1960s or postmodern philosophy of the 1970s as aspects of their time, as expressions of their own culture. Postmodernism, it is clear, is an aspect of the past. How, then, do we account for the term's untimely presence in the context of current right-wing populism?

Right-wing provocateurs like Peterson like to use the term as a description of the present, which, to anyone familiar with the term, is cause for some consternation. The Right's attack on the postmodern present strikes us as profoundly untimely and indeed as confusing, since we seem to be refighting a battle of a different time, one that has been transported into our present. But, of course, the untimeliness of the term's usage is not just a matter of conceptual imprecision and lack of information or inattention to what every student understands as a crucial first step for academic writing, namely to clearly define and map the terms and concepts that an essay or any given piece of writing will deploy. Although all the latter points are, of course, correct assessments of Peterson's usage of the term, this long list of problems is ultimately beside the point. The point, rather, is precisely Peterson's untimely usage of the concept, which operates in unison with the larger logical and rhetorical framework of the Right that is at every point aimed at perpetuating and making use of the nonsynchronous. Shuja Haider senses just this when he reconstructs the strange ghostly logic of the term postmodernism in Peterson's Youtube videos and talks. "A specter is haunting North America," Haider writers, "the specter of postmodernism, Or at least, that's what Jordan Peterson would have you believe."[147] But the way in which Peterson connects the term to the present,

Haider shows, is telling. In his bestselling book *12 Rules for Life: An Antidote to Chaos*, Haider writes, Peterson amasses "bootstrapping pablum and folksy anecdotes" that are a typical aspect of what Peterson's book truly is: self-help literature. However, Haider continues, Peterson also advances "a pointed political argument":

> If his readers are struggling, he says, it is because contemporary society has fallen into disorder. In spite of the abundance and comfort offered by capitalist innovation, we have abandoned the stability of traditional society, one in which the fittest among us held power and resources, in which consensus was self-evident, and in which, to paraphrase a slogan beloved among the alt-right, there were only two genders. But things have fallen apart. To invoke a cliché, which Peterson does not hesitate to do, the center cannot hold. This, he says, is the result of an idea. That idea is postmodernism.

In other words, *12 Rules* illustrates that Peterson is utterly uninterested in the actual meaning of the term postmodernism or in its complex history. The point is not to get the term right or to add anything meaningful to our understanding of it. The point is instead to strategically deploy the most stereotypical versions of the term that emerged decades ago in anti-intellectual positions on postmodernism that refused to engage with the term academically and instead reduced it to ideas of pure relativism, characterizing postmodern accounts of the political and philosophical stakes of ideas like pluralism, diversity and play are mere code words for chaos and disorder. Borrowed from the past, dissociated from its original content, and redefined in order to describe a distorted vision of the present, the untimeliness of postmodernism is a prime example of the nonsynchronous logic of contemporary right-wing thought.

And yet, we must ask, how is it possible that the term can assume a new life and meaning in the present? Peterson's references to postmodernism invoke some of the most well-known reactionary responses that the term has generated over the decades that saw the rise of postmodernism. What is it that causes young men in 2018 to understand their own moment in time through the idea of a concept and its attendant battles that were fought and that ended decades before their time? What is it that makes young men once again turn toward paternalism and claim the need to fight postmodernism, assuming the very position that in the standard texts of the postmodern canon is associated with old white men who hinder the efforts of the young generation to create a new, a better world? Why, in short, are young men today fighting the battles of the old men of a previous generation?

"And these children that you spit on/As they try to change their worlds/Are immune to your consultations," David Bowie writes in 1971, for, as Bowie saw it, "They're quite aware of what they're going through": "Changes." The 1970s, the height of literary postmodernism, saw the publication of novels like Donald Barthelme's *The Dead Father* (1975), which allegorize a time of transition in history when the repressive fathers of old, whose terrible history of war and capitalist exploitation weighs on and limits the freedom and future possibility of young people, are dying. The symbol of the paternalism of old in the novel is a gigantic Dead Father, dead but not yet dead, whom a group of young people accompany to his grave. Out of touch with the times, out of touch with the demands for liberation and for the possibility of a new world and a new generation, the Dead Father rages against the dying of his era. But, it is clear, death is inevitable for him. The novel ends with his burial. Much postmodern fiction deals with the idea that anti-paternalism promises young people freedom: freedom from the rules of the paternalistic structures of the world of their forefathers and from the history of repression with which old paternalism was associated. Novels like that of Barthelme express a desire for liberation from paternalistic laws and rules that underpinned the darkest and most violent excesses of modernity. The anti-paternalist aspect of postmodernism was a central aspect of its historical project, and it was bound up with the joyous anticipation of the possibility of a different world beyond the world of the old fathers that seemed to be coming to an end.

Kurt Vonnegut's *Breakfast of Champions* (1973), for example, begins with a sentence that is emblematic of this key aspect of literary postmodernism: "this is a tale of a meeting of two lonesome, skinny, fairly old white men on a planet which was dying fast."[148] But the dying of old white men and the end of their world is not cause for great sadness in the novel. Instead, the novel is defined by a longing for the apocalypse that will erase the old and make room for the new. The novel humorously, though not without a sense of political consequence, reflects back upon the mistakes that cause the world's impending death, prompting Kilgore Trout to suggest that "humanity deserved to die horribly, since it had behaved so cruelly and wastefully on a planet so sweet."[149] Barthelme's *The Dead Father* echoes this need for the departure from the old and the benefits of the death of old men. While the Dead Father still clings to the hope that his journey will lead him to the possibility of revival, to the group of young people who carry his body it is clear that this mythical reviving of the father will not and in fact must not occur. A section of the novel entitled "A Manual for Sons" leaves no doubt that it is imperative to fight the temptation to find a new father:

> Do you really want to find this father? What if, when you find him, he speaks to you in the same tone he used before he lost himself? Will he again place nails in your mother, in her elbows and back of her knee? Remember the javelin. Have you any reason to believe that it will not, once again, flash through the seven-o'clock-in-the-evening air? What we are attempting to determine is simple: Under which conditions do you wish to live? ... Ignore that empty chair at the head of the table. Give thanks.[150]

The father narrative, as this section insists, cannot be reformed. It will always remain connected to the same logic and the same forms of violence that characterized its past. Repression and violence, in this case directed against women, are not malfunctions of the paternalistic system, Barthelme's novel argues, but rather constitute its fundamental basis. This conclusion regarding paternalistic systems in essence sums up one of the basic tenets of postmodern philosophy: the father narrative must be abolished in a revolutionary act in order to make possible the thought of future liberation from repression. And so, at the end of the group's journey, standing by the side of the grave that the group has dug for him, the Dead Father begins to realize that he will not be revived.

Barthelme's novel ends with the Dead Father desperately pleading for "one moment more" while the bulldozers that will fill in his grave approach.[151] The young people in Barthelme's novel know very well that the way to the future cannot lie in the revival of paternalism, and they know that they must not give in to the Dead Father's pleading for more time. In our moment, however, it seems that young men are willing to grant paternalism's wishes and have lost the insight of the generation of their parents and indeed grandparents who understood very well the risks of doing so. In the 1970s, postmodernism's anti-Oedipalism was a crucial aspect of a young generation's demand for the future, which necessarily involved a departure from the structures of paternalism that had proven themselves to undergird some of the darkest and most horrific excesses of humanity. Today, however, we witness the emergence of a group of young men who consider postmodernism and anti-paternalism the very obstacle to their freedom, and this aspect of contemporary culture is marked by the replacement of postmodernism's joyful accounts of paternalism's death with mournful representations of a world thrown into chaos whose symbol is the absent or weakened father struggling to protect his family from danger.

Italian novelist Elena Ferrante observes this development in our time with grave concern. "I greatly fear the generations who don't proudly leave their parents behind," she writes.[152] "But," she continues:

> I'm also frightened by those who, at 20, leave their parents behind to embrace the mores of grandparents and great-grandparents. I don't understand the young people who would replace the world of today with a golden age when everyone knew their place, that is, in an order based on sexist and racist hierarchies. Sometimes, especially when they declare themselves fascists, they don't even seem like young people, and I tend to treat them even more harshly than the old people who inspired them.

"Dreaming of a return to the past is a denial of youth," she concludes. Looking at her own children, however, Ferrante is filled with hope. "Not a day goes by when they don't tell me, more or less subtly, that I belong to the past," she explains, "not a day goes by when they don't point out that what I say is banal and out of touch with the present, which is their area of expertise." And this is precisely what ought to happen, Ferrante stresses, because young people should "fight to give their time a new form and demand a better life for the entire human race." Ferrante here provides us with an important guideline for dealing with the work of right-wing provocateurs and charlatans like Peterson.

In his examination of Peterson's work, Houman Barekat is struck by the fact that *12 Rules for Life* is not in fact "especially interesting."[153] After closely examining Peterson's book, Barekat finds that it mainly consists of

> a mishmash of sensible but unremarkable observations about the importance of standing up to bullies and respecting yourself, interwoven with trite Darwinist generalizations about the tendency of human society to replicate the brutal hierarchies of the animal kingdom, and a few tidbits of received right-wing wisdom.

How, he is left wondering, "does such banal material wind up at the top of the best-seller charts?" It is true; the sales figures are mind boggling. *The New York Times* reports that, by mid-2018, *12 Rules* has sold 1.1 million copies, and that "thanks to his YouTube channel, he makes more than $80,000 a month just on donations."[154] But precisely because this is so, we must point out the banality, the emptiness, and the vagaries that lie at the heart of self-help literature that seeks to replace critical thought with nostalgia, platitudes, and flattering truisms, with advice that is at the surface aimed at providing easy answers for a chaotic life but that at its heart constitutes a nefarious attempt at fueling dangerous reactionary tendencies. We must call out such banality, and we must be willing to register moments when our own convictions and ideas have turned into banalities that are out of touch with young people, for, as Bloch argues, "banality is the counter-revolution."[155]

The right-wing self-help trend encourages temporal self-diagnosis, and, once routed through the logic of books like Peterson's *12 Rules*, the diagnosis tends to be the same: temporal homelessness. Peterson helps young men make sense of their struggle with the complexities of the present moment. But Peterson is not concerned with structural problems that young people face today, such as the fact that our present in some ways quite literally comes at the expense of the future: we finance our present by forcing young people to borrow against their future, a future that becomes more precarious with every new loan they are forced to take out. But instead of engaging with the substantial systemic problems that leave young people struggling for attainable futures, Peterson's brand of temporal populism is indicative of a general strategy on part of the contemporary Right that encourages nonsynchronism by allowing young men to understand their problems as a result of untimeliness: our world has moved into a chaotic present that leaves no room for those who prefer a world with only two gender, with strong fathers, and simple notions of masculinity. Such a world, this line of argumentation proposes, resides in the past, and it is possible to fix the chaos and disorder of our present by returning to a time when paternalism and masculine rationality provided order and stability. By encouraging temporal homelessness in the now, Peterson amplifies those forms of nonsynchronism that lead to a growing nostalgia for a mythical temporal home in the past. Not surprisingly, none of this is new, Bloch's work shows. It is a crucial strategy of fascism that takes advantage not only of nonsynchronism but that also attaches the logic of the untimely to the logic of masculinity and paternalism. "The taste of this youth," the youth that is backward oriented and that wishes to return to the past rather than taking the more difficult journey into the future, "is very sensitive to well-developed masculine qualities, to strength, openness, decency and purity."[156] And it is the latter qualities that Peterson knows to sell effectively in our time. Thus, in spite of his repeated claim that he is not a right-wing thinker but a classic British liberal, and in spite of his attempt to peddle his right-wing self-help wares as expressions of the kind of rationalism and common sense that we need in our time, it is already at this point quite clear that Peterson takes advantage of some of the most common strategies and logical operations of fascism. Right-wing self-help literature for angry young men, in Bloch's time as in ours, is intellectual and sociopolitical arson, and it is our responsibility to confront its underlying logic, its aims, and its effects if we wish to avoid the spread of its tragic consequences.

Barekat's description of the basic rhetorical strategies of *12 Rules* provides us with a striking example of the link between Peterson's logic and the logic of fascism outlined by Bloch: "masculinist persecution myth? Check. Repeated appeals to Darwinism to justify social hierarchies? Check. A left-wing conspiracy to take over the culture? Check. Romanticization of suffering? Check. Neurotic angst about 'chaos'? Check." The banality and the conspiratorial nature of Peterson's work should disqualify it along with Peterson, since no part of the work meets basic academic standards. Yet, unlike Peterson's other book (on Jung), *12 Rules* is not an academic work, although his followers tend to treat it as such. Instead, it deals knowingly and exclusively in banalities and uncritical exaggerations, and it is precisely this strategy that explains both its project and its success. "Positions assumed have a stronger impact than do teachings," Bloch points out based on his examination of German fascism, adding that "rousing words seem more precise than analytical ones."[157] It is precisely this strategy that Peterson pursues, a strategy that, as for fascists in Bloch's time, aims to drive "youth into past dreams." "Now, when present life has become too unconvincing to whet one's horns on," Bloch writes, "that which had earlier blustered and gushed emptily now stands uninhibitedly apart in the beautiful old."[158] Banality, conspiracy narratives, vagary, and the reduction of analytical complexity in the effort to simplify problems in order to offer simple solutions, these are the strategies that historically characterize fascism and that re-emerge in the contemporary right-wing self-help industry.[159]

One central aspect of this tactic, as indicated above, is the Right's concern with gender and masculinity. In addition to touting paternalism as the necessary corrective to the problems of the present, right-wing agitators like Peterson combine the nonsynchronous aspects of our present with a focus on gender. Put simply, the temporal differences between the present and the lost past appear in Peterson's work as differences between genders. Aside from insisting that "the masculine spirit is under assault," as another *BBC News* story dedicated to his growing influence shows, Peterson also argues that the chaos of the present is related to a problem of gender.[160] In fact, "most of his ideas stem from a gnawing anxiety around gender," concludes Georgina Rannard after having conducted an interview with Peterson. "In Mr. Peterson's world," she elaborates, "order is masculine. Chaos is feminine. And if an overdose of femininity is our new poison, Mr. Peterson knows the cure. Hence his new book's subtitle: 'An Antidote to Chaos.'" The past that harbors lost forms of control, stability and order is the time of masculinity that, on Peterson's account, stands opposed to the chaos and volatility of our feminized present. Young men, this assessment suggests, have not place in such a present, and yet, they hold all of the answers to its problems.

This, then, is the core of Peterson's strategy. He does not actually offer young men a future and solutions to their problems of the present. Rather, he strokes the ego of angry young men by validating and exploiting their belief that history has left behind a better world, one that they still carry within them. The angry young man is therefore left feeling empowered, for he is the key to the restoration of the old that can fix the problems of the new. The solution, in other words, lies not in doing or in becoming but rather quite simply in being—a traditional man. The nonsynchronous contradiction, therefore, becomes precisely the solution that Peterson sells back to those who are happy to see their anger and ultimately themselves validated. We recognize this line of argumentation, of course, in part due to much-publicized remarks by public figures like Donald Trump, whose conclusion from the scandalous confirmation hearing of newly appointed Supreme Court Judge Brett Kavanaugh was that the present is a "difficult" and "scary" time for young men. And, as news outlets the world over reported, Trump further supported the gendered account of the problems of our present by suggesting that our time causes him to be more worried about his sons than about his daughters. The deepest historical irony of this situation possibly lies in the fact that his group of angry young male disciples are in fact in some sense correct. They are indeed victims. Yet, they are not victims of a present that has gone awry. Instead, they are the victims of those who present themselves as their fathers and purport to protect and defend them. For it is those who understand the value and power of the energy associated with the growing nostalgic longing for paternalism, who foster and feed the anger of young men, an anger that they exploit for profit and that they deploy strategically to protect their own interests.[161]

Sentimentalism for men, the musty new scent by contemporary capitalism

How, then do we explain the origins of this anger that creates the impression of a new crisis of masculinity and that gives rise to a new wave of misogyny, xenophobia, and racial hatred? Pankaj Mishra stresses that crises of masculinity are far from rare. Pointing toward the "great terror induced among many men" by the gains of feminists in the late nineteenth century, Mishra argues that "historically privileged men tend to be profoundly disturbed by perceived competition from women, gay people and diverse ethnic and religious groups."[162] The social change that resulted from feminism in the nineteenth century, for instance, created not just a crisis of masculinity but also responses that are all too familiar in our present context: "fears of regression and degeneration, the longing for strict border controls around the definition of gender, as well as race, class and nationality." Mishra traces the crisis of masculinity in our time back to the changes that resulted from the 9/11 attacks, which, she suggests, ushered in "a frenetic pursuit of masculinity [in] public life in the west." Mishra cites *Wall Street Journal* columnist Peggy Noonan, an admirer of Jordan Peterson's, who praises the reemergence of "manly virtues" in the aftermath of the attacks and the return of "masculine men, men who push things and pull things." It is no doubt true, as Mishra shows, that in the context of this development and as a result of the widespread call for a return to "manly virtues" attacks on "women, and feminists in particular, in the west became nearly as fierce as the wars waged abroad to rescue Muslim damsels in distress." However, while the aftermath of the September 11 attacks certainly amplified the call for new forms of traditional and hypermasculinity and fueled the rise of misogyny and violence against women, the origin of the current crisis of masculinity can be traced back to an even earlier period, a transition into a new stage of capitalism that began to reach dominance in the 1980s. Novelists have been grappling with just this relation between a change in capitalism and the emergence of a new crisis of masculinity for a while, and turning to some of these novel will aid us in making sense of the complex underlying sources of current forms of resentment and of the fears and anxieties that opportunistic right-wing salesmen like Peterson exploit.

To reconstruct this development, it is helpful to return to the 1980s. John Cheever's last novel, *Oh What a Paradise It Seems* (1982), is often read as a minor novel in his *oeuvre*. The "late style" of Cheever's novel, however, may also be read historically, as an expression of a historical transition and of the connected sociocultural changes with which the novel's protagonist grapples.[163] The nostalgic opening lines of *Paradise* also introduce something more than lateness: a sense of the emergence of a new form of the sentimental novel. *Paradise* is more than Cheever's last novel, therefore. It marks both an ending and a new beginning, and it gives voice to the sentimentalism and the confusions about gender and masculinity that attend this moment of historical transition. This, while the novel's first line suggests a modest project for the novel ("This is a story to be read in bed in an old house on a rainy night"[164]), *Paradise* is about much more than that. It is a novel about the 1980s as an important moment of change in American culture. The novel's nostalgia for a world that is in the process of passing is complicated by its attempt to engage with the temporal complexity of responses to the newly emerging world. The naïveté of its aging protagonist Lemuel Sears's observations, for instance, give voice to the concerns and untimely observations of a kind of man who believes to have been left behind by the flow of history and who struggles with the temporal disjoint between himself and the new world. Sears continually finds himself simultaneously in and out of time, alienated from his present due to its transformation and utterly aware of the nature of the transformation itself and of its consequences:

> The fact that the firm Sears worked for manufactured intrusion systems for computer containers kept him continuously exposed to the computer memory with its supernatural command of facts and its supernatural lack of discernment, and this may have heightened his concern with sentimental matters.[165]

The new age in which Sears finds himself and that he examines with all the wonder and alienation of a time traveler is a world of digitalization and financialization, of change, complexity, and nonlinearity. "The time in which I'm writing," the narrator of the novel's frame tale tells us, "was a time in our history when the line or queue had been seriously challenged by automation, particularly in banks."[166]

> Customers were urged by newspaper advertisements, television and mailings to make their deposits and withdrawals by inserting cards into responsive machines, but there were still enough men and women who had mislaid their cards or who were so lonely that they liked to smile at a teller to form a friendly line at a bank window.[167]

Sears, however, the narrator knows, is "of that generation who imagined there to be a line at the gates of heaven," and he regards the changing world with a sense of loss and of confusion, which includes a substantial confusion on the level of gender. Thus, the gender confusion of the novel's protagonist is not just the kind of complex engagement with gender and sexuality for which Cheever's novels are famous, but it is directly bound up with a specific moment in history, with the rise of a nonlinear, decentralized, complex world of digitalization and financialization. Connected to this is Sears's fear that he may not only be excluded temporally but also on grounds of his beliefs about gender and sexuality. "When in the movies he saw a man and a woman kiss ardently," the narrator tells us, Sears "would wonder if this was a country which tomorrow or the day after he would be expected to leave."[168]

In Barthelme's *The Dead Father*, the Dead Father's journey to his grave is accompanied by a jubilant procession of young people who understand the death of paternalism and the world with which it was connected as a historically necessary change and as the source of great possibility. Cheever's novel, however, is quite different in this regard. To be sure, it is not simply a conservative novel, a story about a cranky old man narrated from the perspective of a cranky old man. It is, rather, one of the first novels that articulate the return to paternalism historically in relation to the beginning transition into a new logic of material life and a new historical dominant. *Paradise* provides us with an early example of what has become one of the dominant aspects of the general cultural backlash against a transition in capitalism that has become associated with anti-Oedipalism and with feminization, and it is here that we find some of the origins of the currently widespread reactionary, nostalgic desire to return to a paternalistic past. *Paradise* mediates a transition in capitalism that has been widely described as the transition into neoliberalism, as the full embrace of the free market and of unregulated capitalism that we associate with the Reagan and Thatcher era, which was supported by the shift toward finance and digital capitalism. Beginning in the 1980s, we witness the emergence of a backlash against the logic of this new form of capitalism, and in the 1990s and early 2000s we frequently encounter representations of the new material logic of the world that mourns the loss of old versions of linearity, stability, and of paternalistic order while rejecting the complexity, the chaos, and the volatility of life in contemporary capitalism.

A central motif in such novels (and indeed of contemporary culture more generally) is the lost, weakened, or dead father whose absence signals the general loss of stability and the lack of structured "reality" of life in the contemporary capitalist world. For several decades now, novelists have expressed a deep worry that the new structural conditions of our present may cause the return to old narratives of authority, power, control, and paternalism. In the 1990s, Octavia E. Butler's *Parable* novels, for instance, show that a world that is increasingly built upon deregulation, complexity, and instability may cause the fall from grace of the watchwords of progress of previous periods (diversity, difference, and so on, which become directly attached to the perceived chaos of an unstable world). In the place of positive narratives of change and difference, the novels illustrate, we may see the rise of old narratives of paternalism, stability, order, and leadership. As pluralism and diversity become reconfigured as aspects of an unpleasant present (thus no longer denoting progressive change in the future as in the context of postmodern thought and culture), Butler's novels caution us, we may see people turn toward old paternalistic logic in order to recover a sense of stability and identity that the new world seems to threaten. For Bloch, change is a fundamental aspect of utopian thought. "I am. But I do not yet possess myself. Thus we are just becoming," writes Ernst Bloch.[169] "Through this process of becoming, and above all the acceptance that the process of change and becoming is the only unchanging constant in the world," Thompson explains, "we overcome both the objective social and economic barriers to a return to something new and also—and perhaps more important—whatever psychological traumas may be preventing us from letting go of our foundationally static concepts of human existence."[170] But it is precisely in the changed function that the concept of change assumes in our time that, as novels like Butler's *Parable of the Talents* show, some of the most dangerous tendencies of our time emerge. In a moment when capitalism itself is built on the imperative to embrace change, we witness the emergence of a present that is understood as volatile and fragmented, as a time whose seeming opposite lies in the stable structures that paternalism and strong leaders may provide. *Parable of the Talents* is a novel set in a postapocalyptic North America, in a time in which stability and protection are hard to come by and that is defined by chaos and constant change. People deal with this new reality in different ways. Some seek for the protection of walled cities, willingly submitting themselves to the total control of the corporations who own and run these new versions of company towns. Many migrate to the North. Alaska, the novel's protagonist Lauren Olaminah notes, has become the most common destination, having become a "popular dream ... almost heaven" for those who seek to escape chaos and disorder. People "struggled toward it," Lauren explains, "hoping for a still-civilized place of jobs, room to raise children in safety, and a return to the mythical golden-age world of the mid-twentieth century."[171]

Lauren, however, focuses on an intellectual way of dealing with the consequences of the apocalyptic change. She develops a way of reconciling herself with this new reality and to find a way to embrace the inevitability of change. Lauren founds a community, a new religion, called Earthseed, which is built around a central motto: "God is Change." In a book in which Lauren collects the principles that should guide this new utopian community into the future, a book that she calls *The First Book of the Living*, Lauren writes: "All that you touch/You Change./All that you Change/Changes you./The only lasting truth/Is Change./God/Is Change."[172] And yet, while Lauren seems to embrace a form of becoming that bears a striking resemblance to Blochian utopian thought, and while Lauren's new community called Acorn attracts many of those who are fleeing from the violence and exploitation of the postapocalyptic world, Butler's novel also contains a complex set of warnings about this approach in the context of the changing function that the notion of change itself carries out in a chaotic present. Precisely because the new world seems to be a world of change, many, the novel shows, will turn toward authoritarian leaders who promise stability and order. More troublingly perhaps, even the full commitment to change itself, as in Lauren's case, can harbor dangerous tendencies. In a world in which change has become the new norm, Butler's novel cautions us, the concept of change itself assumes a much more complex role than before. It can no longer serve as a simple indicator for progressive or utopian thought, since change itself can become an aspect of domination and alienation.

Butler's novel illustrates the dangers of a world built on change with striking attention to the complex set of troubling responses that such a situation may produce, and she does so in a way that provides us with an important set of insights into the conditions of our present. The apocalyptic change that precedes the events that the novel narrates, we learn, was not an apocalyptic event as we most frequently imagine it. Instead, it was a slow apocalypse, a gradual process of crisis and decline. The apocalypse, "the Pox," as characters in the novel call it, "was caused by accidentally coinciding climatic, economic, and sociological crises." Lauren's partner Bankole remarks that:

> The Pox was caused by our own refusal to deal with obvious problems in those areas. We caused the problems: then we sat and watched as they grew into crises. I have heard people deny this, but I was born in the 1970s ….I watched education become more a privilege of the rich than the basic necessity that it must be if civilized society is to survive. I have watched as convenience, profit, and inertia caused greater and more dangerous environmental degradation. I have watched poverty, hunger, and disease become inevitable for more and more people. Overall, the Pox has had the effect of an installment-plan World War III.[173]

The sociopolitical consequence of the Pox is a general yearning for paternalistic protection and past forms of order that Texas Senator Andrew Steele Jarret knows to use to his advantage in his bid for the presidency. "Jarret insists on being a throwback to some earlier, 'simpler' time." Lauren notes. "*Now* does not suit him. Religious tolerance does not suit him. The current state of the country does not suit him," she explains, adding with grave concern and a sense of foreboding doom that anticipates the horrific authoritarian rule the Jarret institutes after being elected president:

> He wants to take us all back to some magical time when everyone believed in the same God, worshipped him in the same way, and understood that their safety in the universe depended on completing the same religious rituals and stomping anyone who was different.[174]

But while Jarret and his party, Christian America, using the same slogan that 20 years later would stand at the center of Trumpian politics, promise to "Make American Great Again," Lauren knows that the past that Jarret describes is nothing more than a fiction that Jarret wields as a strategic tool: "there was never such a time in this country."[175] The force of Jarret's political project is that he is aware of the ways in which he can take advantage of the widespread existential anxiety that is created out of chaos and change itself. To Lauren his project clearly appears to be founded upon repression and exclusion, resurrecting a centralized father-God to whose law everyone is subjected. She understands that this project stands in polar opposition to the celebration of difference, of change, instead celebrating safety based on structure, order and sameness. Yet, whereas Lauren clearly sees the danger within this desire, the people portrayed in the novel appear to be strongly invested in the idea of forming a stable sense of self and returning to a protected existence. Consequently, Jarret is elected president and soon establishes a theocratic dictatorship and an authoritarian state that seeks to restore order through violent repression, and prison and labor camps, resurrecting the great fascist evils of the twentieth century.

While novelists importantly engage with the emergence of forms of nostalgia for paternalism that seek to trade in our current moment in history for a previous one that, due to its paternalistic organization, is understood as promising control, stability, and that is easier to map and navigate, they also show that historical events like 9/11 further amplify the association of our present with postpaternalism. Not only does capitalism structurally operate on what is perceived to amount to anti-Oedipal logic, but the 9/11 attacks also further amplify the demand for a return to paternalism, which is understood as the idealized source of protection and order. A striking number of representations of the events of 9/11 are therefore also routed through stories of dead or absent fathers or through the stories of fathers (often divorced or single) who desperately attempt to protect their families. Examples of this include the first American novel that engages with the consequences of the 9/11, William Gibson's *Pattern Recognition* (2003), as well as Don DeLillo's *Falling Man* (2007), Ken Kalfus's *A Disorder Peculiar to the Country* (2006), and Jonathan Safran Foer's *Extremely Loud and Incredibly Close* (2005).[176] The death of the father marked in postmodernism the potential to open up spaces for the new. The now of contemporary capitalism, however, is perceived as chaotic, disorienting, and unstable that the return to idealized forms of paternalism emerges as way to recover stability, protection, and control. In the absence of being able to locate futurity in a present that has become too complex to imagine and too deregulated to change, the return to a nostalgically idealized, simpler time of paternalism becomes one central aspect of our cultural imaginary. Novelists, however, have dedicated themselves to precisely this problem for a few decades now and have generated a rich archive of critique that is an important resource in our moment. Examples of such novels include the work of Richard Russo, Annie Proulx's *The Shipping News* (2001), John Irving's *Until I Find You* (2005), Jonathan Franzen's *The Corrections* (2001), Geraldine Brooks's historically poignant retelling of Louisa May Alcott's *Little Women* from the perspective of the absent father in *March* (2006), and, more recently, Jonathan Dee's *The Locals* (2017) and the novels of Willy Vlautin.

We may understand the emergence of this return to paternalism as a response to what Jean Comaroff and John L. Comaroff already in 2001 in *Millennial Capitalism and the Culture of Neoliberalism* single out as one particularly salient site for contemporary cultural critique and political theory: "the experiential contradictions at the core of neoliberal capitalism."[177] Since then, this topic has been of great interest to critics. In her 2011 book *Cruel Optimism*, Lauren Berlant shows in great detail that recent changes in the affective and the general epistemological relation to optimism indicate a historical shift in material reality as "the fantasmatic part of the optimism about structural transformation realize[s] less and less traction in the world."[178] Berlant examines the "fraying" of fantasies such as "upward mobility, job security, political and social equality and lively, durable intimacy" in a present in which "the ordinary [has become] a landfill for overwhelming and impending crises of life-building and expectations whose sheer volume so threatens what it has meant to 'have a life' that adjustment seems like an accomplishment."[179] In *The Culture of the New Capitalism*, Richard Sennett makes a similar argument that understands the present stage of capitalism as directly linked to a crisis of established life narratives. However, unlike Berlant, Sennett does not historicize or analyze the nostalgic longings for the past that this condition produces with sufficient attention to their political consequences. Instead, his book is both diagnosis and symptom inasmuch as it is exemplary of those instances in which progressive critiques of neoliberalism, due to their nostalgic response to the present, run the risk of replicating a set of arguments that are also characteristic of reactionary, right-wing rejections of the current stage of capitalism.

Sennett is interested in a historical transition in capitalism that, he argues, coincides with the loss of viable life narratives. What he terms "the new capitalism" brings about a new economic and sociopolitical reality that, he argues, paradoxically grants the wishes of the countercultural movements of the 1960s. We encounter similar propositions in works like Franco Berardi's *The Uprising*, in which he argues that "today's neoliberal conformists are the perverted heirs of '68."[180] When Berardi and Sennett argue that our present is a moment when "history has granted the New Left its wish" albeit "in a perverse form," they point toward the problem that we have begun to see above: the watchwords of previous forms of cultural and political revolt—difference, pluralism, anti-paternalism—today describe the economic logic of the current stage of capitalism.[181] The goals of the radicals of the 1960s have aligned themselves with those of the "rulers [of] today," Sennett argues, and "history has granted the New Left its wish in a perverse form."[182] No wonder, then, one might add, that the Left has so far been strikingly unable to engage with the relation between the rise of a new Right and new forms of paternalism on one hand and the anti-paternalistic logic of capital on the other. And yet, it is precisely because we may understand the Right's reaction against forms of anti-paternalism, which in particular in the aftermath of the 2008 crash attach themselves to critiques of free market logic and the call for increased regulation, that the Left should heed Bloch's advice to explore those aspects of latent fascist thought that may be rescued, returned to a critique of capital, and thus recovered for progressive politics.

Contemporary capitalism brings with it new forms of alienation, and it profoundly disrupts established forms of social practice and organization. As the logic of capital finally departs from centralization and the paternalistic logic of the Fordist and Taylorist economies of old, and as the complex, decentralized flows of finance capital and the logic of productive instability rise to dominance, even those forms of social arrangements that were previously part and parcel of capitalist regulation—such as paternalism or the nuclear family—are being devalued. And yet, as Sennett's book shows, once the demands for anti-paternalism are indeed being structurally granted by capitalism, we begin to see the rise of a nostalgic attachment to those life narratives that were left behind. How is it possible "to manage short-term relationships, and oneself," Sennett wonders, "while migrating from task to task, job to job, place to place?"[183] Instability weds itself to a critique of capitalism's short-termism in Sennett's analysis, for "if institutions no longer provide a long-term frame," he suggests, then "the individual may have to improvise his or her life-narrative, or even do without any sustained sense of self."[184] The disappearance of stable life narratives unsettles previous forms of teleology and thus results in a crisis of futurity, one that Sennett understands as connected to the loss of established notions of selfhood. Sennett's main concern, thus, is the effect of a large-scale structural transformation on capitalism's social dimension. What we see in Sennett's analysis is not just another facet of the source of some of the most pressing contradictions of contemporary capitalism, such as capitalism's struggle to manage the tensions between its new logic and its social dimension, but also a clear indication of the source of the nostalgia and nonsynchronism that the contemporary Right exploits. It is not surprising, therefore, that in crucial passages of his book, which is clearly a work of Left academic critique, Sennett's observations also bear a striking resemblance to those of Peterson, indicating once more Bloch's point about the value and danger that lies in the fact that both Left critique and utopian thought as well as reactionary response and fascist agitation may emerge out of the same contradictions of capital. "The fragmenting of big institutions," Sennett writes, anticipating current right-wing concerns over the fragmented state of our present, "has left many people's lives in a fragmented state," adding that, "if you are nostalgically minded—and what sensitive soul isn't?—you would find this state of affairs just one more reason for regret."[185]

A range of contemporary novelists explore precisely this relation that Sennett is unable to fully historicize: the emergence of a new form of nostalgia for paternalism in a moment when capitalism transitions to an anti-paternalistic structure, a new logic of capital that Roswitha Scholz strikingly describes "actually existing post-structuralism"[186] Among the most notable of such novels is Jonathan Franzen's *The Corrections*. Franzen's novel begins with a representation of the present as a time of endings marked in particular by the loss of established forms of order. From its beginning, the novel portrays the new moment in history that it seeks to trace as a time that is characterized by "the madness of an autumn prairie cold front coming through. You could feel it: something terrible was going to happen."[187] The autumnal storm brings with it "gust after gust of disorder" that sound the "alarm bell of anxiety" in the house of Alfred, a character whose most prominent attribute is his inability to cope with historical change. Alfred is an old white man fighting for his sanity, a father who is unable to deal with a world that has turned into postpaternalistic chaos in which small, quotidian problems amount to massive experiences of loss and, to Alfred, indicate a large-scale disruption of established power and order: "Alfred's cries of rage on discovering evidence of guerrilla actions—a Nordstrom bag surprised in broad daylight on the basement stairs, nearly precipitating a tumble—were the cries of a government that could no longer govern."[188] Franzen turns to the autumnal storm that is the historical transition of the 1980s to examine the rise to dominance of the present world. The social and political logic of the new stage of capitalism that Franzen's novel explores is at every point bound up with a nostalgic attachment for lost forms of paternalism that replicate the backward orientation in Sennett's work.

The novel's narrative of the loss of previous paternalistic structures is expressed particularly strongly in the story of the takeover of the Midland Pacific Railroad for which Alfred previously worked (and which invokes the same linearity and now outmoded sense of futurity and progress to which Alfred continues to cling but which does not exist in the present). "The Midpac had already repulsed one unwelcome suitor when it came under the acquisitive gaze of Hillard and Chauncy Wroth, fraternal twin brothers from Oak Ridge, Tennessee, who had expanded a family meat-packing business into an empire of the dollar," the reader learns.[189] Over the course of the takeover negotiations with the two brothers, it becomes clear that they, in much the same way as the new world that Alfred now inhabits, have abandoned the family structure and its associated business models in favor of its next historical step: a financial enterprise without paternalistic family ties or values. In fact, the brothers turn this departure from paternalistic logic into a performance of sorts during negotiations, in which they cast this neoliberal gesture as a form of resistance against the limiting and now outdated structures of the previous stage of capitalism. At an earlier exploratory meeting that Alfred attends, Chauncy Wroth insists on addressing the Midpac's CEO as "Dad":

> I'm well aware it don't seem like "fair play" to you, DAD...Well, DAD, why don't you and your lawyers go ahead and have that little chat right now... Gosh, and here Hillard and myself was under the impression, DAD, that you're operating a business, not a charity...This kind of anti-paternalism played well with the railroad's unionized workforce, which after months of arduous negotiations voted to offer the Wroths a package of wage and work-rule concessions worth almost $2—million."[190]

The Wroths purchase the railroad. Subsequently, we learn, "a former Tennessee highway commissioner, Fenton Creel, was hired to merge the railroad with the Arkansas Southern. Creel shut down the Midpac's headquarters in St. Jude, fired or retired a third of its employees, and moved the rest to Little Rock."[191]

The engagement with the present stage of capitalism in *The Corrections* offers an incisive examination of the social and psychological logic associated with the transition into the neoliberal present. Franzen's novel historicizes the ways in which anti-paternalism transitions from a gesture that may signal new and liberating ways of living and also of doing business to the new, more ruthless and more alienating logic of neoliberal capitalism. Meanwhile, Alfred's struggle with items that to him symbolize various aspects of the present illustrates the resulting nostalgic longings for a lost stable, controllable life narratives that the new logic of material reality produces. Alfred's sense of loss of individualism, or, in Sennett's terms, of established narratives of selfhood, emerges particularly memorably in a scene late in the novel in which Alfred struggles with a broken string of Christmas lights:

> It offended his sense of proportion and economy to throw away a ninety-percent serviceable strong of lights. It offended his sense of himself, because he was an individual from an age of individuals, and a string of lights was, like him, an individual thing. No matter how little the thing had cost, to throw it away was to deny its value and, by extension, the value of individuals generally: to willfully designate as trash an object that you

knew wasn't trash ... The circuit was semiparallel in some complex way he didn't see the point of. In the old days, Christmas lights had come in short strings that were wired serially ... He suspected that somewhere, somehow, this new technology was stupid or lazy. Some young engineer had taken a shortcut and failed to anticipate the consequences that he was suffering now. But because he didn't understand the technology, he had no way to know the nature of the failure or take steps to correct it. And so the goddamned lights made a victim of him, and there wasn't a goddamned thing he could do except go out and *spend*.

What we see here is a striking, early example of the backlash against the new logic of our world that have become so prevalent in our time and upon which the Right opportunistically preys. Our new era is perceived as a time of chaos and disorder, a time that victimizes those who remain attached to the old ways, and a time that disrupts established forms of identity. What Franzen's novel illustrates, too, are those relations that are today crucial aspects of the connection between right-wing anti-capitalism (critiques of consumer capitalism, of corporate capitalism, and of global free-market capitalism) and nonsynchronism that gives rise to the new paternalism, and, as we will see in the next chapter, extremist identitarian logic. And yet, the strikingly nuanced and sympathetic portrayal of this historical transition that Franzen's novel offers returns us once more to the important suggestion that right-wing nostalgia and Left critiques of the logic of neoliberalism emerge out of the same contradictions and lie closely together indeed. This realization must therefore commit us to a more substantial version of the call to "work together across political lines" that has become an empty rhetorical move in recent political dialogue and commentary. If the suggestion that it is important to address problems that all sides have in common means anything in our time, in a time when right-wing extremism and fascism once again threaten our societies, then it must mean the common project of a critique of contemporary capitalism that may lead to a better understanding of the contradictions that produce the fears, anxieties, and struggles of which right-wing agitators and demagogues seize hold.

The Corrections is an example of the important function of the novel in this respect. It lays bare the social and cultural pressures that result from neoliberalism's destruction of established social structures. Such critical forms of culture that explore the social contradictions of capital and its political consequences are important, since, as David Harvey and Comaroff and Comaroff show in great detail, neoliberalism is centrally defined by its attempt to stunt established versions of sociability and collectivity by replacing previous forms of individualism that were based on a relation between "me" and "we" with a "radically individuated sense of personhood" that is not defined in relation to social or collective structures but solely in relation to the market and individualized consumption patterns.[192] By engaging with this problem in detail, Franzen's novel is able to show the sources of a form of nostalgia for times in which fathers (in both the familial and the structural sense) created sons as individuals by providing them with a world and with skills that allowed them to make their own, controlled futures. In crucial passages of the novel, Franzen explores the sources of contemporary nonsynchronism in a manner that anticipates the rhetoric of the manipulative right-wing self-help industry:

> You were outfitted as a boy with a will to fix things by yourself and with a respect for individual physical objects, but eventually some of your internal hardware ... became obsolete, and so, even though many other parts of you still functioned well, an argument could be made for junking the whole human machine.[193]

Ultimately, Alfred himself comes to the realization that is so important in our time, the realization that Ferrante urges us all to come to, and the understanding of the relation between past, present, and future that Bloch shows us as one of the most important means of defending society against a new wave of fascism:

> Oh, the myths, the childish optimism, of the fix! The hope that an object might never have to wear out. The dumb faith that there would always be a future in which he, Alfred, would not only be alive but have enough energy to make repairs. The quiet conviction that all his thrift and all his conservator's passion would have a point, later on: that someday he would wake up transformed into a wholly different person with infinite energy and infinite time to attend to all the objects he'd saved, to keep it all working, to keep it all together.[194]

Alfred is aware of the impossibility of returning to past forms of paternalism, and he knows that he must recognize that the futures of the past have died, that history has moved on, and that neither Alfred nor the era of his youth has a place in the present. He is aware of his own conservatism and of the sources of his wishes to preserve the old ways and thereby himself. The future, Franzen's novel shows, lies not in the promise of fathers nor in their continued life but in what Peter Thompson describes as the core of Bloch's notion of utopia. For Bloch, Thompson writes, the process of attaining utopia "is a self-generating one: the process is made by those who are made by the process."[195] Bloch did not see utopia as a "pre-existing programmatic state which had to be reached under wise and all-knowing leadership," Thompson writes, "but as an autopoietic process driven by the labouring, creating and producing human being driven on by their material hunger as well as their dreams of overcoming that hunger." What drives us toward the future is the hunger for change that results from the material contradictions of the present, not paternalistic leadership or the continuation or restoration of the old. Alfred's realization is a sad one, a realization that confirms his untimeliness. But in his realization there is also hope, for what Alfred preserves in his willingness to overcome the urge to protect himself is the core of utopian thought.

It is important, then, to understand this new rise of misogyny not simply as a problem of the Right, as an aberration from an otherwise healthy society. Instead, the current stage of capitalism that operates upon postpaternalistic logic creates attendant social crisis as symptoms of this structural and historical transition, and the new crisis of and nostalgia for masculinity is a widespread aspects of contemporary culture that creates ideal conditions for the rise of right-wing extremism that crucially bills itself as a defender of masculinity and paternalism. The association of the new stage of capitalism and of life in the present with a feminized version of life that comes at the cost of the erasure of paternalistic structures has become a widely adopted narrative in our time, and it forms a crucial logical building block of the underlying criticisms of the present that are frequently invoked in suggestions that our "politically correct age" has "gone too far." This line of logic is particularly dangerous because it transforms a critique of contradictions of the capitalist present into a problem of identity and gender, thus suggesting that it is not capitalism itself that creates a range of pressing social problems but rather a cultural shift toward a "feminized society" that constitutes an attack on paternalism. The answer to the problem thus reframed lies not in the attempt to address the systemic contradictions of capitalism but to wage a cultural war, to defend masculinity, paternalism, tradition, and identity.[196] It is only by replacing a critique of capital with a new culture war that the new paternalism is able to imagine itself as a defense of the present while also assuming the role of historical victim and shrouding the present's pervasive misogyny in tales of resistance against a time of repressive misandry. Our moment in time, therefore, demands Blochian analysis that is able to lay bare this set of problematic relations. For Bloch, the key to our ability to engage with this problem is to understand the relationship between subjective nonsynchronism and the material contradictions of the present. "The *subjectively* non-synchronous element," he writes, "appears today as *accumulated rage*."[197] This rage, however, must not just be denounced but also understood through a critical analysis of contemporary capitalism and in relation to "the *objectively* non-synchronous elements," the "continuing influence of older circumstances and forms of production."[198]

The negative experience of neoliberal temporality and immediacy, of the systemic drive toward abstraction and deregulation, and of capitalism's evisceration of established social models and forms of collectivity factors crucially into both Left and Right critiques of the present and attaches itself in both cases to a discourse that revolves around loss and endings. In such a situation, it is not surprising that what is true for culture also holds true for politics. The politics of the present that positions itself against capitalism is often a politics of recovery and restoration that seeks to put back what we have lost—while the Right demands the restoration of paternalism, the liberal Left also frequently argues for a return to regulation, often taking the form of Rooseveltian structures and New Deal politics. Instead of aiming for the radically new, for the better world that may arise from a courageous and committed critique of capitalism, both sides of the argument often collapse into a nostalgic attachment to the past. For Sennett, for example, this backward orientation emerges in the context of his examination of the emotional reactions that different stages of capitalism create. Previous stages in the history of capitalism (Sennett specifically has Fordism/Taylorism in mind) created dread, he argues. The current stage of capitalism, however, creates anxiety. The difference between anxiety and dread expresses for Sennett the different ways of imagining and relating to the form of life that each capitalist system requires: "anxiety attaches to what might happen; dread attaches to what one knows will happen. Anxiety arises in ill-defined conditions, dread when pain or ill fortune is well defined ... Failure in [Fordism and Taylorism] was grounded in dread; failure in the new institution is shaped by anxiety."[199]

While previous stages of capitalism were violently repressive and exploitative in their own right, the experience of the new capitalism nevertheless causes Sennett to suggest that Fordism and Taylorism were in a number of ways preferable. At least, he reasons, these structures were stable, it was possible to map and comprehend them more easily, and it was possible to know our enemy and to subsequently formulate a future politics of resistance. The rejection of the present becomes for Sennett therefore a matter of mourning the loss of a lesser evil and prompts him to reflect on the lost, slightly less alienating structures of Fordism, ultimately focusing on social concerns over a systemic critique of capitalism in similar was as right-wing thought: "in terms of wealth and power, a paternalist like Henry Ford was indeed as unequal to workers on the assembly line as any modern global mogul. In sociological terms, however, he was closer to them, just as the general on the battlefield was connected to his troops."[200] It is precisely in this line of reasoning—which rejects capitalism's deregulated, decentered, unstable, and abstract structure as profoundly alienating in comparison with which the exploitative structures of paternalist Fordism appear preferable—that we can locate an idealization of lost paternalistic structures that dovetails with similar arguments on part of the Right. If there is a father, a centrally located paternalistic structure, Sennett reasons, then a politics of resistance becomes, at least at its core, easier to imagine. We can try to stick it to the man. What happens, however, once capitalism transitions into a postpaternalistic stage and there is structurally no longer a man to whom we can stick it? In Sennett's case, the answer seems to be to wish for the return to previous forms of paternalistic arrangements. It is a politics of the "at least"—at least paternalistic forms of capitalism and social arrangement allowed us to conceive of politics of liberation in ways that appear absent from the present. But while this politics of the "at least" appears to offer a simpler way to imagine Left politics, it also replicates a narrative about our present that ultimately serves right-wing extremism better than Left critique.

Novels like Cormac McCarthy's *The Road* explore just this problem, asking what happens when paternalism, which we treat as the only structure that allows us to stabilize and evaluate life narratives and ourselves, as the way to stabilize our imagination of the future, disappears. In McCarthy's novel, the logic of the postapocalyptic world is defined by the absence of paternalism: "do you think that your fathers are watching? That they weigh you in their ledgerbook? Against what? There is no book and your fathers are dead in the ground."[201] Everywhere, fathers are imagined as under attack, and already in 1995 Fred Pfeil examines the ensuing male hysteria as bound up with the emergence of a myth that is elevated to the status of an actual insight into the logic of our present: the displacement of the white male subject from the center to the periphery of capitalism. Consequently, Pfeil notes with some amusement, "excitable white-guys" appear to "have become the new subaltern subject of post-Fordism."[202] The alleged new subalterity of the white male subject and in particular of the father in general constitutes a dangerous misreading of both the present and the history of capitalism. After all, while the transition in capitalism is coded as a transition away from a masculine and to a feminized world, and while the logic of the new capitalism is represented in particular on the Right as a loss paternalism that novels like McCarthy's interrogate as central aspects of our current cultural and political imagination, this narrative distorts the actual historical relation between capitalism and paternalism. "Under capitalism, real fathers are disempowered; thus capitalism holds out the promise of freedom," writes Klaus Theweleit in *Male Fantasies*.[203] This fundamental relation to a version of antipaternalism upon which capitalism relies, even in its industrial stage, is merely amplified in contemporary capitalism. There is a history of capitalist antipaternalism, in other words, and while our present no doubt marks the highest stage of this aspect of capitalism, it is by no means a new development, and it does not categorically stand opposed to a lost paternalistic past in the way that those like Peterson who hold out a falsified image of the 1950s as the lost good old times of paternalism.

Right-wing agitation, anti-postmodernism, and anti-Marxism

As Corey Robin shows in great detail in *The Reactionary Mind*, the Right has historically been most successful when it has been able to articulate its logic and politics in opposition to a strong Left. Additionally, Robin argues, twentieth-century fascism understood to sell itself as a source of youthful energy, as an alternative to the establishment that could lead the way into the future. In recent years, however, the new Right, and in particular the extreme Right, has struggled to maintain this narrative. As Robin illustrates, Trump himself recognizes this difference in a campaign book in which he declares that "it's not 'morning in America' ... invoking Reagan's famous tag line from 1984" but that we are now "*mourning* for America."²⁰⁴ Although the extreme Right still works hard to establish itself as a new brand of revolutionaries, as rebels who drain swamps and fight back against the politically correct status quo, the fact that their revolution is only able to confront the current crisis of futurity by pointing toward the old and the past undercuts one of its historically most successful tactics and makes even angry young men, as Ferrante observes, appear untimely and grandfatherly. Additionally, the lack of a strong Left in North American politics over the course of the past years has made it increasingly difficult for the Right to portray itself as the noble force that battles against a resurgence of the Left. The Right has therefore tried to find a stand-in for such a strong Left against which it can position itself: postmodernism. But postmodernism makes for a bad understudy for a strong Left. As Bowles argues, Peterson's claim that "Marxism is resurgent" relies for its intended scary effect more on Peterson's own performance than on historically convincing logic—uttering these words, Bowles describes, is accompanied by Peterson "looking ashen and stricken."²⁰⁵ And while there is something desperate and indeed almost amusing about the Right's attacks on postmodernism, a deeper analysis of the role that postmodernism plays in the logical framework of right-wing thought today reveals that even in its current form that lacks the force and coherence of previous historical instantiations the current push toward the right contains great danger. In fact, the rhetoric and underlying logic of demagogues like Peterson is far more dangerous than it claims. Far from expressing traditional common sense or simply espousing views that could be described as classic British liberalism, the Right's attacks on postmodernism lay bare the protofascist sentiments that characterize its logic.

The Right enlists the concept of postmodernism in the fight against change and, as importantly, in order to reconstruct a Left enemy. The way in which agitators like Peterson go about doing this, however, is notably incoherent. The fact that Peterson is anti-Marxist, Barekat suggests, "would be relatively unremarkable were it not for the fact that, in many of his online disquisitions about what he sees as a left-wing takeover of campus culture, he uses the terms 'Marxism' and 'postmodernism' almost interchangeably."[206] Haider likewise notes that "Peterson traces the dangers of postmodernism to a place of ill repute: Paris. In particular, the École Normale Supérieure, a centuries-old university founded to realize the ideals of the Enlightenment."[207] The Parisian university is of interest to Peterson because he claims that it is at this very institution that Jacques Derrida and Michel Foucault created "a school of thought that has now taken over the world."[208] This school of thought is postmodernism and, as Haider recounts, Peterson claims that the "architects of the postmodernist movement" were "avowed Marxists." Anyone with an even cursory knowledge of postmodernism will be struck by the comically uninformed nature of this conflation of postmodernism and Marxism. "Not only are these two schools of thought very different from one another," Barekat argues, "they are also in certain respects mutually antagonistic." After all, some of the central voices of postmodernism were decidedly conservative ones, including Jean François Lyotard whose book *The Postmodern Condition* (1979) is one of the key texts of the postmodern canon. Moreover, some of the most forceful critiques of postmodernism, the very critiques that also provide us with some of the most influential definitions of postmodernism itself, were generated by Marxist critics, including Fredric Jameson's *Postmodernism or, The Cultural Logic of Late Capitalism* (1991) and David Harvey's *The Condition of Postmodernity* (1989).

As commentators like Haider and Barekat note as well, there is something almost comical about the baffling lack of understanding of the basic terms upon which Peterson's arguments rest. Peterson does not directly engage with postmodernism and postmodern theory. In fact, as Haider confirms, the only relevant citation in Peterson's critique of postmodernism, one that he "customarily recommends at speaking engagements," is Stephen Hicks's book *Explaining Postmodernism* (2004). A free speech advocate and, as Haider notes, "acolyte of Ayn Rand," Hicks seeks to show in his book that postmodernism is little more than a rhetorical strategy deployed by academics on the far left that seeks to compensate for the failure of socialism and communism. Not surprisingly, such an account of postmodernism, aside from its political points, shows such a glaring lack of information about even the most basic historical and intellectual aspects of postmodernism that it is not surprising that it was published (and recently republished) by presses that, even after some thorough research, are difficult to locate and that certainly do not bear even a passing resemblance to accepted publishers of reputable academic work. "Armed with this dubious secondary source," Haider writes, "Peterson is left making statements that are … mired in factual error." Peterson's modus operandi, in Haider's view, is "to take a common misunderstanding at face value, proceeding to build a whole outlook on it."

Of course, as suggested above, the Right's characterization of postmodernism is as incoherent as its account of what they call cultural Marxism, of gender studies, and so on. Accuracy is never the point of these attacks. The tactic of Peterson and his fellow travelers is to merely mimic academic analysis while generating rhetoric and arguments that are not bound by the basic standards of academic inquiry and scholarship. Concepts are therefore not deployed academically, as well-defined and well-researched aspects of a larger project of critique and inquiry, but they are wielded as rhetorical weapons. Their content is not about actual critical meaning in an academic sense but about its mere semblance. What matters, in other words, is not that the term is used in a way that is recognizable to those who study and research it—that is, academically—but that the term carries a popularly recognizable, resignified meaning that is understood by those on the Right who do not seek information but rather concepts and ideas that confirm their already existing perceptions of the present. In short, postmodernism in the work of Peterson and Hicks does not function like an academic concept but as part of a right-wing populist vocabulary. It is invoked in the service of right-wing demagoguery, which means that it is emptied of its actual content, resignified, and endowed with a new, bizarrely distorted life. This new life, therefore, is what should interest us about the term postmodernism today.

To be sure, as Robin stresses, "conservatism … has always borrowed from its enemies on the left."[209] But there is something different about the current Right's efforts in this regard. Whereas the act of borrowing from the Left "once signified a supple and shrewd awareness of the moment," Robin argues, "the Trumpist theft of words and borrowing of gestures signify a conservatism that is exhausted, paradoxically marooned and unmoored."[210] In billing themselves as the defenders of conservatism and reason while clumsily repurposing and ham-fistedly deploying concepts borrowed from the Left, the new wave of pseudoacademic right-wing rhetoric and thought in fact undermines conservatism's stronger version of itself, and it illustrates one of the fundamental differences between contemporary conservative thought and the rebellious alt-right salesmanship of Trump and Peterson. The alt-right's opportunism that is mounted on a mere semblance of serious intellectual engagements with the present, with history, and with political thought is aimed less at a robust conservative political agenda than at crisis profiteering. The new Right's attacks on the Left, and on postmodernism, "theory," the humanities in general and on fields like gender and women's studies in particular are characterized by the deployment of vague and stereotypical characterizations and reductive or obscurantist caricatures of concepts and entire academic disciplines and fields. And yet, as in Peterson's case, this tactic does what it is intended to do: sell. Peterson dresses up fundamentally nonacademic work as academic research in order to lend it credibility. Likewise, the seeming paradox that for all his railing against the vagaries of postmodern discourse Peterson's work exclusively deals in vagaries that present bafflingly simplistic solutions to the complex problems of our time is a crucial aspect of and evidence for his salesmanship. His work is an exercise in simplification, in nostalgia, and in providing his disciples with ways to understand economic critique and complex socioeconomic problems as problems of personality, identity, and naturalized or essentialized gender relations. Such simplification not surprisingly finds eager followers, for few things are easier and more effective than providing the social group who is witnessing a historical change that is questioning their power with a way to feel victimized and with a way to believe that the new system is worse than the old. What could be easier today than continuing to do what Fred Pfeil already diagnosed in the early 1990s: to allow excited white men to revel in their newfound sense of historical victimhood and to understand themselves as the new subaltern subjects of our time?

Whether it is the work of Peterson and other right-wing YouTube personalities like Paul Joseph Watson or the periodically occurring hoaxes that attack academia and that are too obviously self-serving to deserve to be recognized through citations, the most difficult work of the new Right today lies in the attempt to hide the fact that its aims are not the defense of academia or of the future of young men but about personal advancement and profit. Shaking up the establishment from the right is an image that sells, one that exploits the fears and all too real struggles of those on whom the Right preys. In such a situation, academic critique has an important role to play. Academics cannot cede territory to those who seek to erode the foundations of informed political debate and social, cultural, and economic analysis. And although it is clearly successful, the conflation of academic and populist dialogue that we witness as a crucial aspect of the rise of the alt-right must not succeed in its attempt to erase the standards of public intellectualism. The answer to the rise of a new Right does not lie in trying to match the popularity and replicate the strategies of its icons, in spite of the fact that self-promotion and salesmanship is one of the fastest growing demands of the neoliberal university on academics. Rather, we must lay bare the Right's strategies for breeding and exploiting its loyal followers through rigorous critique, and it is this project for which critical theory and the work of Bloch provide us with an invaluable resource. In turn, this also means that modeling what true public intellectuals do is a crucial part of the social responsibility of academics today. Critique is not fan culture, and it is not aimed at spectacularly winning debates or "owning" opponents on YouTube, as though academic inquiry and intellectual exchanges were a spectacle or contact sport. Ultimately, this means to recognize the most significant points of entry into our analysis of the Right, which is not to engage with falsehoods and holes in research. After all, pseudoacademic arguments are never aimed at actual academic debate, which is why attempts to correct mistakes ultimately remain without consequence for those who see themselves as the sons of new right-wing fathers, those who are not willing to be convinced by opposing viewpoints while hiding behind a rhetoric of championing evidence-based reasoning. What is more effective is to examine the phenomenon of the contemporary Right itself and ask what its tactics reveal not only about what is being said but also about what is not being said. Such an approach reveals the Right's use of the term postmodernism not as a matter of an actual analysis of the present but as a strategy for obscuring the actual sources of current forms of nonsynchronism and of the forms of anxiety that define our moment. It is, in short, a way of framing an economic crisis as a cultural conflict. When the Right speaks of postmodernism, it does so in order not to have to speak about capitalism.

Chapter 4 explores the ways in which the Right short-circuits necessary critiques of capitalism as well as structural analysis by reframing economic and structural problems as cultural conflicts and as problems of race, nation, and gender. Still, although figures like Peterson are possibly best understood as salesmen who seize the opportunity to profit from a historical moment of crisis, and although Peterson cannot be accurately described as a fascist, it is important to point out the danger that lies in his rhetoric, which mobilizes protofascist ideas and impulses. The attack on postmodernism itself serves as an example of this. One of the central aspects of fascism is its hostility toward difference. In our moment, as we have seen, difference has been assigned a productive function in capitalism, which creates contradictions that generate a backlash not only against capitalism but also against difference itself. In this context, it is clear that those like Peterson who know to fan the flames of current resentment by attacking difference and pluralism also contribute to the creation of a situation in which fascist attacks on difference may once again flourish. If we place Peterson's opportunistic attacks on postmodernism in the historical context of postmodernism's politics, therefore, we are able to see that Peterson is not only undermining the concepts that he stereotypically associates with postmodernism but also the very attempt to protect humanity from a return of fascism that constituted one of postmodernism's originary projects.

Marci Shore rightly wonders how postmodernism, once "conceived largely by the Left as a safeguard against totalizing ideologies" is now largely wielded as a term "on behalf of an encroaching neo-totalitarianism on the Right."[211] The names Derrida, Foucault, or Deleuze show up in right-wing dialogue in a manner that is utterly dissociated from their actual works or any meaningful, detailed, or academically recognizable consideration thereof, functioning as names that are cynically invoked in order to signal the purported danger and irrationality of postmodernism. The point of this strategic anti-intellectualism is not to voice actual critiques of postmodernism but to create a certain effect. And while, as I argue above, this is part and parcel of the strategy of the new Right, it also erodes one of the forms of thought that emerged in the aftermath of the Second World War as a way to combat those foundations of Western thought out of which fascism and totalitarianism were able to emerge. Although it may by and large be mere opportunistic salesmanship and lack of conceptual rigor, the attack on one of the most significant forms of anti-fascist thought of the twentieth century is a facet of a present in which the return of fascism is once again an all too real threat. Shore reminds us that: "for Derrida the word 'play' was not meant to trivialize our lives and our relationship to the world. On the contrary, 'play' was an affirmation of our creativity, our freedom and our responsibility." Thus, while the Right seeks to reduce postmodernism to relativism, empty pluralism, and the irrational objection to the idea of truth, Derrida's "refusal of all claims to absolute truth," Shore emphasizes, "was meant to protect us from totalitarian terror. Deconstruction, Derrida insisted, had always represented 'the least necessary condition for identifying and combating the totalitarian risk.'"

Likewise, in his introduction to Gilles Deleuze and Félix Guattari's *Anti-Oedipus* (1972), Michel Foucault stresses that the work's "strategic adversary" is fascism.[212] What is at stake in Deleuze and Guattari's contribution to thought, Foucault argues, is not just the opposition to the fascism of Hitler and Mussolini but also to "the fascism in us all, in our heads and everyday behavior, the fascism that causes us to love power, to desire the very thing that dominates and exploits us."[213] It is important to note, therefore, that Peterson's and the contemporary Right's opposition to postmodernism is also an opposition to one of the main forms of anti-fascist thought that emerged in the aftermath of the Second World War and the Holocaust. The fact that Peterson bills himself as a mystical father figure, which invokes the very danger of the "fascism in all of us," and the fact that his work is aimed at a restoration of paternalism and encouraging young men to "desire the very thing that dominates and exploits us," illustrate the dangerous core of his work. And it is possibly due to the fact that Marxism and postmodernism do ultimately have one thing in common—anti-fascism—that they function as interchangeable terms or as similar expressions of the Left in the work of Peterson. In turn, the simultaneous opposition to both Marxism and postmodernism reveals that it is about more than just a clumsy attempt to reconstruct a Left enemy. It contains a substantive attack on anti-fascist thought. The Right's attempt to obscure the anti-fascist aspect of postmodernism while enlisting young men in the restoration of the very forces that postmodernism understood to lie at the heart of fascism, therefore, goes hand in hand with recent attempts to discredit the very term "anti-fascism." Anti-fascism is a term that any society that still takes a stand against fascism must defend, for fascism does not permit equivocation, as there is no aspect of it that can be legitimized or dealt with in separation or isolation from the hatred, the violence, and the death at which fascism is ultimately aimed.

Our aim, therefore, is not to defend postmodernism but to defend against right-wing anti-intellectualism that wields concepts like postmodernism in the struggle against those forces that may keep fascism and right-wing extremism at bay. We must address the fact that anti-postmodernism is bound up with a backlash against anti-fascism itself, with a backlash against those forms of thought, culture, and politics that fight to prevent the return of fascism at all cost. Far from describing the dominant logic of the present against which young men must rebel, we must instead ask ourselves difficult questions about the reasons for the failure of anti-fascist thought to prevent the return of another wave of hatred and violence. Under which conditions, we must ask, is it once again possible to sell racism, misogyny, xenophobia, and small-mindedness as liberation? Of course, right-wing demagoguery is logically incoherent and intellectually fraudulent. After all, the Right manages to out-victim the culture of victimization against which it rages, it out-identities the identity politics to which it supposedly stands opposed, and it out-diversifies the logic of toleration and diversity that it loathes by demanding that right-wing extremist positions be tolerated and given protection under the principles of free speech, claiming protection from the very mechanisms of safeguarding diversity and freedom that it proposes to dismantle. And, of course, in spite of its opposition to postmodernism, contemporary right-wing agitation confirms one of the central suggestions of postmodern thought, namely that the political is today firmly located in the cultural. The duty of Left critique and indeed of all academic work that takes a stand against the threat of fascism in our time is not to address the problem of a new extreme Right by trying to correct errors in thought, for this fails to recognize the centrality of replacing critique and analysis with emotion in right-wing strategy. Instead, it is of crucial importance to examine the structural conditions that make possible the rise of protofascist thought today. We must address the threat of fascism at its most fundamental level, in its connection to capitalism, by taking a step back from the immediate noise created by right-wing anger and by tracing the historical conditions of its emergence and the social and cultural logic of its current manifestation.

4

Mystifications or Lumberjacks without Forests

"Mustiness: we live with it more than ever," remarks Bloch in a section of *Heritage of Our Times* dedicated to the discussion of the reactionary culture that accompanies the rise of German fascism that he observes with great worry. "Children are not taken out of the mustiness. They continue to absorb it or suffer until they become like their father."[214] We, too, as we have seen in the previous chapters, live in an age of mustiness, in an era in which young men look backward for solutions to the problems of a present with which they understand themselves to be out of synch. The contradictions of the current stage of capitalism are bound up with specific forms of nonsynchronism, which centrally include a notable backward orientation into the direction of traditional forms of masculinity and paternalism that are said to have been lost in the present. The reactionary desires that emerge out of our present bind themselves to what Bloch calls the "unfulfilled fairytales of the good old times," which the contemporary Right understands to exploit to its advantage. In previous chapters, I have stressed the importance of tracing the source of these forms of nonsynchronism back to their origins in capitalism and the need to offer rigorous structural and economic analysis in place of opportunistic attempts on part of the Right to construe the source of present problems as matters of culture or gender. Such a project should have become easier in the aftermath of the 2008 economic crash. As Peter Thompson argues, 2008 was "late capitalism's Berlin Wall moment," since the crash itself and the subsequent economic crisis restored our attention to "the social inequality and disparity of wealth distribution [that became] clear for all to see."[215] The crash, Thompson argues, resulted in an "unmasking of the whole political and economic system of ideological control that had prevailed since 1945."[216] And yet, as critics like T. J. Clark note, the fact that capitalism's contradictions were all of a sudden apparent to all of us did not translate into new energy for the Left. In fact, Clark suggests, so little happened in the way of a broader critique of capitalism that he finds himself questioning the very idea of a Left politics. The experience of the past decade, he writes, should be considered proof that "there are *no* circumstances capable of reviving the left."[217]

Leaving aside the problem that Clark's argument in favor of what he calls "a left with no future" only further compounds the presentism and the long now that results from contemporary capitalism in the first place, we must still ask how we can make sense of the fact that a large-scale economic crisis that lays bare the inequality and exploitation on which capitalism rests gives rise more readily to a right-wing turn that to Left critique. What I wish to suggest in this chapter is that we may find a partial answer in the rise of the Right itself, which functions as a protective mechanisms for capitalism. Although in particular the new extreme Right frequently relies on rhetoric that is critical of capitalism, right-wing culture and thought, I will show in what follows, nevertheless serves as a form of capitalist crisis management. In this context, culture's new mustiness counteracts the unmasking effect of events like the 2008 crash and works to veil the contradictions of capitalism. As we will see, the replacement of economic analysis with a focus on matters of identity is a key aspect of right-wing strategy, one that leverages capitalist crises only in order to displace discontent onto the plane of identity. Instead of tracing back the pressing social problems of the present to their origins in capitalism, right-wing agitation directs the anger of the public at discussions about race, nationality, culture, and tradition. The latter strategy of displacement and obfuscation is aided by nonsynchronism, by a new culture of mustiness that maintains a general sense of nostalgia for the idealized good old times. In a situation in which the new Right works hard to turn economic problems and their social manifestations into problems of the erosion of the good old times and of traditional forms of gender and mythical versions of racial, national, and cultural purity and unity, we must regard even the seemingly benign mainstream cultural attachment to the "retro" with great concern, for it enables the more nefarious and dangerous forms of nonsynchronism today. We live in a culture that celebrates the simple life by locating it in the past or in forms of living and working that seem to signal pastness, a culture ripe with the mustiness of good old country life, of the off-grid, and of agritourism, a culture thick with the scent of pomade and beard wax that accompanies the longing for traditional masculinity that is reenacted in axe-throwing bars in the hipster areas of town, in rooms filled with reclaimed barn wood and the rustic décor of the new lumberjack chic. Such a culture and its attachment to masculinity and nature, as we shall see, binds itself troublingly to the nonsynchronist identitarianism, and the new forms of racism and xenophobia that hide the injuries that capitalism inflicts upon the present.

Identitarian attacks on identity politics: A right-wing veil for capitalism's contradictions

"Why do millennials insist on living in the past?" wonders Rhiannon Lucy Cosslett, writing for *The Guardian*.[218] Cosslett takes the revival of Polaroids as an occasion to ask why the millennial generation is, in her words, obsessed with borrowing from previous generations. This practice strikes Cosslett as decidedly strange. After all, she notes, this is "no way to carve an identity." But in a time that is as obsessed with repurposing the old as it is with identity itself, and in a moment when the future seems unavailable for the aspirations and dreams of the current generation, the problem seems hardly surprising. Identity is deeply involved in the crisis of our present and in the turn to the past and to the right. Francis Fukuyama seems to agree. His most recent book, *Identity: The Demand for Dignity and the Politics of Resentment* (2018), is dedicated to exploring the relationship between the sociopolitical crises of our moment, including the rise of populism, and our obsession with identity. Fukuyama's declaration of "the end of history," which, as we have seen, is often associated with the crash of futurity and the creation of a timeless long now, gives way to a different concern in his recent work. As Louis Menand puts it in *The New Yorker*, in his recent book, Fukuyama "postpones the end of history," arguing that liberal democracy and free trade, far from marking the absolute horizon of history, turn out to be delicate structures that are being severely damaged by contemporary identity politics.[219] As Menand shows, Fukuyama understands the demand for recognition as a "master concept" that underlies "all the contemporary dissatisfactions with the global liberal order." Moreover, Fukuyama proposes that this master concept allows us to understand the origins of conflict in virtually every corner of our globe since the time of Plato. The desire for recognition, Fukuyama proposes, creates conflict and poses particular problems for liberalism, since it makes demands that cannot be satisfied by economic change.

Being confronted with a set of sweeping and often stunningly reductive claims may distract from the possibly most dangerous problem that Fukuyama's recent book contains. Fukuyama argues that the problem of our time lies in the fact that the Left continues to frame political struggles as economic problems, as contradictions of capitalism, when the actual source of these problems in his mind lies in identity. "This theme goes back to Plato, who talked about a third part of the soul that demanded recognition of one's dignity," Fukuyama explains in a recent interview, elaborating that this demand "has morphed in modern times into identity politics."[220] "A great deal of modern politics is about the demand of that inner self to be uncovered, publicly claimed, and recognized by the political system," he explains, suggesting that the failure of the Left lies in its inability to understand this centrality of identity. Fukuyama suggests that recent versions of this struggle for recognition emerge out of the social movements of the 1960s and 1970s. A variety of groups, including "African-Americans, women, the LGBT community, Native Americans, and the disabled … found a home on the left." The latter, he concludes, triggers a similar reaction on the Right: "they say: What about us? Aren't we deserving of recognition? Haven't the elites ignored us, downplayed our struggles? That's the basis of today's populism."[221] What we should do in order to address this problem, Fukuyama proposes, is to address the fragmentation that results from the variety of politics aimed at different identity groups. In short, he suggests, "we need to get back to a narrative that's focused less on narrow groups and more on larger collectivities, particularly the collectivity called the American people."[222]

Fukuyama is critical of the fact that the Left has continuously framed problems in economic terms when identity is in his estimation the more important category. And herein lies the crucial problem with his argument. Fukuyama unwittingly reproduces and lends further credence to one of the basic assertions of right-wing agitation. Although Fukuyama claims to have left behind conservatism in recent years and moved to a more "liberal" position (I am inserting the quotation marks around the word liberal in part because the contemporary Right shares a striking affinity for identifying themselves as "classic liberals" or "classic British liberals"), his recent work reproduces a far more dangerous logic that is even more strongly associated with conservatism and indeed with the extreme Right. One of the trademark arguments that is associated with the Right's claim that the present is a time of chaos and disorder is the suggestion that identity politics fragments larger traditional categories, thereby eroding the foundations of traditional social order. It is on the basis of such suggestions, for instance, that Jordan Peterson mounts his appeals to return to the good old times of the 1950s—because, he argues, unlike today, the good old times only knew two big, solidified gender categories. According to Peterson, our nations have withdrawn from tradition and from the religious and national structures that stabilized culture, and we can only fight this meaninglessness that results from the fragmentation of contemporary life by returning to what he describes as "ancient wisdom," to "the great myths and religious stories of the past" that he describes in his book *Maps of Meaning* (1999) and in *12 Rules for Life* (2018).[223] This return will offer what Peterson's book promises: an "antidote to chaos." And this antidote, he explains, is a sense of order that is based on well-understood social norms, on "social structure, explored territory, and familiarity."[224] Opposing the fragmentation of identity and arguing for the restoration of big, stable identity categories is a hallmark of right-wing extremist rhetoric and of contemporary right-wing populism. The Trump government, for instance, tries to position itself as the defender of the idea of the American people in much the same way that the alt-right claims for itself the role of the protector of categories like "American" from fragmentation, seeking to preserve the mythical purity of racial categories as well as the singular association of the idea of the American people with whiteness and Christianity. In far-right rhetoric, large categories like the American people stand opposed to the fragmentation of traditional, purportedly "pure" sources of identity that results from multiculturalism, and it is precisely in opposition to identity politics that the Right presents itself as the defender of a tradition and heritage that it sees as under attack. In a moment when a new wave of white supremacist and right-wing extremist organizations group themselves under the banner of the Identitarian Movement, it is intellectually and politically negligent to simplistically champion big identity categories and opposition to the fragmentation that purportedly results from identity politics as an answer to the rise of a right-wing populism in our time.

It is, therefore, not the Left's embrace of a fragmented form of identity on one hand and its insistence on the need to trade in identity politics for economic critique on the other that is the problem. Rather, the more pressing issue is the centrist position that Fukuyama's recent work represents, a position that ultimately fuels right-wing discourse. Canadian Prime Minister Justin Trudeau presents a striking example of this tension. Trudeau is frequently accused by the Right of threatening Canadian values and Canadian identity by championing identity politics. To the Right, Trudeau represents the excesses of a form of identity politics that in its critics' view erodes national pride, national culture, and traditional conceptions of family, gender, and masculinity. The Left, by contrast, frequently points out the solely strategic mobilization of identity politics and social causes by the Trudeau government in order to veil its callous pursuit of capitalist expansion. Social policy and arguments for inclusion and appeals to the rights of identity groups signal a progressive politics that stands in direct contrast to and that serves to distract from the Trudeau government's commitment to the ruthless exploitation of natural resources in the Canadian North and to pipeline construction with little regard for matters of environmental protection or conservation, and it distracts from its unwillingness to act decisively or with any true substance or consequence on matters of reconciliation with regard to Canada's First Nations. Both the Right and the Left have criticized Trudeau's relation to identity politics, thus, leaving Trudeau noticeably undecided in his response to the topic.

In 2018, Trudeau delivered the commencement speech at NYU, a speech that was clearly intended to address both the Left's and the Right's complaint but that ultimately, in spite of its stated intentions and rhetorical efforts, serviced most strongly the right-wing position on identity. Illustrating the ways in which centrist fence-sitting does little more than exacerbate the polarization of debates while simultaneously enabling the rise of a new Right, Trudeau's politically and logically incoherent speech lays bare the recognition of the centrality of the category of identity in right-wing discourse as well as his ultimate inability to take a clear position on the relation between Left and Right claims over identity. Trudeau urged graduates, "to take up a leadership role against aggressive nationalism and identity politics that make the world a far more complex way to live."[225] At the same time, Trudeau also criticized the fragmentation that may result from a focus on identity and stressed the need to focus on "the leadership that brings people together." And while bringing people together is likely an idea that only very few would readily perceive as a bad thing, what matters here is that Trudeau's logic ultimately collapses into the same line of logic that we also find in right-wing critiques of the fragmentation that results from identity politics and the appeal to turn to strong leaders who can bring us together in the defense of bigger categories (as long as we are white, straight, Christian, and of the correct nationality). Thus, although Trudeau seeks to oppose the Right's version of identity politics, claiming that we should oppose the "polarization" and "aggressive nationalism" that is connected to "the identity politics that has grown so common of late," his logic ultimate replicates the Right's approach to identity. While Trudeau's speech passionately mobilizes the usual banalities of centrist accounts of diversity and identity—common ground, big categories—he misses the point that this is precisely the logical plane upon which right-wing arguments operate.

Like Fukuyama and Trudeau, the Right takes aim at the fragmentation of big, traditional identity categories by contemporary identity politics. But while Left critique would point toward the fact that the fragmentation of established forms of social collectivity is one of the trademark aspects of contemporary capitalism, the suggestion that it is identity, not economic critique, that provides the more fundamental answers here means that Fukuyama's argument remains confined to a choice between two kinds of identity: a variety of smaller identity groups or big categories like the American people. But as soon as analysis and our political options are limited in such a way, we witness the problem that Trudeau's speech indicates, namely that it becomes difficult to dissociate the centrist call for larger identity categories from the Right's demand for the same solution to the same stated problem: the fragmentation of identity. The Right, too, suggests that categories like the American people and associated ideas like American or Canadian culture are damaged by the push toward identity politics. Its critique of fragmentation is aimed at the erasure of individual categories relating, for example, to gender identity and race and at the restoration of the unity of bigger categories like the nation, gender, or masculinity into which all smaller categories must once again be reabsorbed or from which those categories to which the Right objects must be excluded. The Right's appeal to the big categories of identity is not aimed at a liberal politics of inclusion, as is the case in Trudeau's and Fukuyama's argument, but at a flattening of identity, at the erasure of difference. And yet, while there is, of course, a significant logical difference between right-wing and centrist critiques of identity politics and the embrace of bigger identity categories, it is clear that these nuances are lost in the context of a heated public debate that often only deals in sweeping generalizations, catchphrases, and broad observations. In this situation, it is more important than ever to point toward the ways in which confining ourselves to the terrain of identity hinders our attempts at engaging with the structural sources out of which the sense of the fragmentation of the social emerges. And we must note that the embrace of identity serves as a way to distract from precisely such a necessary critique of capitalism.

Identity, therefore, is certainly not the best way to make legible the source of social and political crises in our time. Our continued struggle to develop accounts of and answers to the rise of right-wing populism today does not result from the Left's tendency to privilege economic critique over identity critique, as Fukuyama suggests. On the contrary, it emerges from a lacking understanding of the ways in which identity and identity politics functions in the context of right-wing rhetoric and agitation. The problem is not that we pay too much attention to Left economic critique. The problem is that we have not taken it seriously enough. Instead of committing ourselves to a rigorous critique of the contradictions of contemporary capitalism and to analyses of the relation between the crises in material life and the social and political problems with which these crises are bound up, we have confronted the problems of our present as problems of identity and thus done little more than replicate one of the standard strategies of the contemporary Right, a strategy that is part and parcel of the Trump administration, for instance. By turning to identity and by departing from economic and structural analysis, we participate in the veiling of the contradictions of capitalism and of the structural origins of the new forms of violent resentment that stoke the fires of extremism. We might simply ask ourselves, for example, if problems of identity and culture truly best explain some of the standard demands of the extreme Right today. We are currently witnessing a right-wing turn in rural parts of Canada that have been severely struggling with economic decline, areas that have been hit by new waves of poverty that have largely gone unaddressed by federal and provincial policy makers. In such areas, some of the most common complaints take the form of a resentment against immigrants that laments that Canada seems to have money for immigrants but not for its own poor. The Right understands to obscure the economic concerns out of which such a form of resentment grows and to amplify the hatred against immigrants to which it is connected. The solution that the Right touts is a new culture war, not a matter of addressing the problem of a rapid rise of rural poverty. In such a situation, are we truly best served by abandoning economic critique in favor of a focus on identity? Doing so participates in the obfuscation of some of the important structural problems that make possible a new turn to the Right. And, of course, it is clear that the embrace of identity as opposed to economic approaches also serves those governments who prefer to celebrate identity categories instead of addressing systemic problems such as rural poverty that would require actual economic change and solutions. Additionally, we lose sight of the ways in which identity functions in the context of right-wing populism, and we perpetuate the Right's suggestion that the social and political problems of our time are best understood as conflicts of identity and culture. The latter suggestion is one of the Right's most significant tactics for obfuscating and distracting from the actual source of the actual problems, illustrating the ways in which right-wing identitarianism serves as a protective mechanism for the crises of capitalism.

But while it is undeniable that identity serves the logic of neoliberal capital as much as that of the contemporary Right, it is also quite clear that, in the age of continued police and state violence directed at the black population, at immigrants, and at refugees, and in the context of continued anti-Islamism and new waves of xenophobia, we cannot simply abandon our attention to individual identity categories in favor of economic critique without granting the Right's wishes. After all, these categories and the struggles that they ultimately make legible to us are of important strategic purpose in the effort to stop the spread of and to counteract new forms of racism and xenophobia, and violence against non cis-gender people. To simply abandon identity politics is to lose sight of the important work that it did historically and to grant the wishes of the extreme Right. Asad Haider's book *Mistaken Identity* presents a compelling case for the continued importance of identity politics and shows that it must not simply be jettisoned. Instead of setting up a simple binary choice between identity and economic critique as Fukuyama does, Haider illustrates that we must historicize the dialectical connection between these categories in order to understand the complex ways in which they function. The success of the politically most effective forms of claims over identity, Haider shows, such as in the context of the Civil Rights Movement and in the context of the Black Panther Party, is contained in the fact that they also contained rigorous systemic analysis. Haider shows in his book, for example, that "the civil rights movement was in fact the closest US equivalent to the mass workers' movement in postwar Europe."[226] Although both make appeals to identity, for instance, there is a big difference between the appeals to identity and structural critique that we find in movements like Black Lives Matter and the appeals to identity that over-write the economic source of social problems that we find in right-wing extremist identitarian movements. In order to appreciate this important difference, and in order to understand the precise relation to structural problems that appeals to identity assume in different political contexts, we cannot sever its relation to the economic without unwittingly supporting the logic of the Right over the logic of movements like Black Lives Matter. Fukuyama is certainly correct to foreground the fact that identity politics is notoriously difficult to reconcile with economic or structural critique. Political theorists like Adolph Reed Jr. have long insisted on just this point. But, as analyses such as Haider's illustrate, Fukuyama's analysis arrives a step too late and remains unable to appreciate the fact that, as Haider illustrates, the problem lies not in a choice between economic analysis and identity politics but in fact that identity is precisely not best understood as a transhistorical, universal demand for recognition but instead as standing in a complex relation to economic structures. And it is in relation to this relation that the contemporary turn to the right and its embrace of identity over and against structural arguments is best understood.

I would suggest, then, that one of the ways to understand the Right's claims over identity as part of its basic strategies and political logic is to illustrate the ways in which identity serves as a way to hide underlying economic relations of exploitation, domination, disenfranchisement, and alienation. Critique that aims to make visible that which is hidden by the Right's turn to identity can serve as an important political tool in our time that also allows us to understand one of the central aspects of right-wing thought and rhetoric today. The work of Bloch provides us with a valuable basis for this project of contemporary critique. Bloch shows that the attempt to veil the contradictions of capitalism is one of the central aspects of fascism, one that distinguishes fascism from the workers' movement. "Revolutionary and reformist proletarian organizations shared the assumption that the immediate situation in the production process ... determined the key aspects of a class consciousness which would lead to unified class action," Bloch argues.[227] "As Eberhard Knödler-Bunte shows in his examination of fascism, the National Socialists argued differently:

> Their class theory to the extent that one can speak of theory at all, was limited to phenomena in the sphere circulation (big capital, usury, a Jewish-freemason-Marxist conspiracy, small shopkeepers versus department stores, etc.), to general moods and prejudices, cultural traditions and to immediate experiences in the political and public spheres.[228]

Unlike proletarian movements that were aimed at addressing the underlying structural contradictions out of which social problems emerge, Knödler-Bunte shows, National Socialism aimed for a "personalization of social forces whose mediations were ignored."[229] As Anson Rabinbach insists, we can understand Bloch's analysis here in relation to the logic that characterizes critical theory's account of fascism more generally, anticipating, for instance, Walter Benjamin's suggestion that "fascism sees its salvation in giving these masses not their due, but instead a chance to express themselves."[230] In our time, the Trump regime's well-known and much-repeated opposition to what it calls "globalism" similarly is not a way to actually address the problems of global capitalism but instead serves as a way to reestablish a focus on national pride and identity. Even Trump's America First program operates as a program for the masses primarily on the level of nation, culture, and identity while its economic policies are aimed at creating benefits for the economic elite.

Bloch's analysis of German fascism is of great value for our time also because it allows us to understand the underlying logic of the Right's critique of the fragmentation of society on one hand and its personalization of economic relations on the other, a strategy that invokes economic problems only in the effort to create additional fear and resentment surrounding a purported assault on tradition and culture. Instances in which the Trump administration does address itself to economic problems are also moments in which personalization plays a key role. The anthropomorphization of individual sectors at whom individual decisions are aimed—like Trump's defense of "the coal miner" through the creation of a handful of jobs—is largely a symbolic act intended to signal to workers that their personal struggles will be recognized and valued. In reality, such much-publicized efforts to address the plight of the coal miner address the problems of only a dwindling fraction of the working class while serving as a distraction form the larger systemic problems of contemporary capitalism. Thus, while the Right attacks identity politics for its fragmentation of big identity categories, it simultaneously pursues a politics of personalization and fragmentation that dismantles larger economic categories like the working class. This fragmentation in turn absolves the Right from a politics for the people (say, for all workers). In other words, the Right pursues a double strategy that serves to protect capitalism: it fragments economic categories in order to defend the capitalist status quo to the benefit of the economic elite and at the cost of the worker while simultaneously pursuing an inverse strategy on the level of identity, opposing the defense of individual identity groups and sowing cultural and racial discontent in order to refocus politics on the defense of traditional notions of national, cultural, and racial unity. As in Bloch's time, the contemporary Right replaces a focus on economic problems with a focus on "the people," understood in similar ways as the idea of *Volksgemeinschaft* under National Socialism. The idea of the *Volk* or the people in National Socialism functioned as a depoliticized version of categories like the working class, invoking mythical racial and national unity and purity that the politics of the Right claimed to defend. Today, too, in Germany as in North America, we witness the reemergence of this conception of the people in the rhetoric of the extreme Right. The people, as right-wing rallies readily reveal, is not a category that unifies a diversity of people in pursuit of a liberal politics as in Fukuyama, but it serves as an expression of the cultural traditions and of the racial purity that the extreme Right sees as under attack by identity politics and immigration.

Fascism: Capitalist crisis management

In an article in which he explores the role of the notions of victimization in contemporary right-wing thought, a role that he associates with what he terms "the aggressiveness of vulnerability," Pavlos Roufos notes with some dismay the logical confusion that results from the Right's attempt to take hold of ideas and concepts that we more readily associate with the Left.[231] Roufos notes in particular recent books like Angela Nagle's *Kill All Normies: Online Culture Wars from 4Chan and Tumblr to Trump and the Alt-Right* (2017), which examines the role that idea of "transgression" assumes in right-wing rhetoric. Nagle takes the fact that "the strategy of transgression has been effectively recuperated by the alt-Right" as an occasion to question the notion that "transgressive attitudes have been beneficial to progressive/Left movements in the past" and suggests that "transgression should be abandoned altogether."[232] Roufos is right to be perplexed by this line of reasoning. After all, as Corey Robin shows, "from its inception," conservatism has relied on a mix of "racism, populism, violence, and a pervasive contempt for custom, convention, law, institutions, and established elites."[233] But, Robin stresses, it is of crucial importance to understand that it has done so in order to "build a broad based movement of elites and masses against the emancipation of the lower orders."[234] Far from delegitimizing the notion of transgression tout court, what is required is an analysis of the ways in which specific forms of transgression function in right-wing thought and politics.

As we can also see in Bloch's examination of the German Right, the seemingly paradoxical combination of anti-capitalism with policies aimed at benefitting the ultra-wealthy is a central aspect of right wing strategy. In fact, right-wing anti-capitalism must be understood as a crucial aspect of the Right's function as a safeguard for capitalism. The Nazi, Bloch writes, "pretends to be rebellious" and at times camouflages himself as an anti-capitalist, but his "propaganda must develop sheer revolutionary appearance."[235] In the introduction to a special issue dedicated to the topic of fascism, the editors of the journal *New German Critique* foreground the significance of Blochian analysis for our ability to understand, in Bloch's terms, the ways in which "an authentic tradition of revolt" constitutes one of the foundations of fascism.[236] What Bloch seeks to identify here is the fact that fascism finds its origins in a critique of and opposition to capitalism that is ultimately absorbed and distorted by fascism but that under different conditions may have given rise to a progressive politics. It is with regard to this origin of fascism and its connection to anti-capitalism that Bloch stresses that it is of the utmost importance to examine the root causes of fascism in the contradictions of capitalism if we wish to combat fascism and deploy some of the discontent that enables its rise in the context of a progressive critique of capitalism. What this also means, however, is that we must understand the performance of rebelliousness as the impoverished version of a resistance against capitalism as a crucial part of right-wing politics that we can also trace in the contemporary Right. The Trump administration's claims to wish to "drain the swamp," to protect American workers from unfair trade agreements fair, and to oppose "globalism" are examples of such a performance of rebelliousness.

The co-optation of revolutionary energy and its displacement from a critique of capitalism to broad forms of anger directed at enemies who are said to threaten the integrity of mythical notions of racial and national purity is part and parcel of fascism. Knödler-Bunte argues that this aspect of fascism indicates that fascism is best understood as a "depoliticized mass movement."[237] The "fascist public sphere," Knödler-Bunte contends, is ultimately nothing other than "a politicized public sphere aimed at real depoliticization."[238] This account of the inherently contradictory ground on which fascism operates—establishing a public sphere that encourages politicization while simultaneously reducing political dialogue and thought to impoverished versions of itself—helps us understand the strategy of governments like the Trump administration that strategically lower the bar of public and political discourse in order to replace political dialogue with emotionally charged, vague slogans. Paired with the mere semblance of rebelliousness, this connected set of tactics consolidates the obfuscation of structural problems and puts depoliticized discourse, including pseudopolitical branding efforts and slogans, disinformation campaigns, and conspiracy narratives, in place of political analysis, debate, and programs. The extreme Right has traditionally relied on a semblance of rebelliousness and anti-capitalism that it reduces to populism and racist agitation, and it has billed itself as a political mass movement while ultimately depoliticizing the public sphere. In our time, too, these connected strategies serve to protect the capitalist status quo and safeguard the economic elite whose interests are threatened by the anti-capitalist sentiments that current economic crises generate but that fascism collapses into a concern with culture and identity and depoliticizes by fostering a grotesquely distorted version of a mass movement whose aims are contracted to hatred and violence.

And while he cannot be accurately described as a fascist or a Nazi, the work of right-wing provocateur Peterson displays precisely this coinciding of agitation and depoliticization. Peterson fans the flames of white, male discontent, but he does so by insisting on personalization and a necessary reorientation toward the past in order to recover old values and forms of identity. Peterson blends self-help individualization with the outright rejection of the need for transformative politics, suggesting in the sixth rule of *12 Rules* that young men ought to clean and organize their rooms and houses before setting out to criticize or change the world. By identifying problems of gender and identity as the source of all of the discontent from which young men may suffer, Peterson replaces actual politics with mere anger and uninformed scapegoating. And yet, it is by replacing political discourse and analysis with its empty shell that Peterson allows angry young men to understand themselves as the defenders of reason and political objectivity.

But while the Right's strategy in particular in this regard may appear contradictory and indeed incoherent, it is this aspect that contains its particular danger. The reason that young people turn to fascism instead of Marxism, Bloch argues, is that while Marxism presents them, fascism represents them.[239] The appeal of the focus on identity as opposed to economic critique lies in the sense of personal validation and recognition that it offers, and fascism understands that the desire for representation of those who suffer from the exploitation and alienation of capitalism is a powerful tool for the depoliticization of the working class. Thus, in Bloch's words, fascism depoliticizes the working class by positing "folk and Fatherland as a substitute for their own sinking caste."[240] This depoliticization of the working class and the displacement of the concern of workers onto the terrain of identity has been aided by mainstream and academic arguments that gleefully declare the end of class as a useful category for social critique, arguments that take aim at Marxism while unwittingly aiding those whose investment in the abolition of an interest in class should constitute the main object of our analyses. At the same time, however, Bloch illustrates that vulgar Marxism also tends to play a crucial role in the rise of fascism, serving as an example of the Left's failure to offer an "opposite land" and alternatives to the myths and dreams of fascism.[241] Merely pointing toward economic problems that parts of the population exemplify, the contemporary Left, too, as much as the centrist or social democratic alternative, has failed to offer a true politics for the working class and for the poor, thus leaving many without alternatives and thus ever more susceptible to the appeal of representation over presentation. As Haider insists, it is important for us to understand that:

> [W]hat makes a movement anticapitalist is not always the issue it mobilizes around. What is more important is whether it is able to draw in a wide spectrum of the masses and enable their self-organization, seeking to build a society in which people govern themselves and control their own lives, a possibility fundamentally blocked by capitalism.[242]

Without a Left that is aimed at offering a coherent sense of the form of anti-capitalism that Haider describes, we witness the orientation of those who suffer the harshest consequences of capitalist crises into the direction of the Right, which offers validation and representation and which promises honor and pride in identity in place of substantive changes to the realities of working class life. The underanalyzed public labeling of contemporary right-wing voters as "deplorables" and the denunciation of the recent turn to the Right as simply irrational or uneducated further amplifies the Right's appeal to those for whom no one offers a substantive politics and who thus seize hold of the remaining bare minimum that the political landscape has on offer for them: representation, validation, and flattery. Simply denouncing votes for the Right as "despair and stupidity," Bloch reminds us, is as counterproductive as the attitude of the centrist and the social democrat whose response to the threat of right-wing extremism is to hope for better times and for whom everything passes "by itself."[243] What such approaches miss, Bloch stresses, is that fascist sentiments find their origin in the contradictions of capitalism and the insight that for this reason things could have "turned out differently ... if dialectically transformed."[244]

It is precisely in the Right's appeal to pride, as Bloch reminds us, that not only its power and temptation but also its danger is located. In particular racial pride, Bloch argues, "serves more than ever the craftiest demagoguery: it completely encloses the slavedriven individual in his ring of blood, gives him German honour for bread, thwarts the class struggle."[245] And just like the contemporary Right that offers validation and pride on the level of identity, race, and nation in order to distract from underlying structural and economic problems, German fascism, Bloch shows, understood to deploy the categories of race and nation in a general effort of personalization. Fascism, Bloch writes, "makes the racially interpreted 'nation' just as personal, into the self-esteem of the individual blond body; so that the Teuton, satisfied with his blood, does not crave a share in the ownership of the other riches of the nation."[246] In addition to offering a possibility to redirect anti-capitalist sentiments at concerns with identity that are aimed at pride and honor and thus protect avoid demands for systemic change, the contemporary Right also enlists new forms of racism in order to further its rebellious image. Right-wing provocateurs cast themselves as rebels in a politically correct time that, they claim, has become repressive, as fighters for liberation from the "fascism" of the Left that attempts to silence right-wing speech, invoking free speech as a way to protect racist and hate speech while priding themselves in what they see as their ability to wield the master's tools against him. Racist speech, they claim, is their voice, and their voice deserves to be heard like all others if we believe in tolerance and democracy, an argument that blends two key aspects of right-wing rhetoric that represent its internal strategic incoherence as its ability to point out contradictions in the logic of the Left: rebelliousness (the willingness to say what the "repressive Left" does not want to hear) and victimization (fighting for beliefs that political correctness in spite of its commitment to toleration will not tolerate). In this context, we are reminded of Henri Lefèbvre's insistence that fascist rebellion should be understood as a central aspect of fascism's attempt at political mystification, as part of its attempt to fundamentally disrupt a society's understanding of its economic and social reality. By representing itself as a revolutionary mass movement, fascism's "unreality disguises itself as the supreme reality, and tries to make true reality definitively unreal."[247]

The new forms of racism whose rise we witness in our time and the narratives of racial pride and purity of identity with which they are bound up erase, in Bloch's words, the "inclination toward dismantling, towards analyzing the situation, towards uncovering the causes" of the system that disenfranchises and oppresses the working class, the poor, and so on. But in addition to serving as a protective mechanism for capitalism, racism and xenophobia also replace critique and thought with emotion and fanatical devotion. In one of the most memorable passages of *Heritage*, Bloch recalls a statement by a young Nazi that, in Bloch's mind, expresses just this aspect of fascism that reveals its particular power and danger: "you do not die for a programme you have understood," Bloch remembers the young Nazi exclaiming, "you die for a programme you love."[248] Racism, that is, and appeals to identity, blood, heritage, and honor not only serve as a way to manage the severe contradictions and injustices of capitalism but also as a way to replace analysis with emotion, thus contributing to the general depoliticization of right-wing politics. In such a situation, we must reiterate the need for a return to a form of Left public intellectualism modeled for us by the tradition of critical theory, and we are reminded of Adorno's suggestion that "those who think are in all critique not angry: thought sublimates anger."[249] Additionally, we must understand contemporary racism and xenophobia not simply as aberrations from an otherwise healthy capitalist system. Rather, they are instrumental to keeping the system alive by managing its contradictions. The good old times of blood, race, and nation keep the radically different time of anti-capitalist futurity at bay. In this context, it is crucial to remember Bloch's insistence that "race always looks the way business needs it."[250]

"Whoever is not willing to talk about capitalism," Max Horkheimer writes in 1939 in the *Zeitschrift für Sozialforschung*, "should also keep quiet about fascism."[251] Horkheimer's suggestion reiterates the understanding of fascism as a form of capitalist crisis management that also characterizes Bloch's approach to fascism. And, as the editors of *New German Critique* note, this account of fascism finds expression in the work of later scholars, too, such as Reinhard Kühnl and Peter Sinclair, who conclude that "though fascism was a mass movement, its function remained the rescue of 'capitalism.'"[252] When Eberhard Knödler-Bunte examines fascism as a depoliticized mass movement, he likewise stresses that "the objective content of fascism was the maintenance of the arbitrary regulation and preservation of the functioning of the capitalist socioeconomic systems during periods of crisis."[253] Although "fascism assumed political and public shape as an anti-democratic and at the same time anti-capitalist and anti-Marxist mass movement and as a neutralized popular movement of depoliticized masses," Knödler-Bunte shows, we must move past fascism's initial appearance and examine its relation to capitalism if we are to understand not only its origins and emergence but also its function.[254] Analyses of the function of fascism as a protective mechanisms for capitalism in times of systemic crisis, Bloch shows us, allow us to better understand the sources of fascism, and they provide us with a basis for a political approach to fascism that traces its root causes and that returns discontent to its source. By laying bare the originary sources of the discontent that fascism exploits, we are able to show that fascism serves as a way to disrupt anti-capitalist movements that are aimed at substantive change. One crucial aspect of confronting fascism through rigorous critique of its relation to capitalism, Knödler-Bunte argues, are analyses of the ways in which fascism betrays those to whom it offers protection and validation, illustrating that fascism concentrates "the hopes, expectations and prejudices of broad masses of employees and workers" while ultimately directing them "against the traditional programs and actions of the proletarian movement."[255]

And yet, in spite of the immense importance of such forms of critique in times that witness the rise of a new extreme Right, Knödler-Bunte stresses that simply equating new forms of right-wing thought and politics with fascism may hinder more than it helps our efforts at gaining a better understanding of and at ultimately preventing the spread of new right-wing movements. Of course, this objection points to the general risk of creating false historical analogies. But Knödler-Bunte also stresses the need for precise historical analysis rather than general assertions of relations. After all, he notes, not all forms of capitalist crises lead to fascism. Rather, we must examine "the specific interrelation of economic crises" on one hand and "the constellation of political forces" with which it is connected on the other if we are to understand the specific manifestation of right-wing or authoritarian thought that emerges in a given historical context.[256] In fact, he insists, the term fascism itself has significant drawbacks for political critique and strategy. Rather than deploying the term fascism as "a slogan … in present-day struggles," Knödler-Bunte argues, we should utilize our understanding of fascism as a set of analytical tools that may help us make sense of specific aspect of the contemporary Right. In short, Knödler-Bunte stresses, "battle slogans without analytic content are of no value."[257] It is the task of critical theory today to deploy its archive of tools designed to examine fascism and the extreme

Right in order to identify and ultimately name and conceptualize the specific, complex network of reactionary and dangerous thought and culture in our time. Broad attacks on the Right that wield the term fascism as a mere slogan overwrite the specificity of the specific facets of the contemporary Right that we must seek to understand in detail. Bloch's analysis of fascism, therefore, does not provide us with a universal tool for the diagnosis of any given manifestation of right-wing extremism. Rather, it affords us insights into some of fascism's trademark strategies that may allow us to generate analyses of aspects of right-wing thought today. Instead of giving us a label that we can apply to groups or movements today, Bloch's work on fascism provides us with an archive of analytical tools and approaches that we can utilize in order to gain a better understanding of certain aspects of the contemporary Right. It is, therefore, ultimately not helpful to label Trump a fascist. But it is very helpful indeed to examine the ways in which the Trump administration deploys tactics and forms of logic and rhetoric whose function shares crucial aspects with fascist thought and political strategy.

Romantic anti-capitalism

In his examination of fascism's attempts to veil the contradictions of capitalism, Bloch is particularly struck by the ways in which the logic of blood and race binds itself to the idea of nature. Fascism's pursuit of what he describes as a program of "backward rejuvenation,"[258] Bloch argues, is closely connected to a form of "romantic anti-capitalism" that, instead of yielding a fully developed anti-capitalist analysis and politics, merely rejects aspects of the capitalist present and advocates for the return to an idealized, better past.[259] This idea of a better past, Bloch shows, is often connected to nature that also becomes the site for resurrecting the idea of national and racial purity. Appeals to blood and soil and to what Bloch describes as images of "blood and forests" are expressions of a romanticized notion of the German people, understanding national identity in connection to a sense of mythical racial purity that is directly bound up with and emerges out of German soil. This set of narratives, Bloch argues, was particular persuasive and appealing to those who saw themselves as out of step with their times and for whom the rise of German fascism provided a way to understand themselves as filiated by a lineage that binds soil, blood, and nation together and that must be restored. Bloch here uses the label "Saxons without forests"[260] in order to describe the German petit-bourgeoisie's particularly notable fascination with the past. In our time, we witness a similarly, troubling attachment to the idea of nature as the spatial fix for the temporal problems of the present. The nonsynchronisms of the long now give rise to a widespread form of nostalgia that is also connected to a nostalgia for lost forms of natural existence, and in the context of such nostalgic narratives we frequently encounter the same set of logical connections that Bloch traces in fascist narratives of backward rejuvenation: the return to nature brings with it the restoration of old forms of social and familiar order, restores to primacy lost forms of masculinity and paternalism, and it reestablishes social Darwinist ideas. Such narratives of contemporary culture, which are part and parcel of the nostalgia industry that seizes hold of nature to express its temporal desires, share troubling components with the imaginary that underlies fascist narratives of a revolt against the present. As Rabinbach shows, fascist revolt is in part aimed at "the restoration and actualization of 'authentic experience.'"[261] And by understanding the relation between nonsynchronism and narratives of nature and authenticity that revive mythical notions of racial purity and male primacy, we are able to appreciate Bloch's suggestion that "fascism is the heir to the legitimate and powerful tradition of romantic-anticapitalism."[262]

Contemporary culture is marked not only by new forms of sentimentalism, as the previous chapter argued, but also by a return to the pastoral. In fact, the ubiquitous reality TV narratives that champion off-grid living, homesteading, and the return to Alaska as a form of time travel that reestablishes lost forms of life blend sentimentalism and the pastoral. Additionally, some of the most successful YouTube channels are dedicated to men who act out the present's fetishized investment in "primitive skills" and survival techniques, producing narratives that argue that the reacquisition of such skills, skills that have been historically exhausted in the context of our present, is of the utmost importance for our ability to deal with scenarios that, every viewer ultimately knows, will never occur. Like doomsday prepping, the fascination with primitive skills and survival scenarios is, contrary to the claims of those who advertise these skills, not a way to engage with the future but rather a way to simulate returns to nostalgically idealized forms of life that as such never existed. And while such aspects of contemporary culture appear at first blush rather benign, their popularity, paired with a general idealization of forms of masculinity whose degree of successful re-implementation is once again conveniently visually signaled by beard length, reinforces the nonsynchronous aspects of the now. To be sure, this is not to say that the striking variety of such aspects of contemporary culture ought not be understood as harboring protofascist sentiments. However, we must examine those cultural narratives in the present that problematically bind themselves to and that amplify the force of ideas that ultimately operate in the service of far-right narratives about our present of which what Rabinbach terms "the utopia of völkisch community in nature" is an integral part.[263] The pathos of life in contemporary capitalism causes people to seek salvation in the past, and culture assumes a crucial role in the construction of spaces for this desire. And, of course, since this narrative has proven itself to sell well, the connection between nature and lost forms of the better life has become an integral part of today's nonsynchronism industry that offers a myriad of opportunities for the contemporary subject, for lumberjacks without forests, to play out the narrative of a return to nature that also brings with it the return to mythical ideas of the better life in the good old times. And yet, as we will see, there are aspects of culture that have been addressing themselves to the rise of this set of narratives and that examine the contradictions and the danger inherent in them. Returning to the work of the novel, we can see that novelists have in fact been grappling with this troubling reemergence of the pastoral under the conditions of the present and in the context of romantic anti-capitalism that seeks backward rejuvenations for several decades.

"Much of the pastoral literary genre has long been a solidly bourgeois form of escapism,"[264] writes Steven Poole in a 2013 article in *The Guardian* in which he examines the recent revival and surging popularity of nature writing. "The idealization of the natural world is as old as the city, to the corrupting influence of which a return to pastoral life is always presented as a cure," Poole suggests. Today, "the increasing ... appetite of metropolitan readers for books about walking around and discovering yourself in nature," Poole argues, "is the literary equivalent of the north London 'farmer's market,'" since "both feed on *nostalgie de la boue*—the French term for a kind of rustic-fancying inverted snobbery, which literally means 'nostalgia for the mud.'"[265] Toward the end of the article Poole remarks in passing that the nostalgia for the mud that for him characterizes recent "'Back to the Land' movements" and "today's back-to-nature revival" is "a response to corporations and the financial crisis." Unfortunately, Poole does not offer a precise account of this relation aside from suggesting that "the global machine of mass 'productivity' is broken," which means that "we should retreat to our gardens and tend our organic carrots." But, as we have seen, the matter is not quite that simple, since the relation between capitalism's contradictions and romantic anti-capitalism that attaches itself to the pastoral imagination also stands in an important relation to the central role that such narratives assume in contemporary right-wing discourse. As Poole suggests, the current desire to return to nature is related to a backlash against life under contemporary capitalism. However, this relation does not merely give rise to yet another wave of escapist cultural narratives but also to the dark underside of this nostalgic longing, namely right-wing nonsynchronism. What is significant here, however, is that we are beginning to see one of the origins of the logical connections between anti-capitalism and the pastoral in our time: the tension between capitalism's turn toward abstraction and immateriality and the concreteness and immediacy of reality that life in nature promises. This relation in turn can be understood in its full political import and in relation to similar aspects of the right-wing imagination when we consider the role that the desire for the restoration of authentic experience plays in the *völkisch* racial imagination of fascism in which blood and racial heritage are concretized through notions of mythical rootedness in nature and the soil. As Bloch suggests, the subjective rejection of capitalism gives rise to "pent up anger" that expresses itself objectively in in "romantic anti-capitalism that seeks its future in a better image of the past."[266]

Some of the most striking examinations of the complexities of these relations are contained in the contemporary novel, which seeks to make legible the causes and consequences of such reactionary desires. Far from adding to escapist idealizations of nature in our time that we find in contemporary popular culture, the novel has provided us with crucially important examinations of the dark underside and the political commitments—both overt and unintended— that are part of the current turn to nature and to the land. As early as the 1970s, novelists examine the consequences of the emerging understanding of the present as a time that is defined by new forms of alienation and that creates a crisis for our temporal imagination. Novelists develop detailed critiques of the experiential contradictions that result from contemporary capitalism and of the limitations that it seems to impose on our imagination. One of the earliest novels that dedicate themselves to this project is James Dickey's *Deliverance* (1970), which anticipates the widespread nostalgic turn to nature as a way to restore more authentic ways of life and along with it return to an understanding of masculinity whose reliance on old-fashioned physicality stands opposed to the increasing immateriality of life and work in contemporary capitalism. Lewis Medlock, who organizes the fateful canoe trip of a group of middle-aged men down a river in the rural backwaters of Georgia, represents the lure and ultimate failure of the withdrawal into body and nature that responds to the rise of a new historical dominant. "I believe in survival," Lewis declares at the beginning of the novel in his account of the value of his trips back to nature.[267] Survival is for Lewis a matter of opposing life in contemporary society. Unlike life in the city, surviving off the land allows him to embrace and rely upon the timeless concreteness of the male body, which provides Lewis with a way to escape from the time of virtuality that increasingly characterizes his present. In nature, Lewis claims, "the old human body is the same as it always was. It still feels that old fear, and that old pain."[268] The city is for Lewis the place where "everything [is] dead" and where he is forced to lead a life that is "out of touch with everything."[269] Hunting and surviving, on the other hand, is valuable precisely because it is connected with suffering: "you'd die early, and you'd suffer, and your children would suffer, but you'd be in touch."[270] The trip back to nature is for Lewis a matter of "breaking the pattern" and of transitioning "out of the sleep of mild people, and into the wild rippling water."[271] This transition, Lewis believes, can only be accomplished by restoring the primacy of the male body—and nature, the land is the site of natural masculinity, while the city is the space of emasculated "mildness." The infamous rape scene that is no doubt the most well-known aspect of Dickey novel forcefully undercuts the association between nature and masculinity that Lewis forges and throws the tension between the city and the rural into violent relief, juxtaposing the act of sexual violence with the temporal exclusion of the rural subject from the synchronous present.

What we see in Dickey's novel is an early example of representations of the changed relation between country and city that has become a crucial aspect of contemporary culture. Constructions of nature as the source of mythical pastness and of traditional masculinity go hand in hand with the reversal of modernity's characteristic understanding of the relation between the city as the site of progress and futurity and the country as the site of rural backwardness and stasis. Modernity's futuristic city is the site of change and the space of the energy that drives historical development in opposition to which nature is understood as the space of stasis. As critics like Raymond Williams and Fredric Jameson show in some detail, this account of the relation between country and city underlies studies of this relation reaching to Marx's infamous reference to the tension between the city and "rural idiocy."[272] And although this relation is often reductive and in itself highly problematic, Jameson shows that it is also out of this opposition between country and city that a "proto-Utopian" impulse emerges.[273] What we also see, however, is that this relation today, in particular in its reversed form that abandons the notion that the city serves as the motor of change and as the locus for futurity and that therefore returns to nature as the site of a better life, creates a protoutopian impulse that, as Bloch reminds us, can lead to strikingly different consequences. Dickey's novel illustrates the ways that this critique of life in the capitalist city attunes the narrator to the environmental destruction that capitalism brings with it. The valley through which the river runs that takes the men through their faithful journey, we learn in the early pages of the novel, will soon be flooded as part of the construction of a hydroelectric dam that will provide power for the city. The journey itself is therefore occasioned for the novel's narrator by a sense of urgency: soon, the valley will be destroyed, and this will be their last opportunity to go on this trip. For Lewis, however, as we have seen, the return to nature leads into a very different direction and is entirely bound up with the nostalgic reconstruction of lost forms of life and masculinity. And it is this latter aspect of the turn to nature that we witness with increasing frequency as a stock narrative of contemporary mass culture, which in turn calls for critiques and analyses of this well-established reactionary form of the return to nature.

Dickey's novel at every point places Lewis's reactionary desires in relation to the contradictions of and Lewis's rejection of the capitalist present. The novel's narrator knows that Lewis's true aim is, "to rise above time," and he also understands very well that Lewis's attachment to nature is just "romance."[274]

In particular, Lewis's idealization of the life of farmers and hunters and the mythical pastness of their mode of existence strikes the narrator as a starkly idealized picture that bears little relation to the past or to the lives of those who continue to work and exist under such conditions in the present. To the narrator, Lewis's desire to nature and to live off the land is clearly legible as a present simulation of a life that as such never existed in the past and that distorts the reality of such forms of existence in the present, amounting to a dual temporal myth:

> You'd think that farming was a healthy life, with fresh air and fresh food and plenty of exercise, but I never saw a farmer who didn't have something wrong with him, and most of the time obviously wrong; I never saw one who was physically powerful, either. Certainly there were none like Lewis. The work with the hands must be fantastically dangerous, in all that fresh air and sunshine, I thought: the catching of an arm in a tractor part somewhere off in the middle of a field where nothing happened but that the sun blazed back more fiercely down the open mouth of one's screams.[275]

Lewis's explanations register for the narrator as temporal escapism firmly rooted in the present and clearly reveals itself as based on a simulacrum of past natural purity and harmonious existence in nature. Particularly Lewis's romanticized idea of working the land strikes him as an insult to those whose life, labor, and dire struggles are transformed into an attraction for the middle- and upper-class temporal tourists of the increasingly abstract and immaterial present of contemporary capitalism. Opposed to the immediacy of the metaphorical hand through which Lewis aims to get back in touch with nature stands, therefore, the injured, mangled hand of the farmer indicates the subjective and objective nonsynchronism contained in this scene, and through its absence to hand points to what is missing in the present.

The difference between the two hands—Lewis's hand with which he gets back in touch with nature and the farmer's severed hand—is not a difference of time but of thought and politics. Lewis's desire to get back in touch with the body and nature attaches itself in polar opposition to the "progressive dematerialization" of capitalism and life that Mark C. Taylor analyzes in great detail in his 2014 book *Speed Limits*. "Today's globally wired financial markets," Taylor argues, are defined by the global circulation of financial assets that are no longer "grounded in anything beyond themselves … in nothing real."[276]

Although novelists like Dickey have engaged with aspects of this argument since the early 1970s, the analysis of the social and epistemological effects of the transition into dominant finance capitalism only becomes a central aspect of theoretical discourse in the early 2000s. Jean Comaroff and John L. Comaroff, for example, stress that one of the crucial aspects of neoliberalism is:

> [T]he explosion of new markets and monetary instruments, aided by sophisticated means of planetary coordination and space-time compression, have given the financial order a degree of autonomy from "real production" unmatched in the annals of political economy.[277]

What Comaroff and Comaroff describe as the "spiraling virtuality of fiscal circulation, of the accumulation of wealth purely through exchange"[278] that operates upon abstraction and immediacy registers for theorists such as Franco Berardi as a particular contraction and turn toward immediacy in the context of monetarization:

> [S]igns fall under the domination of finance when the financial function (the accumulation of value through semiotic circulation) cancels the instinctual side of enunciation, so what is enunciated may be compatible with digital-financial formats. The production of meaning and of value takes the form of parthenogenesis: signs produce signs without any longer passing through the flesh. Monetary value produces more monetary value without being first realized through the material production of goods.[279]

Contemporary capitalism can from this perspective be understood as the autonomization of (finance) capital. Finance capital's autonomization from real production and the erasure of the primacy of labor and the commodity from relations of value as money increasingly relates directly to money in the context of the rise to dominance of finance capital is based on an intensification of abstraction and contraction that remove the objective from the surface and that brings with it another form of the obfuscation of class, dissolving, as Comaroff and Comaroff argue, "the ground on which proletarian culture once stood."[280] No wonder, then, that such a situation prompts the desire on the Right as well as on the Left to return to a much idealized "real economy," a desire that seeks to confront financialization's attendant social problems by "re-industrializing" the economy, to once again "make things," or to idealize a return to forms of labor that are understood as more concrete or "real."

We encounter this line of reasoning not just in academic analysis but also in mainstream commentary. In an article in *Adbusters* magazine titled "The Narcotic Abstractions of Finance," Darren Fleet similarly suggests that we might understand the history of Western civilization as "the history of creeping abstraction" that has "reached its endgame" in finance capital.[281] In a moment when our lives "have become a derivative," Fleet argues, "our economic system has taken upon the etymology of apocalypse in the word finance … a word whose Latin root is finis, meaning 'the end.'" What disrupts our lives, Fleet suggests, is the sense that all of life has become subject to full abstraction.[282] As a result, when, as Taylor argues, "financial markets have become almost completely detached from the real economy," we witness the increasing nostalgic idealization of versions of life that seem to provide the opposite of such full abstraction. And since real time turns out to be the time of capitalist abstraction, getting back in touch with (the time of) nature seems to offer way to return to a lost, more concrete, more real version of time and existence. In this context, the physical experience of time is idealized as more real than the experience of capitalist temporality and creates the desire to return to, to use the title of Howard Kunstler's 2008 novel that in this case fuses cause and symptom, "a world made by hand."[283]

It is through this interplay of time and its end, of concrete immediacy and abstraction, that we can understand the relation between nature and romantic anti-capitalism. The experience of capitalism's omnipresent immediacy from which there seems to be no escape results in the development of a nostalgia for a different form of immediacy that expresses itself in the longing for authentic experiences and for the concrete life. Instead of abstraction and presence, nature is understood to promise a sense of both pastness and concreteness, a relation that is expressed in desires to "get back in touch with nature" or generally in the idea to "once again get in touch with x." The "touch" in these expressions underwrites the nostalgia for immediacy as a concrete, unmediated relation between subject and object, and the fantasy of a prior, more direct, more natural relation between self and world that is understood as being disrupted by the abstraction and virtuality of contemporary capitalism. Of course, as articles such as that of Poole indicate, the emergence of a nostalgia for nature that stands in opposition to the new forms of alienation that the contemporary stage of capitalism brings with it is as ubiquitous as it is understandable. But if we analyze this current trend with Bloch, then it becomes clear that this reaction against capitalist might give rise to both progressive economic critique and reactionary idealizations of the past that attach themselves dangerously to the logic of the contemporary Right. Thus, it is of crucial importance for our understanding of the Right's ability to leverage the nonsynchronism and its attached forms of nostalgia to examine the opposition between capital and nature in our time not only as a form of anti-capitalism but as a form of anti-capitalism that takes both progressive and dangerously reactionary forms. The exploitation of the latter, of the appeal of a "remythologized past," as Rabinbach shows, has been one of the key strategies of right-wing politics. Whereas the Left during the rise of German fascism appealed to a "synchronous" utopia of "planning" and rationalized social life, Rabinbach explains, the Nazi image of labor was instead that of "refeudalization," of an idealized return to "a Medievalism in which labor is handicraft, proletariat gives way to the workers' estate (Arbeitertum), and work itself is raised to a moral dimension and spirit of rejuvenation."[284]

Chuck Palahniuk's novel *Fight Club* (1996) may be read as delivering a critique of the collapse of anti-capitalism into the desire to return to a precapitalist or even precivilizational state of things. And, of course, the fact that Palahniuk's novel has become, as Ben Beaumont-Thomas outlines, a "bible for the incel movement" and a key text in the imagination and rhetoric of the alt-right (terms such as "snowflake" are lifted from Palahniuk's novel), makes *Fight Club* a particularly notable text in the context of current right-wing culture.[285] It should be added, too, that Palahniuk's novel is as fascinating as it is frequently misread, for its salient critique of the collapse of anti-capitalism into authoritarianism and fascism, in spite of frequent references to the making of soap out of parts of the human body that should be easy giveaways of its critique, has largely gone unnoticed in right-wing idolizations of the novel. Instead of the credit card companies and banks that collapse at the end of David Fincher's no doubt more well-known 1999 movie adaptation of Palahniuk's novel, the object of the professedly anti-consumerist, anti-capitalist Project Mayhem in Palahniuk's novel is to attack the Museum of Natural History—the group seeks to destroy history itself. The novel's unnamed narrator comes to an important realization while mercilessly beating a member of Fight Club because he is "in a mood to destroy something beautiful": one way of dealing with the present world that he dislikes so much is to make "the whole world ... hit bottom."[286] The morning after this realization, the group founds Project Mayhem, the activist branch of Fight Club, and begins to set out to accomplish their ultimate aim: "to blast the world free of history."[287]

The aim of Project Mayhem is to destroy the present and return the world to a better, earlier state in which men live in and directly relate to nature:

> Tyler said, picture yourself planting radishes and seed potatoes on the fifteenth green of a forgotten golf course. You'll hunt elk through the damp canyon forests around the ruins of Rockefeller Center, and dig claims next to the skeleton of the Space Needle ... It's Project Mayhem that's going to save the world. A cultural ice age.[288]

Project Mayhem's desire to return the world to a state of natural purity is the direct conclusion of the desire that led to the founding of Fight Club: to once again give the male body a concrete purpose and immediate use value. From the beginning of the novel, it is clear that this desire is directly associated with a crisis of masculinity that is aimed at an escape from the present and a return to nature and to a less alienated existence in the past. Project Mayhem's escapism is further connected to a reactionary longing for a mythical time in the past during which the weight of the world rested on the laboring male body or was held in the hands of men. The source of this present crisis of masculinity is already visible in Dickey's novel, which situates the men's return to nature in the context of a historical situation that is defined by the effacement of the centrality of the male laboring body in the new structure of capitalism. It is not coincidental, one might add, that the rise of the bodybuilding industry historically emerges inversely to the fall of the role of the male laboring body— the more the male laboring body and its physicality is removed from the center of production and life, the more we see the turn to alternative ways of using the body: tanning it, strengthening it, reducing it to a survival or fighting tool, and, as in *Fight Club*, lamenting the "feminization" of the present while jubilantly enacting a return to the past utility of the male body by grooming it for the next fight. The return to the male body is therefore also bound up with a profoundly misogynistic understanding of the present that we already encountered in the previous chapters and that binds itself even more forcefully to the longing of a new paternalism and its associated restoration of traditional masculinity. Tyler Durden, the unnamed protagonist's alter ego, claims that the men of Fight Club constitute "a generation of men raised by women." "I'm wondering," he adds, describing life for men in the present as marked by a "great spiritual depression," "if another woman is the answer."[289]

The reactionary desires that Palahniuk's novel lays bare are, of course, as irrational and fantastic as the vision of the past for which they long. And yet, such narratives harbor great danger in our time and must be understood as feeding into those aspects of our present that contribute to the rise of right-wing thought. As Jordy Rosenberg insists, it is important to remember that "fascism doesn't operate through reason." Rather, he explains, "it unleashes horrible fascinations, ensnaring the subject in what Bloch called a 'warlike erotic[s].'"[290] The wish for a world made by a masculine hand that stands at the center of Palahniuk's novel and that constitutes an important aspect of its critique of the present is fittingly expressed in a little-discussed scene that is missing entirely from Fincher's adaptation: the first meeting between the narrator and Tyler. The narrator recalls (or more accurately imagines himself) having met Tyler on a beach. In this first meeting, Tyler is in the process of constructing a sundial whose shape reminds the narrator of a hand, an action that registers for the narrator strikingly in its physicality and in the immediacy of the relation between Tyler and nature that finds expression in this act of manual labor. The sundial here functions as a symbol of the temporal atonement of man and nature, of the immediacy and concreteness of the relation between self and world that is coded as entirely masculine:

> I took a vacation. I fell asleep on the beach, and when I woke up there was Tyler Durden, naked and sweating, gritty with sand, his hair wet and stringy, hanging in his face. Tyler was pulling driftwood logs out of the surf and dragging them up the beach. What Tyler had created was the shadow of a giant hand, and Tyler was sitting in the palm of perfection he'd made himself.[291]

What we see here once more is the centrality of the image of the hand that invokes a different relation between self and world than that upon which contemporary capitalism rests. Tyler gives human form to the narrator's reactionary desire to return to the past, to escape contemporary capitalism by seeking communion with nature, a desire that is connected not only to the idealization of masculinity and to the forms of misogyny that are central to the novel but also to the very desires that cause the men of Fight Club to willingly submit themselves to an authoritarian structure and a paternalistic leader. One might suspect, therefore, that such desires for a return to a mythical world made by the hands of men are involved in the reason that fascists are obsessed with dramatic displays of hands in salutes that serve to reassure each other of the identity and masculinity that their hands are said to hold.

Getting back in touch with the homeland

Bloch shows that fascism centrally operates on a strategy that invokes the idyll and the pastoral as aspects of the nonsynchronous that are bound to ideas such as that of "natural rights" and of the natural, original purity of identity, race, and nation to through a relation that he describes as "mythical *enchantment* by the soil."[292] Fascism strengthens the attachment to the comfort of the known and to the past by simultaneously fostering a "deep antipathy towards moving into the unknown." Stressing the "grounding" effect of nature while connecting race and national identity to mythical notions of "rootedness in the soil," Bloch argues, fascism is able to create a culture in which "even in the town the soil has triumphed over motion and a very old space over time."[293] The myth of natural origin and purity in turn binds itself to "folkish (völkische) doctrine of family, caste and nature" and serves as yet another aspect of the obfuscation of capitalist contradictions and a fully developed anti-capitalist politics since it "lacks every connection with the way of life of the workers."[294] This function of myth as obfuscation is a crucial aspect of the right-wing imagination, as is the construction of the images of the Right's new paternalistic figureheads, as we saw in Chapter 2, as mystical fathers. The problem of the veiling function of myth and the mystical as a response to present and to history is reiterated in Jean-Paul Sartre's famous suggestion that "mystical ecstasies are our only means of escaping from the temporal world; and a mystic is always a man who wants to forget something."[295] Bloch urges us to subject the function of myth to close analysis for this reason. In the aftermath of the Second World War, having witnessed the evils of fascism that in his mind were characterized by "obfuscation combined with stupidity" and that gave rise to previously unseen forms of barbarism, Bloch argues that in the context of fascism myth revealed itself "in all its foulness."[296] This, Bloch argues, is "reason enough to be wary of the mythical sphere in its entirety."[297] In this context, Bloch emphasizes the importance of Marxist critiques of myth that have alerted us to the very danger that myth harbors in the context of reactionary thought. In particular myth's attachment to nature in the attempt to obfuscate the contradictions of the present, Bloch argues, must receive special attention, for, as German fascism shows, there lies great danger in myth's "most primitive version, which Engels once called the 'Imbecility of the primeval forest.'"[298]

But to be critical of myth and to regard it with great suspicion, Bloch stresses, is not to suggest that it should be rejected altogether. After all, he suggests, there lies in myth also a positive core. For all its obscurantist aspects and in spite of the dangers associated with this function, myth also contains what Bloch calls the *"utopian light of comprehended futurity,"* a form of the utopian imagination that points the way to the future precisely because it has "burst forth from the myths of the *past*."[299] Bloch points here specifically to subversive myths "like those relating to eating from the tree of knowledge, the tower of Bable, or even the rebellion of angels," and he argues that "just as the fairy tale lends its genial proportions to every salvation of myth, likewise the quietest and most enchanting of fairy tales may end up serving as an authentic means of disenchantment."[300] Foregrounding the fairy tales of Hans Christian Andersen, tales in which nothing "stands in need of salvation, except for ourselves," Bloch indicates here another version of the same conviction that we have encountered in previous chapters, the conviction that even in myth, as in the nonsynchronous or in the gruesomely distorted pseudoutopia of fascism, there is something worth saving, something that contains a utopian core that may be recovered.[301] In our moment, too, we can trace such forms of recovering utopian thought precisely by exploring its distorted other, the obfuscations and myths of our time, in order to recover authentic means of disenchantment. Novels such as Nathaniel Rich's *Odds Against Tomorrow* (2013) illustrate this very idea of the recovery of utopian thought and of critique from its seeming ruins. Rich's novel utilizes the stock narrative of the mythical return to nature in order to return its underlying impulses to the contradictions of capital and thus explores the temporal crises of our time, nonsynchronist desires, and the nostalgic idealization of a return to nature in their complex relation to contemporary capitalism.

Odds Against Tomorrow follows protagonist Mitchell Zukor, a talented young mathematician, from his time in university through his career as a budding corporate "futurist" to his withdrawal into a pastoral life in the marshes of the Flatlands (a neighborhood in Brooklyn) after the destruction of New York City by a gigantic hurricane. The novel introduces Mitchell as a young man who is notable for his talent for mathematics and for his tendency to fantasize about disasters:

> [T]he way other people fantasize about surprise inheritances, first-glance love, and endless white empyreal pastures, Mitchell dreamed of an erupting supervolcano that would bury North America under a foot of hot ash. He envisioned a nuclear exchange with China; a modern black plague; an asteroid tearing apart the crust of the earth, unleashing a new dark age. Such singularities didn't frighten him, he claimed; they offered freedom. They opened wormholes to a sublime realm of fantasy and chaos.[302]

Mitchell's fantasies of destruction are the result of his struggle to come to terms with his historical context: "he may have understood numbers, but everyday life was too complex for him."[303] Imagining large-scale disasters offers Mitchell a way to imagine simpler ways of life that succeed the disastrous destruction of a life that he often finds bewildering, which expresses itself in his ultimate withdrawal into a life in nature at the end of the novel.

After leaving university, Mitchell is initially recruited by a company in New York City, Fitzsimmons Sherman, that tasks Mitchell with calculating worst case scenarios and their financial impact on the company:

> Mitchell's assignment, it soon became clear, was simple: he was to calculate the price of each Fitzsimmons employee's life, in dollars ... His job was not to predict longevity ... For the purposes of his assignment, a person's value meant the value of his life to Fitzsimmons Sherman.[304]

Mitchell's new job requires him to constantly engage with the future. His tendency to imagine apocalyptic future scenarios in this context becomes an asset, because his assignment requires him to imagine the future apocalyptically. The service that Fitzsimmons Sherman provides to its customers is in fact connected to the effort to limit futurity to apocalyptic scenarios. And this strategy pays off for the company, since contracting the imaginative engagement with and anticipation of the future to the threat of possible apocalyptic destruction in the future serves as an effective way of generating value in the present. In the company's strategy, one that it exports to larger corporations who seek to develop future strategies based on a clear assessment of future risk, destruction and capitalist accumulation become directly linked: "the work often required him to type the word 'future' into his search engine—as in 'future holdings' or 'future cost of' or 'future mass destruction.'"[305] In the context of his research Mitchell encounters an online ad, which his search engine continually recommends for him, whose tag line greatly intrigues Mitchell: "FIND OUT WHAT THE FUTURE WILL COST YOU."[306] After visiting the company's website and discovering that the ad is for a company called "FutureWorld" that offers "consulting services in 'future prediction'" Mitchell decides to write to the company, inquiring: "what *will* the future cost me? ... Can I afford it? Will I pay with my life?"[307] This initial email initiates an exchange with FutureWorld founder and director Alec Charnoble (a suitably disastrous-sounding last name) who ultimately convinces Mitchell to leave Fitzsimmons and join FutureWorld.

One of the guiding principles of Charnoble and his company is that "chaos breeds financial opportunity."[308] And since "this [is] a chaotic time," he argues, FutureWorld aims to position itself in order to profit from the present's chaos. A chaotic present that appears consumed with "fear of a great danger coming on," Charnoble suggests, is fertile ground for the service his company offers.[309] Companies can enlist the services of FutureWorld to study the particular risks and potential disasters a company may encounter, quantify how likely they are to occur, and how much a given disaster may cost the company. This, Charnoble argues, allows companies to make specific, strategic plans now for the likely disaster of tomorrow. Mitchell's brilliant mathematical abilities paired with his sense of impending doom make him an ideal candidate for FutureWorld, Charnoble knows, not only because he is able to imagine and calculate potential disasters, but because he is able to frighten clients. "It's essential, in this line of work, to frighten clients. To convey a sense of implacable doom, in a manner of speaking," Charnoble tells Mitchell, adding:

> It's not difficult to frighten people during hard times ... The challenge is to scare them during the hopeful times, in the lulls between catastrophic events, when FutureWorld's services start to seem like an unnecessary luxury. When I look at you I start to believe that another disaster is fast approaching.[310]

The apocalyptic imagination that helps draw the future into the present becomes a strategic tool for capitalism. The odds against tomorrow, the act of betting on future destruction, functions as a different facet of speculation in finance capitalism that transforms the future into an asset of the present, an aspect of Rich's book that examines in detail the connection between the disastrous consequences of financial speculation on our social and cultural imaginary that commentators like Fleet foreground. In Rich's novel, futurists are defined as specific agents of capitalism who amplify existing fears and anxieties by projecting them onto projected future scenario in order to be able to market solutions to or forms of protection from future catastrophe in the present. The futurist's gaze, Rich's novel shows, is fully fixed on the present, and the success of futurist strategy lies in the ability to amplify conservative desires for protection and for extending the present into the future.

Mitchell's increasing success as a futurist, however, runs into a philosophical barrier with which Mitchell struggles to come to terms. Mitchell has an old friend, Elsa Bruner, who suffers from a medical condition that without advance signs or symptoms may cause episodes which, if not immediately treated by medical professionals, will lead to her death. Yet, in spite of this, Elsa decides to relocate to a removed rural area to begin a "utopian agricultural experiment" (65), starting a collective farm with a group of friends, a decision Mitchell cannot understand. In the context of his work, the fear of death and destruction prompts his clients to do their best to protect themselves from potential catastrophes, to engage in corporate doomsday prepping. Why, then, does the actual threat of death not cause Elsa to do the same? Why, Mitchell wonders, would she choose to pursue what strikes him as the least logical route? Throughout the novel, Elsa's choices and her view of the future, of fear, and of utopia stand opposed to Mitchell's. Her choices and rationale lay bare the flaws in Mitchell's logic, illustrating that his particular view of the world replaces future possibility with world that is entirely constructed in the image of the fears and anxiety that Mitchell conjures up in and that emerge out of and point back toward the present. Elsa's view of the present strikes Mitchell as a matter of "wishful thinking" and as such as "negligent, dangerous."[311] Still, in crucial moments in the novel, Elsa, who embodies the core logic of what we may understand as Blochian utopian thought, exerts an influence on Mitchell that encourages him to engage in self-critical examination of the consequences of how work and worldview:

> [T]he young, low-level financial associates who met with him suddenly seemed pitiful. They didn't realize what they'd gotten themselves into. Like him, they had come from distant cities and towns to New York, hoping to make their fortune. Out of their element, without anyone to advise them, they bunked in dormitories dressed up as apartments in overpriced midtown high-rises and spent excessively on sushi, online dating, tailors, executive haircuts. But they were blind to their fate. They didn't realize they were being fed like virginal sacrifices into the maw of history, of twenty-first-century capitalism, of vast, complex systems that were wildly beyond their control.[312]

The fascination with the end times and large-scale disasters, Mitchell realizes in these moments, functions in part as a mechanism for hiding the end times, the disasters, and the destruction of the future that capitalism itself creates. His activity as futurist, in other words, is a matter of relocating disasters that are altogether part of capitalism itself in external relation to the system and replacing them with the fear of "expected" natural disasters that creates the desire to protect the very system from which the actual danger to human life originates.

The constant corporate and private doomsday prepping that Rich's novel portrays reveals itself as part and parcel of a broader problem: the displacement of our focus on capitalism's own disasters and onto natural disasters whose influence on the world represents the last shred of history that the characters in the novel can imagine. But this logic represents a withdrawal from the responsibility for change and history, as becomes clear throughout the novel as a result of Elsa's choices that chart a different path. But for Mitchell and for the majority of those who surrounding him in everyday life, only nature itself is capable of making a difference and of creating future change in a present that is otherwise fully subsumed under capitalism. Nature, in this sense, becomes not only an aspect of the present's nostalgic desires for immediacy but it is also transformed into the only force that is able to bring about change in a present whose timelessness is further reified by the turn to nature itself. The attachment to natural disasters and apocalyptic destruction is centrally involved in creating the impression of an a-historical and static present in opposition to which it is simultaneously mobilized, reiterating the underlying contradictions of the problem of the long now that we encountered at the beginning of this book.

Eventually, however, after expecting the big storm for some time, disaster actually does strike, and, following a long drought, a large Hurricane devastates New York City and large swathes of the surrounding area. Initially it seems as though the destruction might mark the beginning of a different now and a point beyond which restoring the old is not possible, which Mitchell understands as the definite and inescapable timelessness of omnipresence with which his futurism had been toying: "for the long term was now upon them. According to the scientists, these would become the presiding conditions."[313] Faced with life in the long term, Mitchell's friend Jane convinces him to see this as a great professional opportunity for futurists and persuades him to found his own company, FutureDays. "Jane, of course, was right," Mitchell realizes after initial hesitation:

> This was where the futurist came in. Essentially a futurist was asked to prevent the future from happening. He was paid to devise solutions that might halt change … Those in power wanted to be told that everything will stay just as before—as long as you purchase a little insurance. And this was the service that Future Days would provide. In the short term, it would be a lucrative business. And the short term was all that mattered. He was beginning to think there would be no long term.[314]

Mitchel begins his work for FutureDays in FEMA trailer number 2199, but he soon regards this number with some discomfort. To Mitchell it does not invoke a year in the future but instead signals that "the future had arrived," a future which "assumed the shape of a long white rectangular box with two windows looking out over the narrowest part of the East River. A coffin with a view."[315] FutureDays, he knows, merely serves to confirm that death and the end of time and long-term change have become the new way of the world. Consequently, Mitchell abandons FutureDays and decides to flee the destroyed city. Together with a group of refugees Mitchell follows now unused railroad tracks east to the Flatlands, an area utterly devastated by the storm, flattened and devoid of any recent architecture. Only a few old buildings remain standing after the storm, and an abandoned bank building becomes Mitchell's new home.

Mitchell soon realizes that the fear of the apocalypse that had defined his life up to this moment has disappeared. Sensing the beginning of a new way of life, Mitchell concludes that he also needs a new way of looking at the world. Finding himself to be "without belief," now that he has "forsaken the cult of fear" and "abandoned the order of the futurist," Mitchell decides that he needs a new belief: "yes, a new faith was required, something rigorous, ascetic, all-encompassing."[316] Mitchell finds this new faith in nature itself. Laboring the land and surviving in the marshes of the Flatlands, Mitchell trades in the time and futurity of neoliberal capitalism for the time of nature and his body. But, it becomes clear, his attempt to atone self and world, to replace a world that is defined by utter abstraction with a world of the immediately concrete, does not lead to any form of insight into his current life. In fact, the retreat into the absolute immediacy of body and nature are a way for Mitchell to avoid any intellectual or interpretive relation to the world. His new faith that addresses Mitchell's initial metaphysical lack, the alternative to the world of the capitalist long term that he decided to abandon, lies ultimately in the rejection of a metaphysical engagement with the world altogether. His new life in nature, he finds, creates a striking "general sensation," namely "mindlessness."[317] Still, Mitchell labors on, trying hard to disregard the mindlessness resulting from his return to nature and focusing instead on laboring the land itself: "he'd be away from the world, yet in it more intimately than he had ever known. *Doing finally.*"[318] The return to nature, Rich's novel shows, replaces the problem of the absorption of the future into the long now of capitalism with the withdrawal into a mythical relation to the land out of which emerges only a stunted relation to and understanding of the world as well as an impoverished future in which the nostalgia for concreteness reveals itself as a drudgery of mere survival: "this was a future. It might not be the best possible future or even a particularly comfortable future, but it was a future that he could see."[319]

Yet, while Mitchell is utterly unable to see the logical flaw in his plan for a new existence, it is the novel's female character who is able to understand that which remains hidden to her male counterpart, unearthing the incoherence of both the romanticized return to nature as a way to confront the problems of the present and the idealized notion of masculinity to which it is attached. In the final paragraphs of the novel, we see Mitchell struggling with the contents of a letter that is delivered to him. The letter is from Elsa, who, Mitchell learns, is alive. Elsa has chosen to undergo open-heart surgery to correct her condition and is preparing for university, where she will study environmental law. Mitchell is confused by this information and remarks that this does sound like "the Elsa Bruner [he] knew."[320] The letter from Elsa also contains an old postcard that Mitchell had sent her when he first began working for FutureWorld:

> It read 'By the time you get this, I'll be a futurist.' It was in Mitchell's handwriting, with his signature. Only Elsa had crossed out Mitchell's name and signed her own. 'What the hell is that supposed to mean?' said Mitchell (303).

What Mitchell tragically still cannot comprehend at the end of the novel is the distinction between two forms of futurism that Elsa wants to communicate to him. Elsa has embraced the risk that is associated with the present and, by confronting the contradiction and dangers of the present head-on, she is able to develop a sense of futurity. Mitchell's own futurism, though seemingly consisting of two different choices, ultimately fails, and the seeming difference between the choices—turning risk itself into an aspect of financial speculation on one hand or avoiding the risks and dangers of the present entirely by reducing existence to the risk of mere survival—reveals itself as only two sides of the same problematic coin, as connected desires that together reiterate the limiting sense of a timeless present without future. Novels like *Odds against* therefore examine the sources of contemporary forms of nonsynchronism in relation the contradictions of finance capitalism while also laying bare the illogic of the desires and responses that such forms of nonsynchronism generate of which the desire to return to the land is a particularly prevalent manifestation in our moment. The critique of the nostalgic attachment to nature as a way to resolve the contradictions that emerge in the context of life in contemporary capitalism in Rich's novels therefore echoes contemporary theorists like Judy Wajcman, who argues that "resisting technological innovation and calling for deceleration or a digital detox," a form of resistance that frequently leads to the idealization of nature, "is an inadequate intellectual and political response." "Indeed," Wajcman stresses, "wistfully looking back to an idealized slower time and mourning its passing has long been the preserve of conservative political theory."[321]

"All previous history," Bloch insists in *Subjekt-Objekt* (1949), "is still human prehistory."[322] Most of this history, he adds, "still shows 'Nature' in the Hegelian sense, in the sense of a being-outside-oneself, in which the powers produced by mankind, but not comprehended as produced, have broken away and become reified. Hence, they appear as an uncontrollable fate, which they have in fact been in previous history." The tragedy of Mitchell's understanding of the world lies in just such an understanding of the relation between nature and the reification of the power produced by mankind, most notably the reification of the logic of capital to which a similarly reified conception of nature serves as a mythical "outside" to capitalism while, as Mitchell remains unable to understand, ultimately further reifying the status quo. The problematic forms of relating to nature that we have encountered in this chapter are characterized by the intersecting and mutually reinforcing logic of reification and of what Bloch calls "the emptiness of diversion," the escape from and obfuscation of the contradictions of our present through the intoxicating effect that Bloch associates with instances in which the nonsynchronous binds itself to idealized returns to nature.[323] Such "exoticism at home," Bloch writes, is part and parcel of the attempt to resurrect "national myths" in the context of a culture in which myth "has its fantasy not in the distance but, as it were, vertically beneath the native soil."[324] The mythical association of identity with the land, of racial constructions of the relation between soil and nation, possesses a striking power in the contemporary North American context, in spite of the fact that the absence the longer lineage of "national and racial heritage" to which German fascism appealed. The colonial history of North America itself assumes an important role in new forms of white nationalism and white supremacy, since they not only display a longing for precisely those narratives of race and nation that Bloch outlines but also reconstruct the brutal history of colonization into a story of European supremacy over North America's indigenous peoples, reimagining murder and ethnic cleansing as expressions of racial superiority and reconstructing North American as the native soil for new myths of national and cultural purity and superiority.

But while such hateful and cynical revisions of the history of colonialism and of the relation between race and land that are a central aspect of new forms of white nationalism must be vehemently opposed, Bloch's work also encourages us to analyze the sources of contemporary forms of romantic attachments to the past, to nature, and to masculinity. Doing so will allow us to better understand the origin of these desires and their current power, and it may allow us to trace aspects that can be rescued or redirected toward a critique of the underlying structural sources of the discontent out of which they emerge. "Romanticism has no other future than at best that of the undisposed-of past," Bloch writes, adding that "it does have this kind of future, and it ought to be 'resolved' (Aufgehoben) for it, in the precise dialectical multiple sense of the term."[325] It is in this way that we see a concrete example of what it may mean when Bloch suggests that the Left ought not simply reject reactionary impulses but instead trace their origin and thereby offer the underlying anger and resentment a different home. And in this way, too, Bloch stresses, we can recover the idea of home itself for a different project. Instead of serving in the context of romanticized idealization of lost ancestral homes or ideas of a mythical homeland that fuse race and soil, there lies in the idea of home, once differently conceived, a source of utopian thought. For Bloch, the idea of home is not a matter of nostalgic longing or of restoration. Rather, Thompson illustrates, it is a matter of "a still unimaginable idea and reality of Heimat or home as utopia," an anticipatory understanding of the idea of home, which understands the concept not as "one of an eternal return to some prelapsarian idyll" but as the utopian longing for a home that is not yet, a home that is "still being created."[326] In the final chapter of this book, I will illustrate the immense value of just such an understanding of home, of futurity in a present without time, that Bloch's work gives us. For in particular in the time of the long now that brings with it a new moment of danger and the rise of new forms of nonsynchronism and of reactionary thought, Blochian thought redirects our attention from the desire to return to lost notions of home, self, land, and nation and instead establishes a different relation to both past and present. The answer to the problems of the present lies not in myth or in the greatness of a lost past but in the attempt to reclaim the true utopian futurity that lies in the abandoned or silenced demands for a better life that the past contains and that may guide the way toward the future.

5

Completing the Thought of the Past: Literature as Utopian Method

Where do we turn when it seems as though the future can no longer offer us improvements or changes to the existing world, when everything that lies ahead of us seems like a mere extension of our present? As we have seen throughout this book, this problem is a common one today. In a world in which virtually every part of life has become subsumed under capitalism and in which change itself does not bring about future alternatives to capitalism but merely new iterations of its presence, the future disappears into a long now. In such a situation, we witness the emergence of a specific form of reactionary thought that seeks answers in the past when the future is understood as offering only more of the same. But such returns to the past inevitably create and are aimed at versions of a past that never existed. Nostalgic idealizations of ways of life that are understood as having been lost ultimately reveal themselves as nothing more than simplistic solutions to or ways of avoiding the fears and anxieties of our present that are projected onto the past. Between such simulations of the past and a future that is understood as inaccessible or devoid of change and difference, where might we locate possibilities for politics, thought, and art?

Novels like Cormac McCarthy's *The Road* (2007), which engage with this struggle between the past and the future, appear to confirm the deadlock that results from this situation. In the novel's early pages, the narrator, who relates to us the arduous journey of a father and his son through a postapocalyptic wasteland in search of a future, poses a striking question: "how does the never to be differ from what never was?" Throughout the previous chapters, we have seen that the work of Ernst Bloch provides us with a different way of imagining not only past and future but also time itself, one that is of crucial importance for our ability to engage not just with the contemporary crisis of temporality itself but also with its social and political consequences. Examined from a Blochian standpoint, the question that McCarthy's novel poses identifies the difference that may allow us wrest the remnants of hope from the grip that the capitalist long now has on the utopian imagination. For it is in what never was rather than in what will never be that Blochian utopian thought is located. Utopia, Bloch shows us, lies not in lofty dreams of a future that will never come to pass but in a different understanding of the past. That which never was restores our attention to those demands for liberation that went unheard, to the dreams of a better world that were repressed, and to those projects and ideas whose time had not yet come but that seek to be completed in the future. The never to be is a politically and philosophically empty category and form of our imagination. What never was, however, indicates that which is not yet and that which may yet be. Thus conceived, the past offers us a source of hope beyond naïve utopianism and reactionary turns to the past. In the context of the long now, this understanding of the relation between past and future may be experiencing its most timely instantiation.

Previous chapters have indicated this important aspect of Blochian thought. In this final chapter, I will illustrate the significance of Bloch's conception of nonsynchronism and of excess synchronism for our time. Bloch provides us with a different conception of the relation between past, present, and future than the one that has come under severe crisis in the context of the capitalist long now. Bloch's work asks us to imagine time beyond the linearity and standardized homogenization of capitalist standard time, and it thereby indicates a source of hope and futurity that dialectically sublates both time's purported exhaustion and the reactionary turn to pastness that characterizes recent right-wing thought. Bloch shows us that we should not simply understand the past as the time of what was. Moreover, understanding the past as the time of what we wish had been, Bloch shows, harbors great danger, particularly in historical moments of crisis when it is difficult to imagine paths to a better future. Instead, Blochian thought provides us with a way of understanding the past as an archive of unfulfilled dreams that reach into the present and that anticipate the future. The present, in turn, contains the latent potential that points toward possible futures. As Peter Thompson argues, the present contains those "preilluminations, of a better world, messages of hope sent to us from a not yet possible future reality but already known to us from our own need for the fulfillment of past desires and memories as 'anticipatory consciousness.'"327

Blochian thought, however, does not just provide us with an alternative to the dangerous forms of nonsynchronism and reactionary attachments to the past that emerge out of the contradictions of our moment. More than that, Bloch's work explores the origins of reactionary nonsynchronism, which, Bloch shows, is often the distorted result of what originally emerged as a protoutopian impulse and as a demand for change. Bloch urges us to engage with right-wing nonsynchronism beyond critique, denunciation, and ridicule. In addition to laying bare the hatred, the violence, and the mystification of actual social and economic crises that are part and parcel of right-wing extremism, Bloch stresses the importance of exploring those aspects of right-wing thought that may be rescued for progressive projects. Bloch's work urges us to remember that, under different conditions, matters could have been quite different and the original demands for change and the backlash against the contradictions of capital that underlie right-wing extremism and fascism may have given rise to progressive utopian thought. For this reason, too, as I will demonstrate through a reading of Cherie Dimaline's 2017 novel *The Marrow Thieves*, Blochian thought is of great value to the pressing project of decolonizing the present. In particular in those passages of Bloch's work that directly address the multiple timelines and notions of temporality that are bound up with the history of colonialism, passages that have received too little attention thus far, we find a form of thought and critical analysis that allows us to trace those timelines and those dreams of freedom and demands of liberation that have been silenced by colonialism and that remain repressed in the colonial long now. Bloch suggests that the anticipatory energy of the now, the latent potential in the present that emerges through an engagement with the past, is contained nowhere as strongly as in art. In our moment, this chapter argues, Indigenous and First Nations literatures are particularly powerful expressions of this form of utopian art and imagination. In particular in the North American context in which a new wave of white nationalism attach settler identity to the violent history of colonialism, Indigenous and First Nations artists who model for us what it may mean to activate the past as a way to formulate the "not yet" through an engagement with that which was not permitted to be constitutes one of the most striking manifestations of the kind of utopian thought as well as one of the most significant forms of contemporary political art. We find the other of white racism's temporal imagination in novels like *The Marrow Thieves*, which model for us concrete examples of the great value and political urgency of decolonizing the long now by understanding futurity as the anticipatory consciousness that results from the unfulfilled wishes and desires for liberation of the past that continue to exist in the present and that tear at the fissures of colonial presence, the purportedly homogeneous, uniform long now.

Hope: Material hunger for what's missing

It is not a bad idea to look backward. How we do so, however, makes all the difference. We can look to the past in order to find utopian impulses. But we can also look to the past in order to service reactionary desires. Situations in which the latter happens, Bloch stresses, may be best addressed not by discrediting retrospection itself but by offering a better version thereof. In particular since the displacement of discontent and rebellious energy from the level of intellectual analysis to that of emotion is a crucial strategy of the Right, Bloch's emphasis on the act of dreaming as a pathway to utopian thought and progressive politics is helpful in our time, for it illustrates a way to engage with the relation between past and present that bridges emotion and analytical thought. Oskar Negt reminds us that "it was precisely the mechanistic intellectualism of many German socialists which ultimately drove many people into the arms of the Nazis."[328] And although "they did not gain there an understanding of their situation," Negt stresses, "they did find a language—no matter how shabby and deceitful—that was directed at an emotionalism (Gefühlsstand) characterized by poverty, instability, and susceptibility to rapture."[329] In order to counteract this right-wing strategy and the Left's tendency to reinforce it by insisting on addressing the matter via "mechanistic intellectualism," the very intellectualism that has proven itself to further alienate its intended audience and that the Right easily reconstructs as an expression of class privilege, we may turn to Blochian thought. Negt writes: "it is necessary everywhere to occupy concretely the dream areas of the imagination instead of neglecting them altogether and thereby abandoning them to those who are bent on deception and the destruction of reason."[330] The danger of moments in which we witness the rise of the extreme Right, Bloch argues, call for something more than critique, opposition, and ridicule of the nonsynchronous desires and of irrational and hateful thought and rhetoric. The Left, Bloch stresses, must also be able to offer alternatives, forms of utopian thought that reclaim the territory of dreams from the Right.

Anson Rabinbach foregrounds that Blochian thought is marked by the conviction that we have an obligation to understand the relation between the competing temporal dimensions that together make up the present, which in our time most notably contains the tension between reactionary turns to the past, the perception of the temporal exhaustion of the present, and the latent utopian potential that lies in the present as a residue of the past, as a dialectical relation. In Bloch's work, in particularly inasmuch as it is marked by nonsynchronism, the present is understood as always multiple, as constituted by the "the temporal and multi-layered contradictions within a single present."[331] This immanent temporal multiplicity of the now can be understood as the result of "the sedimentation of social experience" that creates, for instance, the desire for the "resurrection of the past among those groups most susceptible to fascist propaganda."[332] But, Rabinbach shows that Bloch insists on the value of Marxist analysis in this context, since Marxism understands fascist ideology not simply as "an instrument of deception" but as fundamentally bound up with fragments of "an old and romantic antagonism to capitalism, derived from deprivations in contemporary life, with a longing for a vague 'other.'"[333] In other words, instead of limiting the focus of analyses of fascism to the irrationality of surface rhetoric or action and to the distorted version of the past that it mobilizes, Bloch argues for the importance of locating the reasons for a turn to fascism in the contradictions of capitalism. But rather than redirecting the discontent that the present produces toward romantic anti-capitalism and constructions of a "vague other," as is the case in right-wing thought, Marxist analysis asks how rejections of the contradictions of the present might be returned to their sources in order to encourage fully developed critiques of contemporary capitalism. Since the turn to fascism originates in the contradictions of capital, Bloch emphasizes, there lies positive potential even in fascism, a potential may be rescued and turned into a basis for progressive politics.

"Not everything that is irrational can be dismissed as stupidity," writes Bloch in *Heritage of Our Times*.[334] Rabinbach fittingly describes *Heritage* as a "polemic against the irrationalism of the rational," foregrounding the limits of analyses of fascism that "fail to grasp what is 'rational in the irrational.'"[335] Bloch's insistence on the need to trace the irrational in the rational, the protoutopian thought that lies at the heart of fascism but that is distorted and all but entirely hidden by fascism's irrationality and hatred, also contains a self-reflexive critique of Marxism. As Rabinbach shows, Bloch is convinced that Marxism will remain unable to reckon with this aspect of fascism's origin and that it will remain unable to comprehend the urgency of tracing the rational in the irrational "as long as it represse[s] its own history as a prescientific utopia."[336] "There can be no successful attack on the irrational front," Bloch writes, "without a dialectical intervention."[337] Ultimately, therefore, Rabinbach argues, *Heritage* "is not only an appeal for the rescue of the emancipatory content of other traditions, rather it is an appeal for the rediscovery of these roots in Marxism itself, for its own "genuine nebulae" to become explicit."[338] In other words, Blochian thought provides us with a way of analyzing right-wing thought that at the same time serves as a reflection on Marxist critique. It therefore identifies a critical method and a political strategy that seeks to undo fascist thought from within while simultaneously engaging in an examination of the limits and possibilities of Marxist thought and politics.

Blochian critique is aimed at the demystification of those underlying contradictions that fascism veils. But while it is of crucial importance to foreground the ways in which fascism is dependent upon and functions as a form of mystification, Bloch's engagement with fascism does not stop there. As Douglas Kellner puts it, Blochian thought is also a means of recovering those "unrealized dreams, lost possibilities, abortive hopes … that can be resurrected and enlivened and realized in our current situation."[339] "For Bloch," Kellner explains, "ideology is 'Janus-faced', two-sided: it contains errors, mystifications, and techniques of manipulation and domination, but it also contains a utopian residue or surplus that can be used for social critique and to advance progressive politics."[340] A critique of fascist thought that contents itself with simply dismissing fascism as irrational is on Bloch's account foreshortened. "Bloch would dismiss this purely denunciatory practice of ideology critique as 'half-enlightenment,'" Kellner writes, adding that Blochian critique instead seeks to "criticize any distortions in an ideological product, but then goes on to take it more seriously, to read it closely for any critical or emancipatory potential."[341] The limit of approaches that focus only on the exposure of the irrational in fascism lies in Kellner's view in the assumption that eliminating error alone is not a sufficient or effective engagement with fascism. After all, Kellner reiterates, Bloch shows that part of the reason why the Left was defeated by the Right in Weimar Germany "is because the Left tended to focus simply on criticism, on negative denunciations of capitalism and the bourgeoisie, whereas fascism provided a positive vision and attractive alternatives to masses desperately searching for something better."[342]

In particular in a moment when the Left struggles to formulate effective responses to a new rise of right-wing extremism, it is important to take seriously Bloch's emphasis on the importance of recovering the progressive content that may be contained in irrational right-wing or fascist thought in addition to denouncing it. Openly and strongly denouncing it is no doubt absolutely vital and necessary to do, for critique must never give way to apologism or equivocation when it comes to its engagement with fascism. And it is certainly of the utmost importance to distinguish Bloch's call for the critical engagement with those parts of right-wing thought that may be rescued for progressive projects from efforts to normalize or tolerate dimensions of fascism, or from attempts to treat fascism as merely one of many political positions that deserve to be heard or taken seriously. The latter is not what Bloch has in mind, and it must, to be sure, never enter into Left strategy or critique. But the fight against fascist hatred and irrationality must also include a dimension that moves beyond denunciation by exploring the ways in which understanding fascism's core, its root causes, and those forms of discontent that, once dialectically reconstructed, may give way to progressive projects. The most significant aspect of latter project lies in critical theory's ability to lay bare the ways in which capitalist exploitation, alienation, and repression creates those forms of discontent that fascism exploits. What is possible in such a situation is a project that illustrates that the allegiance of those who suffer under such conditions and who demand a better world cannot lie with fascism, for fascism ultimately safeguards the very system that oppresses them. Instead of the hollow validation and representation, and instead of the hatred directed at others in the attempt to veil the origins of systemic discontent that are the only "solutions" that fascism can provide for those whose suffering it purports to address, Left critique must offer an alternative by returning discontent to its source and its ultimate object: the system out of which it originated. Left critique must explore ways to turn romantic anti-capitalism and the stunted forms of capitalist critique that fascism contains into fully developed anti-capitalism. Simply put, Left critique must denounce fascism and lay bare its mechanisms of mystification while also illustrating that the hardships and injustices, the everyday struggles with disenfranchisement and alienation that define the lives of those on whom fascism preys are not solved by a fight against a "vague other" but by a fight against capitalism.

Moreover, in particular in our moment, which as we have seen in some detail is marked by a severe crisis of temporality and futurity, the way forward for Left critique cannot lie in reiterating well-worn accounts of the long now, of the presentism that purportedly defines our time. Every time we refer to the suggestion that it is easier to imagine the end of the world than making even a modest progressive change to the structure of capitalism, a suggestion that is by now almost stereotypically associated with our moment in history, and every time we reiterate the idea of a pervasive crisis of futurity without offering a radical critique of the very logic of capital and of the relation between capitalist time and the crisis of futurity out of which this crisis emerges, we cede further territory to right-wing demagogues and agitators. Accepting the presentism of real-time capitalism as the only time, and confining our conception of temporality and possibility to those constricted and standardized versions of these concepts that capitalism itself offers means that we also relinquish our ability to engage with the forms of nonsynchronism and the latent potential that our present contains, and we abandon the past to right-wing rhetoric. Bloch's work models for us a way to offer a different understanding of the time of our now and a different understanding of the relation between past and future that is also aimed at offering a politics to those who suffer most severely from the presence of capitalism.

Reclaiming the past from the Right and understanding the present not as a time of foreclosure but as a time defined by lack allows us to understand the way forward as charted for us by what Rabinbach with Bloch describes as "the hunger for happiness and freedom" that emerges not just from dreams but also from the recognition of past and present instances of being denied happiness and freedom.[343] For Bloch, Rabinbach argues, "the past is a beacon within the present, it illuminates the horizon of that possibility which has not yet fully come into view, which has yet to be constructed." The archive of unfulfilled possibility and of silenced demands for liberation that the past contains extends into the now as temporal multiplicity. In this plural now, presence stands opposed to absence inherited from the past, and the absences in the present confront us as tasks, as projects and demands that seek to be realized in the future. To assume that the present is indeed temporally uniform, to assume that our time is fully present and devoid of futurity is to deny those demands of the past that reach into our present and into the future. It means to accept the limits of the capitalist imagination and to abandon our duty to confront the myriad of contradictions in the present and to recover the silenced and repressed cries for liberation that the past contains as unrealized potential.

Bloch's work contains an unapologetic belief in the concept of hope. Even in historical moments of seeming foreclosure and regression, and even in times when the extreme Right and fascism are on the rise, Bloch argues, there is hope as long as critique is able to recover those possibilities for utopian thought that may be redeployed in the context of progressive projects. As we have seen, Bloch has received far less attention than most other major Western Marxist thinkers. Bloch's commitment to hope plays a central role in the persisting lack of serious engagements with his work. Jean François Lyotard's discussion of the function that the concept of hope assumes in Bloch's work serves as a building block of Lyotard's attack on critical theory tout court. Lyotard characterizes Bloch as a naïve thinker whose embrace of utopia and hope is nothing more than "a token protest raised in the name of man or reason or creativity, or ... of some social category—such as Third World or the students—on which is conferred in extremis the henceforth improbable function of critical subject."[344] Against his own pragmatism, Lyotard reads Bloch's work—cursorily and reductively—as a sign of the decline of critical theory, which, Lyotard argues, "in the end lost its theoretical standing" and, in his view, was reduced to claims about utopia.[345] Lyotard reads the focus on hope as an abandonment of the concrete social content and material reality of a given situation, as betraying the very aims that underwrote the beginnings of Marxist positions. This foreshortened reading of Bloch, however, is particularly notable and indeed poignant in the context of our present in which the ideas of Lyotard have been transformed into central aspects of the structural logic of capital and are crucially involved in the crises of change in a present built upon that structural integration of difference itself into the mechanisms of capitalist valorization. After all, it is precisely in opposition to the present crises that are merely confirmed by the logic of Lyotard's work that we can deploy Blochian thought today, turning Lyotard's cynical reductivism into a matter of notable historical irony.

In recent years, we encounter similar engagements with Bloch in the work of critics like Terry Eagleton. In his 2015 book *Hope Without Optimism*, Eagleton suggests that Bloch might be "reasonably accused of excessive cheerfulness," echoing Lyotard's reduction of Blochian thought, in spite of the fact that Eagleton at least dedicates the better part of a chapter to Bloch's work instead of merely a few pages.[346] And yet, despite the fact that Eagleton commits significantly more space to his engagement with Bloch than Lyotard does, his account of crucial Blochian concepts, first and foremost that of hope, is strikingly underdeveloped. "Bloch certainly writes as though hope is built into the structure of the world itself," Eagleton notes, adding: "it is as though Being itself is hope in its very essence."[347] Providing one brief decontextualized quote as evidence, Eagleton claims that Bloch is "writing as though motion, dynamism, mutability, transience, instability, productivity, openendedness, possibility and the like are unequivocally positive, which is clearly not the case."[348] The latter suggestion is, of course, correct: this is indeed not the case, and, as we have seen, Bloch's work suggests just that. Eagleton seeks to reduce Bloch's conception of hope to the simplistic, almost vulgar notion that hope is "an objective dynamic in the world—not only in human history, indeed, but in the cosmos itself."[349] Jubilantly casting this reading as evidence of the fact that he has caught Bloch in a severe conceptual and logical error with regard to Bloch's relation to the history of Marxist thought, Eagleton juxtaposes Bloch with Marx, who "by contrast may trust to the evolution of the productive forces, but he does not claim that this unfolding is somehow inscribed into the stuff of the world."[350] Just a few pages earlier, Eagleton remarks that Bloch is "one of the luminaries of Western Marxism" but that "he is also the most neglected of that band."[351] And yet, noting that Bloch's work has not been treated in detail and received sufficient attention does not prevent Eagleton from treating Bloch's work so reductively and cursorily that one is confused about the stakes of Eagleton's intervention. Certainly, Eagleton's chapter on Bloch does little to help us understand Bloch better, and it does little in the way of helping us fill the gap in scholarship to which Eagleton himself points. One cannot shake the suspicion that Eagleton recognized that a book on hope would be incomplete without a discussion of Bloch but ultimately remained not very excited about having to engage in that discussion, thus causing him to deliver the bare minimum, glossing over a few basic concepts and reducing complex ideas to clichés.

As we have seen, there is less cheerfulness than absolute urgency in Bloch's conception of hope. Instead of being built into the logic of the cosmos itself, Bloch's idea of an autopoietically constructed sense of utopia is bound up with the complex, nonlinear, and discontinuous notion of a world in its becoming that through the critical engagement with the contradictions of the present constantly folds back on the past and thus lays bare latent potentiality and future possibility. Bloch's account of both hope and temporality is therefore much more complex that Eagleton outlines. In fact, Eagleton misrepresents the basic logical coordinates of Blochian thought in locating hope simply in the stuff of the world and in its material development, concluding that "it follows that hope flows with the tide of the universe rather than moving against the current."[352] Rather than a matter of a simple objective dynamic that relates to the unfolding of productive forces, hope lies for Bloch in the hard-won and constantly threatened ability to deploy critical thought in the effort to lay bare the sources of those contradictions and absences in the past and present that may keep alive the work of realizing a better world. Bloch's understanding of the principle of hope is not a matter of naïve cheerfulness but of his steadfast commitment to hope as dialectically connected to the refusal of the existing and of the limits of thought and possibility that requires an always temporally multiple and complex relation between present and past. Hope in Bloch is also that which tears at the fissures of the foreclosures of the now and that allows us to rescue political and critical possibility by engaging with the root causes of even the darkest excesses of humanity. Returning to Marx, we can find precisely this logical conception of hope that underlies Bloch's engagement with the relation between past and future in one of Marx's letters to Karl Ruge, the importance of which for Marx's understanding of temporality Massimiliano Tomba foregrounds: "it will become plain," Marx writes, "that it is not a question of drawing a sharp mental line between past and future, but of *completing* the thought of the past."[353] What this means, Tomba shows, is that Marxist thought is fundamentally wedded to the importance of turning to the past in order to recover "previous attempts at liberation [that] await their completion."[354] And it is this basic operation of Marxist thought and politics that Bloch develops to its highest form.

Far from a naïve belief in hope as an integral part of the flow of the cosmos and of material development, Bloch stresses that hope is inherently fragile, constantly under attack, and always threatened. But it is precisely because this is so that hope maintains its force and importance. To be sure, Bloch argues, the "kind of hope that consists only of dreams always can and will be disappointed."[355] True hope, hope as understood in the context of his work, on the other hand, "must be unconditionally disappointable" because "it is open in … a future-oriented direction: it does not address itself to what which already exists."[356] "For this reason," Bloch concludes, "hope … is committed to change."[357] Only if we understand that hope must inevitably hold "the condition of defeat precariously within itself," and only if we insist that hope is at its heart not confidence, we can develop and understanding of hope that stands "fully within the topos of objectively real possibility."[358] Thus, Thompson reiterates, hope as a principle in Bloch "demonstrates that it is something linked not just to optimism but to the tendencies present in a material world that is constantly in flux."[359] Precisely because Bloch gives us the most substantial and fully formulated Marxist account of utopia as hope without optimism, Eagleton's misreading of Bloch is notable, for Eagleton's own convictions and logic lie much closer to those of Bloch than his chapter tries to suggest.

Bloch understands hope as immanently connected to the project of finding something that is missing. However, this search for what is missing is decidedly different from and in many ways serves as the dialectical completion of right-wing nostalgic relations to the past as the time that harbors lost mythical ways of life and tradition. The search for what is missing is joined to Bloch's conception of consciousness and of our relation to the world itself, which Bloch understands as incomplete and as at every point marked by the lack that results from and that points toward the contradictions of material reality and the repressed and excluded aspects of the past that are carried forward into the present. Especially in moments when the present seems repressively complete, when we struggle to imagine alternatives to the existing, Bloch's conception of consciousness and of our relation to material reality is of great importance. "That which lives is not yet alive to itself. Least of all in its own functioning. Is not aware by what and in what it has its beginning; is still in the lower depths; yet in every moment that is a moment now, is there, throbbing," writes Bloch in *A Philosophy of the Future*. "To be perceived is only that it hungers and is in need," he continues, "thus it moves ... so it all begins."[360] Hope, Bloch shows, emerges out of a world thus conceived as the material hunger for that which is missing, and it is in this sense, in its connection to lack and not presence, bound up with the hunger for a better life that emerges out of the contradictions of the present and the absences that are carried forth from the past that hope and consciousness both emerge not out of the given of the material world but through the struggle with its foreclosures and absences. "All being is still built around the Not which induces hunger," Bloch writes in "Dialectics and Hope."[361] "There does not yet exist a food which could calm and fill up the lack entirely,"[362] Bloch argues, and it is in its connection to this lack that "hope seeks the truth of history."[363]

As opposed to the impoverished form of hope that right-wing thought locates in the return to a mythical past, hope in Bloch's work lies not in the restoration of something that has been lost but in the realization of something that was never allowed to be. The material hunger that Bloch describes originates out of and lays bare the contradictions of material life, of a present that is characterized by unfulfilled wishes and dreams and by cries for justice that have been silenced. This relation to nonsynchronism, the attempt to recover and mobilize the hope and utopian potential that lies in the not yet, stands polarly opposed to the opportunistic and dangerous nonsynchronism of right-wing agitation and propaganda, the sort of attachment to the past that harbors nothing but dark reactionary anger and violence that replaces a critical relation to the present. Right-wing nonsynchronism obfuscates and distracts from that which hope traces in our present, from the material hunger that demands a better world, a world that realizes that which is missing from our present and that fulfills the past's repressed desires and unexplored possibilities. Bloch's work is needed today more than ever, because it is aimed at tracing hope in pessimistic times, in an era in which cynicism and reaction reign. Bloch shows that pessimism can give rise to hope if we understand hope, as Thomson stresses, not as "happiness and bland optimism" but as "what gives us strength in the face of the knowledge of entropy and death."[364]

The phrase "something's missing," Thompson argues, is not only significant because it was one of Bloch's favorites, but also because it "contains within its apparent simplicity a philosophical depth" that examines the dialectic of presence and absence in the construction of the now and allows us to focus our analyses of the present on "what is possible and what might become possible in today's world."[365] The question of what is missing is of crucial importance for our engagement with the problems of foreclosure and of reactionary thought in our own time, for it allows us to examine the sources out of which the renewed threat of fascism and the hateful opportunism of right-wing nonsynchronism emerges as much as it opens the door to a different, direly needed form of utopian thought that allows us to think beyond the confines of the long now. Bloch's work also gives us an important account of presence and of the now that transcends well-worn notions of a present that is understood as either the vanishing, imperceptible moment between past and future or as the time that is pregnant with the future. After all, the logic of both these conceptions of the present is exhausted in the context of the current crisis of temporality. Bloch instead understands presence as attention to that which is missing in the now, which is also the core of Blochian utopian thought.

"All being is built around the Not, which cannot bear to remain at rest," Bloch writes.[366] This restlessness of the now that emerges out of what is missing establishes the dialectical relationship of dissatisfaction. The negative relation to this lack, Bloch argues, the dissatisfaction that is "restlessly impelling" our relation to the totality—and "the same content is represented positively in hope," which is "restlessly illuminating."[367] Utopia, he argues, is at work in both dissatisfaction and hope. "Hegel, who wanted much to keep his distance from any dissatisfaction, even unwarranted hope," Bloch notes, "nevertheless stated, in his idealist way, that the truth of hope is simultaneously that of freedom."[368] "Little abstracted sparks of utopia exist all around us in everyday life, but they cannot yet add up to a utopian process until and unless they become radicalized, grasped at their roots," Thompson argues.[369] Thompson foregrounds that "the truth of history" emerges in Bloch's thought therefore not as an abstraction but as "the ongoing process of the emergence of the concrete and the growing together of contingency into necessity."³⁷⁰ What Bloch's thought gives us, Thompson emphasizes, is "a concrete utopia," one that "has existence only as a possible outcome of an autopoietic process" and that "contains within it shards of past and present utopian images ... that we carry forward with us on the journey but that also carry us forward, giving us the will to keep pushing forward and to become what we might be."³⁷¹

"To Speak of the unspeakable": The novel as utopian thought

Without those seeds of the future that are contained in the now, without what Bloch calls excess synchronism (*Übergleichzeitigkeit*), Beat Dietschy argues, synchronism is merely a matter of being up to date.³⁷² But truly inhabiting the now means to assume a critical, and analytic relation to it, and such a relationship may emerge by examining the present as the time that lays bare the past's abandoned or repressed projects. Bloch's interest in the now is therefore aimed at the ways in which what is missing and what demands realization points beyond the existing and therefore creates an excess or surplus that makes possible the present's transcendence. This anticipatory surplus in the present, the excess synchronism that Bloch describes, is contained most notably in art. Art provides us with aesthetic pre-illumination, and as Dietschy argues, this aspect of art, its anticipatory quality, also emerges through art's engagement with the past's unfinished projects that beg to be realized.³⁷³ With Bloch, Dietschy describes this utopian core of art as emerging out of the sense of "rebellious lack" (*rebellisches Vermissen*) in the now, the recognition of what is missing in the present that critiques the existing and demands a better world.³⁷⁴ In this sense, Dietschy argues, Bloch shows that futurity does not exist without a nonsynchronous present. This suggestion allows us to further hone our understanding of the current crisis of temporality, for a Blochian analysis foregrounds the disruption of the utopian imagination that results from the associated of our time with absolute presence and temporal homogeneity. We can also see that the desire to salvage a conception of nonsynchronism from such a foreclosed present produces both the protoutopian impulse that gives rise to futurity and the protoutopian impulse that underlies and is ultimately distorted by right-wing nonsynchronism. The importance of the work of art lies in this context in art's ability to create true excess synchronism out of its engagement with the contradictions of the present and in its capacity to reveal the irrational core of right-wing nonsynchronism.

Douglas Kellner argues that "no philosopher since Hegel has explored in such detail and with such penetration the cultural tradition, which for Bloch contains untapped emancipatory potential."[375] Thus, Bloch's work is also of great interest to contemporary cultural and literary critics, since it draws our attention to the value of art for our ability to confront the new forms of alienation and the crises of our imagination that result from the transition into real time capitalism. Kellner shows that Blochian utopian thought relies on art and culture, which create a "cultural surplus" that "preserves unsatisfied desires and human wishes for a better world" and that aids us in the effort to translate these wishes into reality.[376] For this reason, I have turned to literature throughout this book, and I hope to have shown not only that literature has recognized and addressed itself to the urgent problems that new forms of nonsynchronism pose in our moment but also that literature provides us with an form of critique and with a way of exploring the contradictions of our time that concretely carries out the work of utopian thought that Bloch outlines. In the work of Bloch as in the context of critical theory more widely conceived, art assumes a central role in the project of critique and in political praxis. While Bloch found his understanding of utopia most strikingly realized in music, Walter Benjamin and Theodor W. Adorno, for example, bestow particular significance on literature. In particular lyric poetry, Benjamin and Adorno argue, stands opposed to capitalist alienation and, through its critical examination of the existing, through its "distance from mere existence," as Adorno argues, poetry "becomes a measure of what is false and bad in the latter."[377] Through its critique of the existing, the literary work also recovers the social dimension of what is at its core the form of negation that underwrites the project of utopia as understood by Bloch. "The universality of the lyric's substance," Adorno writes, "is social in nature," adding that "only one who hears the voice of humankind in the poem's solitude can understand what the poem is saying."[378] In his examination of the novel, in the context of which we encounter a further example of the direct logical link between the work of Bloch and Adorno, Adorno foregrounds the centrality of art for utopian thought and for politics, one that echoes Bloch's notion of cultural surplus that emerges from an engagement with what is missing in the present: "what is reflected in aesthetic transcendence," Adorno writes, "is the disenchantment of the world."[379]

Well aware of the problems that the current crisis of temporality poses not just for politics but also for art and culture, Timothy Bewes argues that the effort to "temporalize the present" is one of the most pressing projects of our time. For Bewes, such an effort may take its energy and direction from "a new critical commitment to the singularity of literature, a form whose truths and insights seem ever less transferable to, or comprehensible within, standard historical, scientific, or political vocabularies."[380] I would add to Bewes's suggestion that it is specifically in the novel that we find examples of a form of thought that, through its distance from the standard vocabulary and the standardizing temporal episteme of contemporary capitalism, allows us to retemporalize the long now. In his essay "In Praise of the Novel," Carlos Fuentes foregrounds the particular work that the novel does, which provides us with some insights into why exactly the novel should be accorded a central role in our time and why it might, I would argue serve as one of the most significant expressions of Blochian utopian thought today. "Fiction is ... a way of appropriating the world, giving the world the color, the taste, the sense, the dreams, the vigils, the perseverance, and even the lazy repose that, to go on being, it claims," Fuentes writes.[381] In our moment in history, Fuentes knows, "time has been pulverized," which throws into crisis "both the imagination of the past and the memory of the future."[382] There are those, he explains, who accept the purported limitations of our now and "who believe that we live in the best of all possible worlds because they have been told that the indispensable is impossible."[383] Against such a relation to the present, against such defeatism and hopelessness, "the novel tells us that art restores the life in us that was disregarded by the haste of history."[384] And in a passage that bears striking resemblance to Blochian logic, Fuentes praises the novel for its ability to salvage the utopian dimension of our imagination by "mak[ing] real what history forgot."[385] "And because history has been what was," Fuentes concludes, "literature will offer what history has not always been."[386] This ability of the novel to provide us with a form of utopian imagination that breaks through the foreclosures and limits of our time, he argues, lies in the strength of the medium literature, for literature gives us a vocabulary through which we may speak that which is not yet. "For how can history end," Fuentes asks, "as long as we have not said our last word?"[387]

Milan Kundera suggests that we might understand the novel as a "cemetery of missed opportunities, of unheard appeals."[388] Kundera's conception of the novel allows us to understand the novel's function as an expression of the Blochian not yet, as a form of thought that aids us in the project of recovering the future from the cemetery of history. Through the novel's anticipatory engagement with the past, we get a glimpse of a form of thought and of a relation to time that is aimed at returning to life and intellectually and politically reactivating those aspects of the past that were abandoned or repressed and whose time of realization may yet come. The graveyard of unheard appeals that Kundera describes is the novel's site of utopia. It is the soil that nourishes flowers that are not mournful signs of death but hopeful signs of a life and beauty yet to come. And in the context of the rise of a new Right that sketches out morbid images of a distorted better life and that promises to find solutions to present problems in a cemetery that only contains empty graves, Kundera's account of the novel contains a connected, important suggestion. Because the novel serves as a way to make knowable to us the world in its progress and the potentiality that lies in the present, it is, Kundera insists, "incompatible with the totalitarian universe."[389] "The world of one single Truth," which is the world of totalitarianism, and the "relative, ambiguous world of the novel," he explains, "are molded of entirely different substances."[390] "Totalitarian Truth," Kundera argues, "excludes relativity, doubt, questioning; it can never accommodate what I would call the *spirit of the novel*."[391] The novel's ability to make legible the limitations of the present and to break through the existing by giving us the tools to engage with the rebellious lack of the now foregrounds that the novel does not merely serve as a way to reflect or represent the conditions of the present. Instead, the novel functions as a form of critique and as a form of praxis that anticipates the transformation of material reality by giving us the kind of utopian thought that creates change through a confrontation with what is missing. Alain Badiou argues that precisely because literature is able to "open up to the realm of thought the singularity of whatever takes place outside that realm," it ought to be considered a "form of thought."[392] "Literature," he adds, "is a direct contradiction of Wittgenstein's axiom ('Whereof one cannot speak, thereof one must be silent')," since what Badiou calls "literature's first axis" is "the imperative to speak of the unspeakable."[393] Because it speaks the unspeakable and thereby points beyond the foreclosures of the now, we can understand literature in general and the novel in particular as one of the most forceful expressions of the particular form of thought that is utopia.

Fredric Jameson reminds us that "the Utopian text does not tell a story at all." Instead, he argues, "it describes a mechanism or even a kind of machine, it furnishes a blueprint rather than lingering upon the kinds of human relations that might be found in a Utopian condition or imagining the kinds of living we wish were available in some stable well-nigh permanent availability."[394] Likewise, rather than sketching out for us futures that will never come to pass, the utopian core of the novel lies in its ability to establish the basic mechanisms of utopian thought itself. The novel provides us with a concrete example of this mechanism, and it is in this sense that it can be understood as a form of thought and as a form of the utopian imagination that is aimed at the transformation of the existing. The novel's relatively ambiguous relation to the world that Kundera describes is an expression of the novel's formal core that is simultaneously bound up with the form of utopian thought that Bloch outlines. The novel is the art form that is aimed at making the world historically thinkable to us. This means that the novel makes legible material reality in its progress, and, by narrating our relationship to a world that is always understood as in a constant state of development, it allows us to understand our relationship to the world as constantly in flux and as a process of historical development. This understanding of our relation to the world that the novel fosters can be found particularly in those forms of realism that are central to the novel's own history. Novelistic realism and the conception of the world and of our relation to it, Bloch argues, contain the basic architecture of utopian thought. Bloch writes:

> Where the prospective horizon is continuously kept in sight, reality appears there as what it is concretely: as a network of paths (*Wegegeflecht*) of dialectical processes that take place in an unfinished world, in a world that would be totally unchangeable without the enormous future, the real possibilities within it.[395]

Novelistic realism provides us with an understanding of the totality of the world in process that is not a matter of trying to "represent the isolated entirety of each part of a process," as Bloch puts it, but of representing a crucial aspect of that which lends the engagement with reality in the novel an anticipatory function: the representation of "the entirety of the matter that is pending in the process in general."[396] What we find in realism, Bloch concludes is a form of thought that is aimed at uncovering the "tendentious and latent" in the present, and it is precisely in this sense that we can understand the important function of the novel today. In addition to developing detailed accounts of the problems that plague our present, the novel furnishes us with a set of critical and analytical tools and with a method for imagining the present otherwise. The novel is the art form that categorically stands opposed to the exhaustion of our imagination in the long now.

In this way, the novel offers us what Bloch understands as a complete critical relation to reality. "Reality without real possibilities is not complete," he argues.[397] "The world without future-bearing (*zukunftstragende*) qualities deserves as little regard ... as the world of the philistine does."[398] The continued function of the work of art figures centrally into our ability to critically engage with the present and to keep alive the utopian imagination. In our moment, our ability to engage with the temporal crises that shape our present and our ability to oppose and undo the advances of the Right is therefore also dependent upon our defense of art's critical function. It is not surprising, in other words, that we witness the rise of new forms of right-wing imagination in a time when art and its study are also structurally devalued and strategically curtailed by market pragmatism. The latter is a direct expression of a set of tactics aimed at safeguarding the capitalist imagination, tactics that are structurally and logically bound up with the Right's effort to safeguard capitalism by veiling its contradictions and by erasing those forms of thought and dissent that stand opposed to capitalism. Contemporary capitalism and the right-wing imagination join forces in strategic philistinism that seeks to erase the future-bearing qualities of the present, thus contributing to the consolidation of the long now as the definitive temporal logic of our era. In such a situation, we may need the work of the novel more than ever, for, "as a social form," J. M. Bernstein stresses, "the unhappy consciousness of novel fictions should remind us of a different alternative reality."[399]

Peter Boxall provides us with an account of what this may concretely mean, and he illustrates that this particular function of the novel—its ability to give us a way of imagining the world in its historical progress that also serves as a form of anticipation that arises from its engagement with the present's rebellious lack—is deeply connected to the novel's temporal imagination. "The end of the nineteenth century," Boxall writes, "sees massive changes to the way that time and space are produced and experience, as capitalist modernity enters into a new phase in its development."[400] As a result of this historical transition, Boxall shows, we witness the emergence of a range of crises that originate in a crisis of imagination that creates ripple effects in culture, politics, and society. And just like in our time in which we are seeing a structural transformation in capitalism that throws into crisis the ways in which we imagine our basic, temporal relation to material reality "the culture of the fin du siècle," Boxall argues, should be understood as a cultural mediation of the "experience of temporal rupture."[401] In this context, novels like H. G. Well's *The Time Machine* perform important work. In addition to functioning as a way to interrogate the logic and consequences for our temporal imagination of the historical transition that Wells's novel mediates, *The Time Machine*, Boxall shows, also "demonstrates the capacity of narrative fiction ... to occupy a moment, to narrate a rather extraordinarily mobile present and to place that moving present within a larger completed narrative."[402] The value of Wells's novel, in other words, lies in its ability to develop a form of thought that is suited to making sense of the new historical context of a changing world and to understanding the crises of its time as dialectically connected to larger historical transformations in the world's material structure.

In fact, Boxall argues, the value of the novel as an art form is connected to "its capacity to critique the regimes that determine the passing of time, and in its ability to help us know the contradictions that living in time produces."[403] Additionally, he proposes, the novel also "has a particular capacity to craft new time signatures, new temporal forms which enable or even require us to think the time differently."[404] "This, then," Boxall concludes,

> is the double gift of the novel to our understanding of time. It both offers a critical analysis of the processes which shape our being in time, and allows us to conceive new kinds of temporality, to imagine a different kind of relationship to passing time than that which is produced by our existing senses.[405]

Boxall shows that "it has always been a special talent of the novel to fashion a means of 'reckoning time' at key moments in the history of modernity" that is of great importance in our own historical period, which, Boxall suggests, "is perhaps a transformative moment, a moment in which modernity is entering into a new phase."[406] And Boxall is precisely right, I would argue, for the novel assumes a crucial role not just in the context of the temporal crises that result from the transition into real-time capitalism but also in relation to the connected crises of our temporal imagination and of utopian thought that defines the era of the long now. To be sure, reading novels alone will not change the world, and it will neither keep at bay the advancing forces of a new extreme Right nor wrest the concept of change from the grip of contemporary capitalism. However, since the political crises of our time and the Right's ability to leverage the frustrations and resentment that emerge in the context of the long now are directly connected to a crisis in our imagination—to our purported ability to imagine the world otherwise, beyond the confines of the capitalist present—the novel does model for us the kind of thought that refuses the constricting narrative of capitalism's eternal present and that reinvigorates utopia and anticipates a better world by laying bare and critiquing the present's limits and contradictions. At its heart, critical theory is aimed at providing us with a form of thought that is also a form of praxis, since critique is aimed at the transformation of material reality and the transcendence of the existing. This kind of thought-as-praxis underlies the work of Bloch (and to a substantial degree also that of Adorno) and that of the novel, and it is time, I would argue, to return to the critical and political force of both.

Occupy dreaming: Decolonizing the future

"Africa and Asia. For these continents the past of the white races is only negligibly their own too; for those nations who in various ways have enjoyed no future, history as a whole is something that begins tomorrow," writes Bloch in *A Philosophy of the Future*.[407] Bloch's emphasis on the temporal imagination that is bound up with the history of colonialism highlights a particularly salient site for critical inquiry in our time. After all, the notion of an eternal capitalist present, a global long now can only be maintained if we continue to disregard those forms of repressed temporality that are bound up with the history of colonial domination and that constitute forms is nonsynchronism that continue to be maintained in the present. Moreover, the struggle with the sense of a disruption of futurity, of suffering from a situation of absolute confinement that erases established ways of imagining the future as difference, must register as a deep historical irony and as a cynically unhistoricized account of the present for all those whose past is determined by colonial domination and suppression that was bound up with an erasure of futurity. How ironic must the emergence of the narrative of a crisis of futurity that defines the Western imaginary seem to those who were historically denied a future by Western colonialism? Any examination of the utopian imagination, Bloch argues, must also contain an examination of the history of colonialism as a history of temporal domination and of a colonization of the future. The memory of colonialism's denials of the future, in other words, is one crucial aspect of the present's rebellious absences, of the timelines that are connected to repressed dreams of freedom that show quite clearly why, as Bloch emphasizes, not all of us live in the same now. Foregrounding the presence of the temporalities of colonialism that reach from the past into the present and that demand the future that the colonial subject has been denied makes our now a far from uniform time. In fact, the history of colonialism, Bloch argues, registers in the present as an indication of "non-linear historical time" and of the fact that the time is "not fixed and monodic."[408]

Opposed to the Western narrative of progress that is understood as a linear form of temporality aimed at Western conceptions of the future stand, as Bloch shows, the repressed timelines and hopes for the future of colonized people that ask us to understand progress itself as "polyrhythmic" and as a "polyphonic chorus."[409] Progress, Bloch argues, must be understood not as the temporality associated with a Western vanguard that continues to colonize the global imagination of time and of the future but with the plural temporality resulting from the multiplicity of demands for liberation that exist in our present and that together demand "a better Earth for all men."[410] The concept of progress and the temporal imagination with which it is bound up, Bloch argues, assumes a central role in colonialism as well as in capitalism. "Any consideration and analysis of the concept of progress," therefore, "must bear on its social function—its why and its wherefore."[411] In this context, Bloch insists that the idea of progress itself must not be conceived as a matter of a "reactionary nailing down of time and space."[412] It requires not unilinearity but a broad, flexible, and thoroughly dynamic "multiverse": "the voices of history joined in perpetual and often intricate counterpoint."[413] The dynamic multiverse that Bloch associates with utopian thought, one that presents a counterpoint to the time and history of colonial domination and that is aimed at "a human content that is not yet clearly defined, not yet manifest."[414] In this sense, Bloch shows, the colonial past exists in and temporally multiplies the present while also containing those forms of futurity, those demands for liberation and those conceptions of the future, that colonialism sought to erase and that the capitalist present, in part through its continued attempts at standardizing our (temporal) imagination, continues to overwrite. The critique of the long now must also be a project that aims to decolonize the present and that aims to reclaim and decolonize the future by mobilizing the suppressed temporal imaginaries of the past and the unfulfilled wishes that contain transformative possibilities in our present and that reach beyond and break the constraints of the notion of a long now. Decolonizing the future begins by breaking the stranglehold that the notion of a uniform long now has on our present imagination, for the long now preserves and consolidates historical denials of presence and futurity by erasing those imaginaries and forms of temporality that stand in a radically different relation to the now of Western capitalism.

The work of restoring to the surface and of making legible these repressed forms of futurity has in recent years been particularly notably carried out by postcolonial and multiethnic literatures. Of particular note in this context are new forms of speculative fiction that have emerged in postcolonial and multiethnic literature and that contain striking political significance. As David M. Higgins illustrates, speculative fiction in general and science fiction in particular do important work in the context of the temporal crises of our time. And critics have begun to engage with this work. Critics like Sherryl Vint, Higgins shows, foreground the political value of science fiction in our time. Against aspects of contemporary culture that contain a "strained nostalgia" for previous moments in history and their future imaginaries, such as for "seemingly innocent 1950s versions of the future," recent science fiction "bitterly exposes the exploitative corporate fantasies and totalitarian inclinations" of "industry-oriented future[s]."[415] Science fiction, Higgins argues, is able to break the seeming deadlock between "naïve retrofuturism and critical fatalism" and foreground the need for "genuinely open and new futures" as well as the need to "reclaim the power to imagine the future outside of industry-produced advertising images." In recent years, Afro-Futurism has received increasing attention, and critics have pointed out is significant critical and political force. From early authors like Octavia E. Butler and Samuel R. Delany to the new generation of writers including N. K. Jemisin and Nalo Hopkinson, Afro-Futurism has generated a wide variety of powerful examinations of the relationship between our temporal imagination and the mechanisms of colonialism and racism. Multiethnic literature more widely conceived has witnessed a rise of speculative fiction in recent years, and authors like Sesshu Foster have given us striking novels that explode the history of the colonial imaginary through the deployment of narratives that trace alternate temporalities and histories.[416]

And yet, while we are seeing increasing interest in multiethnic and postcolonial speculative fiction, one area in this wider field remains relatively underexamined: Indigenous speculative fiction. Not surprisingly, Indigenous speculative fiction and Indigenous futurisms continue to have a difficult standing in a present that is defined by the temporality of the Western imagination. Even novels like Tracey Lindberg's *Birdie* (2015) that are formally by and large not experimental but that bring to the novel form a different understanding of temporality than the linear time of the history of Western colonialism continue to face difficulties in their reception precisely due to their desire to trace a time beyond that of the settler now. Even mainstream reviews in major news outlets do very little to mask their lack of appreciation for Lindberg's project. In a review for *The Globe and Mail*, for instance, Carleigh Baker writes about Lindberg's construction of the complex relation of the novel's central character, Bernice, to both time and the past that "we spend a lot of time in Bernice's head and a lot of time exploring her past. It gets exhausting. The novel's timeline is a mess. I suspect that's by design, but it doesn't make the reading any easier."[417] While they are willing to celebrate the arrival of a new Indigenous author, critics like Baker remain tellingly unwilling to explore the significance of a different temporal imagination and connected understanding of past and present that novels like *Birdie* give us. What is striking about such reactions is the tension between the dominant temporal imagination and the temporalization of the Indigenous subject that they entail. While the linear understanding of progress (and the progression of narrative plot) and of time continues to be upheld as normalized temporality, the continued construction of the Indigenous subject as nonsynchronous cements the exclusion of Indigenous understandings of temporality from the present and denies recognition to Indigenous futures and futurisms. After all, the standard Western imagination continues to associate the Indigenous subject with an eternal past, confining Indigenous subjects and culture to a timelessness that is maintained through romanticized narratives of the "natural" relation to the timeless land that is understood as definitive of Indigenous culture and subjectivity. As a result, both Indigenous culture and subjectivity are associated with a constitutive pastness that collapses into a-historical timelessness and is thereby excluded from the capitalist settler-contemporary and denied autonomy and futurity.

In recent years, facets of North American indigenous art, in particular new forms of speculative fiction, have emerged that deploy a focus on matters of temporality, futurity, and utopia as part of the struggle against the deep-seated tradition in North American culture of including Indigenous art into the present only insofar as it performs a required constitutive pastness or temporal stasis. Reduced to a stereotypical version of itself that is praised in particular for what Western culture and discourse celebrates as its nonsynchronism, its eternal pastness, Indigenous art is largely repressively tolerated and integrated into the present, since it is reduced to performing an act of temporal exclusion. Confining Indigenous art to the repetition of cultural clichés amounts to a denial of presence, as the cultural dimension of a general strategy that is aimed at the continued exclusion of the Indigenous subject from the now. Through the turn to speculative fiction, however, Indigenous artists have confronted repressive nonsynchronism head on. This form of aesthetic and cultural resistance does important political work, since it illustrates the fallacy and historical sources of the notion of the purported uniformity of the present. By stressing the relations of power and domination that underwrite narratives of the (omni)presence of a long now and by trying to make legible alternative ways of being in and imagining time, such artworks model for us a politics of change in the present and of demanding the future that is one of the most notable contemporary expressions of utopian thought as conceived by Bloch. "Past desire, past experience does not cease to exist or to influence, even when it is not immediately conscious," Bloch writes in *The Spirit of Utopia*. "In dreams, above all," he adds, "returns the desire that has subsided during waking hours, and takes control, excited yet no longer exciting anything, of the hallucinated contents of memory."[418] It is precisely the utopian function of dreaming and to the political project to which this understanding of utopia is connected that novels like Cherie Dimaline's *The Marrow Thieves* explore. *The Marrow Thieves* is a story about a not too distant future in which Indigenous people are subjected to new forms of exploitation, violence, and murder. Having lost the ability to dream as a result of the diseases that result from the apocalyptic environmental destruction of the entire North American continent, the white North American majority resurrects and redeploys well-known horrors of the past as solutions to their problem. Dimaline's novel tells the story of a near-future North America that witnesses the reestablishment of a system of schools, modeled on the gruesome history of the Canadian residential school system, that serve to "harvest" the dreams of the only group of people who are still able to dream and imagine hopeful futures: Indigenous people.

"The earth was broken," remembers Miigwans, one of two elders who lead a group of young Indigenous fugitives on their way to the Canadian North in search of safety. The group is running from teams of "Recruiters" who scour the country in search of the last surviving Indigenous people in order to capture them and take them to "the schools," where their dreams will be harvested.[419] "Too much taking for too damn long, so she finally broke," Miigwans recounts, adding that Earth

> went like a wild horse, bucking off as much as she could before lying down. A melting North meant the water levels rose and the weather changed. It changed to violence in some cases, building tsunamis, spinning tornadoes, crumbling earthquakes, and the shapes of countries were changed forever, whole coasts breaking off like crusts. And all those pipelines in the ground? They snapped like icicles and spewed bile over forests, into lakes, drowning whole reserves and towns. So much laid to waste from the miscalculation of infallibility in the face of the planet's revolt.[420]

The continent "sank into a new era," an era that brought with it "The Water Wars." "Americans reached up and started sipping our lakes with a great metal straw," he tells the group, which set off the first wave of disappropriation: Indigenous lands were stolen by large water corporations.[421] The massive scale of environmental destruction, however, also brought with it disease, Miigwans remembers, which caused mass fatalities—"people died in the millions." But, he notes, such a time of chaos and death was not new to Indigenous people, and they soon developed ways to respond to it. After all, Miigwans notes, "it was like the second coming of the boats."[422] In the early years of the new era that Miigwans describes, Indigenous people witness the repetition of the horrors of colonization: the spread of disease and the large-scale destruction of land, animals, and Indigenous communities.

Being able to draw upon their knowledge of this past allows Indigenous people to survive, but this very ability to survive, the ability to look toward the past in order to find hope for the future, to dream, also brings with it great danger, for it is precisely this ability that the white populations lacks and seeks to recover. "Half the population was lost in the disaster and from disease," Miigwans remembers. The ones that were left "worked longer hours, they stopped reproducing without the doctors, and worst of all," he notes, "they stopped dreaming."[423] The absence of futurity, of hope, and of dreams on part of the nonindigenous population initially generates an interest in Indigenous culture and ceremony. "People turned to Indigenous people the way New Agers had, all reverence and curiosity, looking for ways we could help guide them," Miigwans recalls. But after a while, he adds, people changed: they began "looking for ways they could take what we had and administer it themselves," and they tried to determine how they could "best appropriate the uncanny ability we kept to dream" and how to "make ceremony better, more efficient, more economical."[424] Indigenous people faced yet another wave of disappropriation. "We were moved off lands that were deemed 'necessary' to that government," Miigwans tells the group, "because no one cared about long-range things life courting votes for the next election and instead cared about things like keeping valued, wealthy community members safe."[425] Dimaline's novel serves as a forceful reminder that the negative consequences of short-term thinking and the violence that is associated with defending the power relations and economic interests of those who are invested in maintaining the status quo are most significantly felt by minorities and by those groups who have historically been oppressed and disenfranchised. Little is new in the future world of *The Marrow Thieves*. All of the hatred, the opportunism, the violent disregard for both humanity and the environment, and the exploitation that maintain the power relations of the present, as even the young travelers in the group already know, are merely the latest iteration of a long history of violence and of exclusion. When colonial power looks to the past, it sees effective strategies for domination, well-established horrors that can be redeployed to do their old, horrific work even under different conditions.

Indigenous people, however, remain hopeful, and they draw their strength in part from that which has completely broken down in non-Indigenous society after the collapse: community. "Even after our way of life had been commoditized," Miigwans tells the group, "after our lands were filled with water companies and wealthy corporate investors, we were still hopeful. Because we had each other. New communities started to form, and we were gathering strength."[426] But soon things take a turn for the worse. Through a collaboration of church and scientists, Miigwans tells the group, "they found a way to siphon the dreams right out of our bones."[427] While Indigenous people look to the past to keep alive community, culture, and hope, the remainder of the country, he remembers, "turned to history to show them how to best keep us warehoused, how to best position the culling. That's when the new residential schools started growing up from the dirt like poisonous brick mushrooms."[428] The schools are part of a network of institutions in which the dreams of Indigenous people are extracted from their bone marrow, a process that results in a slow, painful death for those who are captured by the Recruiters and transported to a school. Turning to the past and recovering some of its greatest horrors, in this case the Canadian residential school system, is the only way in which the majority of the North American population is able to imagine solutions to the problems of their time. In the schools, "they leach the dreams from where our ancestors hid them," Miigwans tells the group, "And us? We join our ancestors, hoping we left enough dreams behind for the next generation to stumble across."[429]

Unlike the cruel return to a past that is at best able to extend the present, the Indigenous characters in Dimaline's novel understand that dreams must be aimed at the next generation. The novel's narrator, Francis, finds the to him most striking representation of the power of dreaming and of utilizing the past as a reservoir of futurity in Rose, a rebellious young woman and fellow member of the group that is fleeing to the Canadian North in search of a better life. To Francis, Rose represents the logic of the path that lies ahead: steeped in the past and well aware of the dangers of the present, Rose anticipates a future that gives Francis hope. The group loves the way she rebels, Francis notes, since it is a particular, nonsynchronous form of rebellion: "having been raised by old people, she spoke like them. It made us feel surrounded on both ends—like we had a future and a past all bundled up in her round dark cheeks."[430] Francis regards the periodic retelling of the history of the most recent wave of violence and war on part of Miigwans in the same way that he understands Rose's relation to both past and future. Miigwans's attempt at keeping history alive, such as during times when the group pauses on their journey to hear Miigwans tell what they simply call "Story," Francis knows, is an important way to prepare the group for the future. "We needed to remember Story," Francis explains, adding that it is Miigwans's "job to set the memory in perpetuity."[431] "It was imperative that we know," Francis stresses, for only through knowing history can the group maintain hope, navigate their way into the future, and build toward a future community. Moving into the future by keeping alive the memory of past injuries and injustice, Francis knows, is "the only way to make the kinds of changes that [are] necessary to really survive."[432]

The Marrow Thieves is a novel about the power of memory and the significance of stories and language for our ability to maintain hope in even the darkest of times, and it is a striking narrative about the resilience and ability of those to maintain hope and keep alive the utopian imagination who have suffered the most from a long history of violent denials of futurity. A constant threat to the group of traveler's in Dimaline's novel is the loss of language, the tool through which it is possible to keep alive the knowledge of past injustice and denials of demands for liberation, to speak to and make legible what is missing in the present, and to thereby anticipate the future and dreams of a better life. Those who seek to enslave and exterminate Indigenous people in the novel, by extension, Francis understands, know that one of the most effective tools of domination is to "suck the language right out of your lungs."[433] The young members of the group are always excited to learn "new words," by which they refer to the old language and knowledge with which the elders provide them, words that lend the group power and strategic tools in their fight for freedom. Dimaline's novel is therefore also a work that foregrounds the crucial role of narrative in utopian thought, for it is through language, by having a vocabulary that reaches beyond the words that merely continue to confirm the existing, that the characters in the novel are able to speak to past and present injustices. It is through narratives that preserve the memory of violence and dispossession and through narratives that speak of that which the present system of domination seeks to render unspeakable that the characters in the novel and that we are able to imagine alternatives to what is now and maintain hope for the future through our engagement with that which is not yet.

The novel's emphasis on the power of language, of memory, and of stories, the tools that allow us to trace the aspects of the past that serve as pre-illuminations of the way toward a better life, is particularly memorably expressed in the act of rebellion of the second elder that leads the group northward: a woman named Minerva. In one of the novel's most moving scenes, Minerva sacrifices herself to save the others. She is captured by Recruiters, and is taken to a school where her dreams will be harvested and she will be killed. On her journey to the school, Minerva begins to sing, and her singing reaches a point of climax as the scientists and priests who run the school connect her to the extraction system:

> She sang. She sang with volume and pitch and a heartbreaking wail that echoed through her relatives' bones, rattling them in the ground under the school itself. Wave after wave, changing her heartbeat to drum, morphing her singular voice to many, pulling every dream from her own marrow and into her song. And there were words: words in the language that the conductor couldn't process, words the Cardinals couldn't bear, words the wires couldn't transfer … As it turns out, every dream Minerva had ever dreamed was in the language. It was her gift, her secret, her plan. She'd collected the dreams like bright beads on a string of nights that wound around her each day, every day until this one.[434]

Singing the story of her past and turning herself into a representative of her people's history, Minerva unearths a powerful force, a flow of words and of dreams so strong and so unrecognizable to the system that seeks to exploit her that it brings down the school's walls and destroys the mechanisms that they house, leaving only "a broken system, torn down by the words of a dreaming old lady."[435] This crucial moment in Dimaline's novel emphasizes the power of words and of stories to turn the knowledge of what never was and what was repressed into the power that underlies those dreams and those hopes that are able to undo the violent structures of the present. And yet, Minerva surrenders herself so fully to the future of her community that her own life is lost as a consequence of her singing and dreaming, in the rebellion that her act subsequently inspires. One of the novel's characters anticipates Minerva's death a few pages earlier, foregrounding the novel's understanding of dreaming, of futurity, and of utopia not as a matter of individual improvement but rather as a gift that can be given to the community of the future: "sometimes you risk everything for a life worth living, even if you're not the one that'll be alive to live it."[436] Minerva dies, giving the gift of hope to the future community who can live the life that Minerva's dreaming and that her words make possible, a community who love their language, as one character notes, "the way Minerva loved us, with pride and an enthusiasm of old potential repurposed."[437]

Through a series of shifts in narrative time, a technique that also features prominently in Indigenous novels like Lindberg's *Birdie* or in Louise Erdrich's 2017 novel *Future Home of the Living God*, *The Marrow Thieves* returns to the past in order to weave it back into the present and thus delivers its messages of hope for the future. Dimaline's novel therefore also foregrounds a relation to the past that offers an alternative to nostalgic, reactionary attachments to the past. The group of travelers in the novel take great pride and joy in being "real old-timey," in being able to put to new use past knowledge or strategies, and the ultimate act of rebellion, of fighting for the freedom and future of Indigenous people, is likewise marked by a temporally plural mix of a clear understanding of the present and the strategic redeployment of knowledge and tools of the past. The distinction between two different forms of returning to the past in the context of a severe crisis in the present that Dimaline's novel illustrates also lies at the heart of the temporal and utopian thought of critical theory. As S. D. Chrostowska shows, Adorno's work, which, as we have seen in previous chapters, is deeply indebted to Bloch's conception of utopian, contains an important critique of nostalgia that shows what it may mean to keep alive the utopian imagination. "One must not forget," Chrostowska writes, "that nostalgia and utopia are complementary concepts and, in a sense, stand back-to-back, as dialectical inversions of each other," and it is this particular dialectical relation of nostalgia and utopia that Adorno's work foregrounds.[438] Adapting Svetlana Boym's distinction between "restorative" and "reflective" nostalgia, Chrostowska argues that, as opposed to restorative nostalgia that "spatializes time" and that "repristinates" a "transhistorical reconstruction of the lost 'home,'" reflective nostalgia, which corresponds to the dialectical inversion of nostalgia in which Adorno locates the core of utopian thought, "dwells in longing as such and does not seek restoration qua 'homecoming.'"[439] Reflective nostalgia in Adorno, Chrostowska shows, functions, "as a means of critical-philosophical insight into, and so a mode of resistance to, the present."[440] It is precisely this account of utopian thought that we also find at the heart of Blochian thought and at the core of the utopian politics of novels like *The Marrow Thieves*, in Minerva's dreams that contain the hope and enthusiasm of "old potential repurposed." In Adorno's work, this dialectical connection of nostalgia and utopia serves as "a critical principle that brings thought to the point of awakening, at which time utopian desire takes over as the principle of social-political transformation."[441] This utopian relation to the past that reactivates it for the purpose of critique and in order to recover hope and futurity in the time of the long now in our time stands opposed to restorative nostalgia that underwrites that logic of right-wing thought and culture. And, as Dimaline's novel shows, too, such a relation to the past harbors great danger, for, as Chrostowska emphasizes, "unreflected nostalgia breeds monsters."[442]

In his essay "Traces of Hope," Jack Zipes foregrounds the significance of Ernst Bloch's distinction between *anamnesis* and *anagnorosis* for our understanding of the relation between memory, history, and futurity. Bloch argues that *anamnesis* is fundamentally bound up with stasis and conservatism. In *anagnorosis*, on the other hand, Zipes argues, Bloch locates the work of utopian thought, since it creates a "shock of recognition" that "brings back a trace or fragment from the past in such a new way that it can be reactivated and transformed for future action."[443] In fact, Zipes argues, it is important to foreground that Bloch's notion of the *Novum* itself depends on recollection, which "must be re-utilized as historicized memory that anticipates and guides political action."[444] In his essay "Remembering the Future," Vincent Geoghegan elaborates upon this aspect of Bloch's thought. "In *anagnorosis*," he writes,

> memory traces are reactivated in the present, but there is never simple correspondence between past and present, because of all the intervening novelty. The power of the past resides in its complicated relationship of similarity/dissimilarity to the present. The tension thus created helps shape the new.[445]

Similarly, while the white majority in Dimaline's novel turns to the past to reactivate past mechanisms of domination and violence, the relation to the past that guides the actions of and that keeps alive the dreams of Indigenous people is always temporally complex. The past, though it may seem "real old-timey," enters the present critically in the context of the struggle for freedom of Indigenous people, and the past's content is thereby transformed and turned into anticipatory, transformative thought itself. Dimaline's novels shows, in the words of David Kaufmann, that "the past is not an open treasure-trove" but that "it has to be claimed," since "progress is not the self-actualization of the world—it is, at its best, a product of human choice and bravery in the face of terrible odds."[446]

Zipes considers the work of Bloch of the utmost importance for our time to no small degree because Bloch "militantly insists that we continue to look for utopian signs in our heritage and do not tolerate the abandonment of hope in overcoming the alienating conditions of capitalism."[447] And in particular in a moment when the idea of heritage itself is claimed and distorted by right-wing rhetoric and demagoguery, the understanding of the relation between past, present, and future that we find in the work of Bloch and Adorno and that novels like *The Marrow Thieves* concretely model for us, must constitute a central aspect of our critical and political response to the crises of the long now. Futurity, we learn, lies not in simple linear, naïve notions of a future that may never be. Instead, futurity emerges out of the past, out of those repressed, abandoned, and forgotten aspects of history that continue to exist in our present as nonsynchronous, rebellious lack and that point toward a better life. Futures may crash, and futures may be repressed, but they do not simply disappear. In fact, old futures can reemerge strengthened and with renewed force under new historical conditions, and it is here that we find the core of the Blochian utopian imagination that is so important in our time. "The tradition of all dead generations weighs like a nightmare on the brains of the living," Marx famously writes in *Eighteenth Brumaire of Louis Bonaparte*.[448] And yet, Tomba shows, it is important to remember that "the past tradition can also be revitalized in order to change the present."[449] Returning to Marx's letter to Ruge, Tomba emphasizes that one of the fundamental commitments of Marxian thought emerges from this way of activating the past politically: "it will become plain that mankind is not beginning a *new* work, but is consciously bringing about the completion of its old work."[450]

This relation to the past is not only modeled for us in novels like that of Dimaline, but the very act of re-reading may serve as a concrete example of the ways in which the new emerges precisely out of visitations of the past under new conditions. In his analysis of futurity, Marc Augé argues that we can get a sense of the mechanisms that underlie our imagination of the future whenever we re-read a book. During re-readings, "we come across forgotten details, or aspects that passed unnoticed the first time," Augé argues, because "we don't necessarily have the same gaze."[451] What we experience in these moments, he stresses, are moments of intensity that consist of "the private upsurge of a future which had been put behind us."[452] Afro-Futurist author and literary critic Samuel R. Delany offer us a similar defense of the importance of engaging with the relation between futurity and re-reading. Delany locates in re-reading a glimpse of the utopian imagination, for re-reading "reveals what could not be seen and what could not be said in previous presents, inflecting the instantaneity of the present with ambivalence, complexity, repression, and re-vision."[453] In the context of the rise of new forms of right-wing extremism, in the era of Trump, and in a time when the capitalist long now seeks to mystify the possibility of a better life beyond the age of capital, we must remind ourselves that we are able to find hope and futurity in the past. Critical theory in general and the work of Bloch in particular offer us conceptions of utopia that are most timely and of great importance in our moment. By re-reading this tradition of thought and by aiding in the process of its completion, even in the face of terrible odds, we are able to find hope and futurity in our time while taking a strong, unwavering stance against the rise of a new Right that seeks to collapse both past and future into a violent present. Against the rise of right-wing extremism that mystifies the contradictions of capital and thereby safeguards the capitalist quo, we must follow the example set particularly effectively by Indigenous and multiethnic art and defend hope and utopia. The utopian imagination is the antidote, the reification of time and futurity in the long now. It gives us hope by showing us what could have been, what is not, and what may yet be. Let us then fight for hope and for those dreams of a better life that lay bare what is missing and that anticipate the future by radically refusing the limits of the present.

Notes

Chapter 1

1. "The 10,000 Year Clock: Introduction." http://longnow.org/clock/. The information on the project provided in this book can be found on the same companion website: The Long Now.
2. Michael Chabon, "The Future Will Have to Wait," *Details*, January/February 2006, 90–92. http://longnow.org/media/djlongnow_media/press/pdf/0200602-Chabon-TheFutureWillHavetoWait.pdf.
3. Bruce Mau and Jennifer Leonard, *Massive Change* (London: Phaidon, 2004): 14.
4. Ibid., 139.
5. See http://longbets.org/about/.
6. Nathaniel Rich, *Odds Against Tomorrow* (New York: Farrar, Straus, and Giroux, 2013): 236.
7. Ibid., 195.
8. Ibid., 236.
9. "The Forever Now: Contemporary Painting in an Atemporal World," The Museum of Modern Art, New York, December 12, 2014–April 5, 2015. https://www.moma.org/calendar/exhibitions/1455?locale=en.
10. Peter Thompson, "Introduction: The Privatization of Hope and the Crisis of Negation," in Peter Thompson and Slavoj Žižek (eds.), *The Privatization of Hope: Ernst Bloch and the Future of Utopia* (Durham: Duke University Press, 2013): 2.
11. Ibid., 3.
12. Steward Brand, *The Clock of the Long Now: Time and Responsibility* (New York: Basic Books, 2000).
13. See http://longnow.org/about/.
14. See, for example, Slavoj Žižek, *Living in the End Times* (New York and London: Verso, 2010).
15. Sean Illing, "If You Want to Understand the Age of Trump, Read the Frankfurt School," *Vox*, December 26, 2017. https://www.vox.com/conversations/2016/12/27/14038406/donald-trump-frankfurt-school-brexit-critical-theory.

Chapter 2

16 Jacob Brogan, "'Flying Cars in the Future' Is the Perfect Meme for This Dumb Year," *Slate*, August 24, 2017. https://slate.com/technology/2017/08/i-bet-there-will-be-flying-cars-in-the-future-is-the-perfect-meme-for-2017.html.
17 Douglas Coupland, "What if There's No Next Big New Thing?" *e-flux*, 74, June 2016 (n. pag). https://www.e-flux.com/journal/74/59778/what-if-there-s-no-next-big-thing/.
18 David M. Higgins. "Salvaging the Future," *Los Angeles Review of Books*, May 31, 2016 (n. pag.) https://lareviewofbooks.org/article/salvaging-the-future/.
19 Ibid.
20 Ibid.
21 Bruce Gibney, "What Happened to the Future?" https://foundersfund.com/the-future/.
22 Harry Harootunian, "Remembering the Historical Present," *Critical Inquiry* 33 (2007): 474.
23 Ibid., 474.
24 Ibid., 472.
25 Ibid.
26 Thompson, "Introduction," 1.
27 Ibid., 1–2.
28 Ibid., 2.
29 Amy Elias, "Past/Future," in Joel Burges and Amy J. Elias (eds.), *Time: A Vocabulary of the Present* (New York: New York University Press, 2016). Kindle edition. Locations: 2655–2658.
30 David Harvey, *The Limits to Capital* (London and New York: Verso, 2007): xxi.
31 Barbara Adam, *Time* (London and New York: Polity, 2004): 40.
32 Bliss Cua Lim, *Translating Time: Cinema, the Fantastic, and Temporal Critique* (Durham: Duke University Press, 2009): 72.
33 Ibid.
34 Ibid., 73.
35 Norbert Trenkle, "Value and Crisis: Basic Questions," in Neil Larsen et al. (eds.), *Marxism and the Critique of Value* (Chicago and Edmonton: MCM Prime, 2014): 5.
36 Ibid., 6.
37 Massimiliano Tomba, *Marx's Temporalities* (Chicago: Haymarket Books, 2013): ix.
38 Cédric Durant, *Fictitious Capital: How Finance Is Appropriating Our Future*. Trans. David Broder (London and New York: Verso, 2017).

39 Paul Virilio, *The Futurism of the Instant: Stop-Eject*. Trans. Julie Rose (Cambridge: Polity, 2010): 70. Emphasis original.
40 Ibid., 70–71.
41 Adam, *Time*, 39.
42 Ibid.
43 Mark McGurl, "Real/Quality," in Joel Burges and Amy Elias (eds.), *Time: A Vocabulary of the Present* (New York: New York University Press, 2016). Kindle edition: location 4503–4590.
44 Ibid.
45 Bernard Stiegler, *For a New Critique of Political Economy* (London: Polity, 2010): 4–5.
46 Ibid., 5. Emphasis original.
47 Jared Gardner, "Serial/Simultaneous," in Joel Burges and Amy Elias (eds.), *Time: A Vocabulary of the Present* (New York: New York University Press, 2016): 161–176.
48 See, for example, Carlo Rovelli, "'There Is No Such Thing as Past or Future': Physicist Carlo Rovelli on Changing How We Think About Time," *The Guardian*. April 14, 2018. https://www.theguardian.com/books/2018/apr/14/carlo-rovelli-exploding-commonsense-notions-order-of-time-interview; and "The End of Time," *Nautilus*, September 6, 2018. http://nautil.us/issue/64/the-unseen/the-end-of-time.
49 Christian Marazzi, *Capital and Language: From the New Economy to the War Economy*. Trans. Michael Hardt and Gregory Conti (Los Angeles, Semiotext(e), 2008).
50 Franco Berardi, *The Soul at Work: From Alienation to Autonomy*. Trans. Giuseppina Mecchia (Los Angeles: Semiotext(e), 2009).
51 Kristin Wong, "The Imaginative Powers of a Brain on Autopilot," *The Cut*, January 25, 2018. https://www.thecut.com/2018/01/how-to-be-more-creative.html?utm_campaign=nym&utm_source=tw&utm_medium=s1.
52 Paulo Virno, *A Grammar of the Multitude: For and Analysis of Contemporary Forms of Life* (Los Angeles: Semiotext(e), 2004): 102–103.
53 Ibid., 103.
54 Julie Von, "Unstructured Time," *The Fullest*, April 4, 2017. http://thefullest.com/2017/04/04/unstructured-time/.
55 Sheila Marikar, "The Rich Are Planning to Leave This Wretched Planet," *The New York Times*, June 9, 2018. https://www.nytimes.com/2018/06/09/style/axiom-space-travel.html.

56 Cat Moir, "Beyond the Turn: Ernst Bloch and the Future of Speculative Materialism," *Poetics Today* 37.2 (2016): 340.
57 Ruth Leys, *Utopia as Method: The Imaginary Reconstitution of Society* (Basingstoke: Palgrave Macmillan, 2013): 41.
58 Peter Thompson, "Bloch, Badiou, Saint Paul, and the Ontology of Not Yet," *New German Critique* 40.2 (2013): 33.
59 Guido Mazzoni, *Theory of the Novel*. Trans. Zakiya Hanafi (Cambridge: Harvard University Press, 2016): 366.
60 Ibid., 368.
61 Ibid., 369.
62 Ibid.
63 Ibid., 372.
64 Rita Felski, *Doing Time: Feminist Theory and Postmodern Culture* (New York: New York University Press, 2000): 82.
65 Carolin Levine, *Forms: Whole, Rhythm, Hierarchy, Network* (Princeton and Oxford: Princeton University Press, 2015): 50.
66 Ibid., 49.
67 Ibid.
68 Judy Wajcman, *Pressed for Time: The Acceleration of Life in Digital Capitalism* (Chicago: University of Chicago Press, 2014): 62.
69 Ibid.
70 Harootunian, "Remembering the Historical Present," 472.
71 Ibid., 476.
72 Ibid., 490–491.
73 Ibid., 478.
74 Ernst Bloch, "Nonsynchronism and the Obligation to Its Dialectics," Trans. Mark Ritter, *New German Critique* 11 (1977): 22.
75 Ibid.
76 Ibid.
77 Frederic J. Schwartz, "Ernst Bloch and Wilhelm Pinder: Out of Sync," *Grey Room* 3 (2001): 55.
78 Bloch, "Nonsynchronism," 31.
79 Ibid., 32.
80 Ibid.
81 Ibid.
82 Ibid., 31.
83 Ibid.

84 Ibid., 32–33.
85 Ibid., 33.
86 Ibid., 33.
87 Ernst Bloch, *Heritage of Our Times*. Trans. Neville and Stephen Plaice (Cambridge: Polity, 2009): 28.
88 Ibid., 31.
89 Thompson, "Introduction," 16.
90 Ernst Bloch, "Dialectics and Hope," Trans. Mark Ritter, *New German Critique* 9 (1976): 8.
91 Ibid.
92 Ibid., 10.
93 Ernst Bloch, *Literary Essays*. Trans. Andrew Jordon (Palo Alto: Stanford University Press, 1998): 250.
94 Ibid., 253.
95 Ibid.
96 Ibid., 254–255.
97 Bloch, *Heritage*, 33.
98 Ibid.
99 Ernst Bloch, *The Utopian Function of Art and Literature: Selected Essays*. Trans. Jack Zipes and Frank Mecklenburg (Cambridge: MIT Press, 1988): 216.
100 Jacques Rancière, *Bela Tarr, The Time After*. Trans. Erik Beranek (Minneapolis: Univocal, 2013): 9.
101 Moir, "Beyond the Turn," 347.
102 Ibid.
103 Bloch, *The Utopian Function of Art and Literature*, 17.
104 Ibid.
105 Moir, "Beyond the Turn," 341.
106 Peter Thompson, "Bloch, Badiou, Saint Paul, and the Ontology of the Not Yet," *New German Critique* 119 (2013): 49.
107 Honoré de Balzac, *Un Prince de la Bohème* (Paris: Michel Lévy Fréres, 1865): 189.
108 Thompson, "Bloch, Badiou, Saint Paul, and the Ontology of the Not Yet," 39.
109 Ibid.
110 Quoted in Thompson, "Bloch, Badiou, Saint Paul, and the Ontology of the Not Yet," 52.
111 Jean-Paul Sartre, "Time in Faulkner: *The Sound and the Fury*," in Frederick J. Hoffman and Olga W. Vickery (eds.), *William Faulkner: Three Decades of Criticism* (New York: Harcourt, 1969): 231.

112 Ibid.
113 Max Blechman, "'Not Yet' Adorno and the Utopia of Conscience," *Cultural Critique* 70 (2008): 194.
114 Ibid.
115 Theodor W. Adorno, "The Handle, the Pot, and Early Experience," in Notes to Literature II. Trans. S.W. Nicholsen (New York: Columbia University Press, 1992): 211–212.
116 Ibid., 212.
117 S. D. Chrostowska, "Thought Woken by Memory: Adorno's Circuitous Path to Utopia," *New German Critique* 118, 40.1 (2013): 93.
118 See "Something's Missing: A Discussion between Ernst Bloch and Theodor W. Adorno on the Contradictions of Utopian Longing," in Ernst Bloch, *The Utopian Function of Art and Literature: Selected Essays*. Trans. Jack Zipes and Frank Mecklenburg (Cambridge: MIT Press, 1988). Quoted in and modified by Blechman, "Not Yet", 100.
119 Ibid.
120 Ibid., 95.
121 Quoted in Chrostowska, "Thought Woken by Memory", 95.
122 Ibid., 95.
123 Ibid., 98.
124 Moir, "Beyond the Turn," 339.
125 Ibid., 340.
126 Ibid.
127 Jack Zipes, "Ernst Bloch and the Obscenity of Hope: Introduction to the Special Section on Ernst Bloch," *New German Critique* 45 (1988): 3.
128 Ibid.
129 Ibid.
130 Schwartz, "Ernst Bloch and Wilhelm Pinder," N. pag.
131 Ibid.
132 Ibid.
133 Anson Rabinbach, "Unclaimed Heritage: Ernst Bloch's *Heritage of Our Times* and the Theory of Fascism," *New German Critique* 11 (1977): 5.
134 Peter Thompson and Slavoj Žižek, "Preface," in Peter Thompson and Slavoj Žižek (eds.), *The Privatization of Hope: Ernst Bloch and the Future of Utopia* (Durham: Duke University Press, 2013): xx.
135 Ibid.

Chapter 3

136 Nellie Bowles, "Jordan Peterson, Custodian of the Patriarchy," *The New York Times*, May 18, 2018. https://www.nytimes.com/2018/05/18/style/jordan-peterson-12-rules-for-life.html.

137 Jordan Paterson on the "Backlash against Masculinity," *BBC News*, August 6, 2018. https://www.bbc.com/news/av/world-us-canada-45084954/jordan-peterson-on-the-backlash-against-masculinity.

138 Bloch, *Heritage*, 53.

139 Ibid., 99.

140 Ibid., 98.

141 Ibid., 112. Translation augmented.

142 Ibid., 53.

143 Ibid.

144 See, for example, Andrew Hoberek, "Introduction: After Postmodernism," *Twentieth-Century Literature* 53.3 (2007): 233 or Jeffrey T. Nealon, *Post-Postmodernism or, The Cultural Logic of Just-In-Time Capitalism* (Stanford: Stanford University Press, 2012).

145 See, for example, John Frow, "What Was Postmodernism?" in Ian Adam and Helen Tiffin (Eds.), *Past the Last Post: Theorizing Post-Colonialism and Post-Modernism* (Calgary: University of Calgary Press, 1990): 139–159; and Raymond Federman, *Critifiction: Postmodern Essays* (Albany: SUNY University Press, 1993): 105.

146 See, for example, Ihab Hassan, *The Postmodern Turn: Essays in Postmodern Theory and Culture* (Columbus: Ohio State University Press, 1987); Jean François Lyotard, *The Postmodern Condition: A Report on Knowledge* (Minneapolis: University of Minnesota Press, 1984); David Harvey, *The Condition of Postmodernity: An Enquiry into the Origins of Cultural Change* (London: Blackwell, 1989); and Fredric Jameson, *Postmodernism or, The Cultural Logic of Late Capitalism* (Durham: Duke University Press, 1991).

147 Shuja Haider, "Postmodernism Did Not Take Place: On Jordan Peterson's *12 Rules for Life*," *Viewpoint Magazine*, January 23, 2018. https://www.viewpointmag.com/2018/01/23/postmodernism-not-take-place-jordan-petersons-12-rules-life/.

148 Kurt Vonnegut, *Breakfast of Champions* (New York: Dial, 1999): 7.

149 Ibid., 18.

150 Donald Barthelme, *The Dead Father* (New York: Farrar, Straus and Giroux, 2004): 138.

151 Ibid., 177.
152 Elena Ferrante, "Dreaming of a Return to the Past Is a Denial of Youth," *The Guardian*, March 24, 2018. https://www.theguardian.com/lifeandstyle/2018/mar/24/elena-ferrante-leave-parents-behind-daughters.
153 Houman Barekat, "A Messiah-cum-Surrogate-Dad for Gormless Dimwits: On Jordan B. Peterson's '12 Rules for Life,'" *Los Angeles Book Review*, March 8, 2018. https://lareviewofbooks.org/article/a-messiah-cum-surrogate-dad-for-gormless-dimwits-on-jordan-b-petersons-12-rules-for-life/.
154 Bowles, "Custodian of the Patriarchy."
155 Bloch, *Heritage*, 148.
156 Ibid., 23.
157 Ibid.
158 Ibid.
159 Ibid.
160 Georgina Rannard, *BBC News*, October 4, 2018. https://www.bbc.com/news/world-us-canada-45738409.
161 See, for example, reports like Michael Carpenter's "Russia Is Co-opting Angry Young Men," *The Atlantic*, August 29, 2018. https://www.theatlantic.com/ideas/archive/2018/08/russia-is-co-opting-angry-young-men/568741/, which illustrates the global prevalence of utilizing angry young men, including Fight Clubs, neo-Nazi soccer hooligans, and motorcycle gangs, for political and economic gain.
162 Pankaj Mishra, "The Crisis in Modern Masculinity," *The Guardian*, March 17, 2018. https://www.theguardian.com/books/2018/mar/17/the-crisis-in-modern-masculinity.
163 I invoke here Edward Said's notion of "late style," a perspective via which it is possible to foreground the ways in which Cheever employs this particular style strategically as a way of making legible a particular moment of historical lateness. See Edward Said *On Late Style: Music and Literature against the Grain* (New York: Vintage, 2007).
164 John Cheever, *Oh What a Paradise It Seems* (New York: Vintage, 1992): 3.
165 Ibid., 10.
166 Ibid.
167 Ibid., 10–11.
168 Ibid., 11.
169 Ernst Bloch, *Tübinger Einleitung in die Philosophie* (Frankfurt: Suhrkamp, 1985): 13. Trans. mine.

170 Thompson, "Bloch, Badiou, Saint Paul, and the Ontology of Not Yet," 45–46.
171 Octavia E. Butler, *Parable of the Talents* (New York: Aspect, 1998): 52.
172 Ibid., 3.
173 Ibid., 8.
174 Ibid., 19.
175 Ibid.
176 In a longer list of novels that examines 9/11 in relation to fathering and the disintegration of the nuclear family in general, we might also include novels such as Claire Messud's *The Emperor's Children* (2006), Joseph O'Neill's *Netherland* (2008), and John Updike's troubling addition to this field, *Terrorist* (2006).
177 Comaroff Jean and John L. Comaroff (eds.), *Millennial Capitalism and the Culture of Neoliberalism* (Durham: Duke University Press, 2001): 8.
178 Lauren Berlant, *Cruel Optimism* (Durham: Duke University Press, 2011): 3.
179 Ibid.
180 Franco Berardi, *The Uprising: On Poetry and Finance* (New York: Semiotext(e), 2012): 164.
181 Richard Sennett, *The Culture of the New Capitalism* (New Haven: Yale University Press, 2006): 2.
182 Ibid.
183 Ibid., 4.
184 Ibid.
185 Ibid., 2.
186 See Roswitha Scholz's essay, "Patriarchy and Commodity Society: Gender Without the Body," in Neil Larsen et al. (eds.), *Marxism and the Critique of Value* (Chicago and Edmonton: MCM, 2014).
187 Jonathan Franzen, *The Corrections* (New York: Harper Perennial, 2003): 3.
188 Ibid., 7.
189 Ibid., 69.
190 Ibid. Emphasis original.
191 Ibid.
192 Comaroff and Comaroff, *Millennial Capitalism*, 15. See also David Harvey's introduction to the updated 2006 version of *Limits to Capital* (Verso).
193 Franzen, *The Corrections*, 461–462.
194 Ibid., 462.
195 Peter Thompson, "Ernst Bloch and the Principle of Hope," *The Guardian*, April 29, 2013. https://www.theguardian.com/commentisfree/belief/2013/apr/29/frankfurt-school-ernst-bloch-principle-of-hope.

196 *Lost Fathers—The Politics of Fatherlessness in America*, a collection of essays edited by Cynthia R. Daniels, provides a valuable entry into the variety of ways in which contemporary "fatherlessness" is being discussed across the disciplines. Particularly Robert L. Griswold's contribution to the collection "The History and Politics of Fatherlessness" provides an interesting basic outline of the historical and socioeconomic reasons for the widespread association of the contemporary historical period with the central trauma of fatherlessness. Suffice it to say at this point that fatherlessness (literally and as an extended metaphor for the breakdown of paternalistic structures on the level of economy, national security, etc.) is frequently discussed as the universal explanation for a multitude of social and structural problems the United States currently experiences. Consequently, the defense of paternalistic structures and the defense of the father is constructed as the universal cure for a multitude of "social ills". One indicator of this regressive trend to construct paternalism as in dire need of defense that emerges out of the experience of contemporary capitalism is the recent surge in organizations dedicated to the defense of fathers rights and the sociopolitical function of fathers. Representative examples of such organizations are The American Coalition for Fathers and Children (www.acfc.org), The Fathers Rights Foundation (www.fathers-rights.com), the National Fathers Resource Center, home to the organization Fathers for Equal Rights (www.fathers4kids.com), and resource ad information centers such as www.fathersrights.org, www.dadsrights.org, and www.fathersrightsinc.com. It is not surprising that surge in popularity of these organizations coincides with the rise of narratives of fatherlessness that parallel the rise to dominance of neoliberalism in the late 1980s and early 1990s.

197 Bloch, *Heritage*, 108.

198 Ibid.

199 Sennett, *New Capitalism*, 53.

200 Ibid.

201 Cormac McCarthy, *The Road* (New York: Alfred A. Knopf, 2006): 165.

202 Fred Pfeil *White Guys: Studies in Postmodern Domination and Difference* (London and New York: Verso, 1995): 7.

203 Klaus Theweleit, *Male Fantasies, Vol. 2: Male Bodies: Psychoanalyzing the White Terror* (Minneapolis: University of Minnesota Press, 1989): 373.

204 Corey Robin, *The Reactionary Mind: Conservatism from Edmund Burke to Donald Trump* (Oxford: Oxford University Press, 2017): 244.

205 Bowles, "Custodian of the Patriarchy."

206 Barekat, "On Jordan B. Peterson's '12 Rules.'"
207 Haider, "Postmodernism Did Not Take Place."
208 Ibid.
209 Robin, *The Reactionary Mind*, 271.
210 Ibid.
211 Marci Shore, "A Pre-history of Post-Truth, East and West," *Eurozine*, September 1, 2017. https://www.eurozine.com/a-pre-history-of-post-truth-east-and-west/.
212 Michel Foucault, "Preface," in Gilles Deleuze and Félix Guattari (eds.), *Anti-Oedipus: Capitalism and Schizophrenia* (Minneapolis: University of Minnesota Press, 2000): xiii.
213 Ibid.

Chapter 4

214 Bloch, *Heritage*, 12.
215 Thompson, "Introduction", 2.
216 Ibid.
217 T. J. Clark, "For a Left with No Future," *New Left Review* 74 (2012). N. pag. https://newleftreview.org/II/74/t-j-clark-for-a-left-with-no-future.
218 Rhiannon Lucy Cosslett, "Why Do Millennials Insist on Living in the Past?" *The Guardian*, September 26, 2017. https://www.theguardian.com/commentisfree/2017/sep/26/millennials-living-in-the-past-polaroids.
219 Louis Menand, "Francis Fukuyama Postpones the End of History," *The New Yorker*, September 3, 2018. https://www.newyorker.com/magazine/2018/09/03/francis-fukuyama-postpones-the-end-of-history.
220 Evan Goldstein, "What Follows the End of History? Identity Politics," *The Chronicle of Higher Education*, August 27, 2018. https://www.chronicle.com/article/What-Follows-the-End-of/244369.
221 Ibid.
222 Ibid.
223 Jordan B. Peterson, *12 Rules for Life: An Antidote to Chaos* (New York: Penguin Random House, 2018): xxviii.
224 Ibid.
225 Mia Rabson, "Trudeau Uses NYU Graduation Speech to Criticize Growth in Identity Politics," *CBC News*, May 16, 2018. https://www.cbc.ca/news/politics/trudeau-nyu-speech-intolerance-1.4666476.

226 Asad Haider, *Mistaken Identity: Race and Class in the Age of Trump* (London and New York: Verso, 2018): 15.
227 Bloch, *Heritage*, 44.
228 Ibid.; Eberhard Knödler-Bunte, "Fascism as a Depoliticized Mass Movement," Trans. Russell Berman, *New German Critique* 11 (1977): 44.
229 Ibid.
230 Rabinbach, "Unclaimed Heritage," 14.
231 Pavlos Roufos, "The Aggressiveness of Vulnerability," *The Brooklyn Rail*, July 11, 2018. https://brooklynrail.org/2018/07/field-notes/The-Aggressiveness-of-Vulnerability.
232 Ibid.
233 Robin, *The Reactionary Mind*, xi.
234 Ibid.
235 Bloch, *Heritage*, 64.
236 The Editors, "Introduction: Fascism as Cultural Synthesis," *New German Critique* 11 (1977): 3.
237 Eberhard Knödler-Bunte, "Fascism as a Depoliticized Mass Movement," Trans. Russell Berman *New German Critique* 11 (1977).
238 Ibid., 3.
239 Bloch, *Heritage*, 60.
240 Ibid., 59.
241 Ibid., 62.
242 Haider, *Mistaken Identity*, 16.
243 Bloch, *Heritage*, 60.
244 Ibid.
245 Ibid., 44.
246 Ibid.
247 Michael Trebitsch, "Preface," in Henri Lefèbvre (ed.), *The Critique of Everyday Life, Vol. 1*. Trans. John Moore (London and New York: Verso, 1991): xvi.
248 Ibid., 59.
249 Theodor W. Adorno, "Resignation," in Hermann Schweppenhäuser (ed.), *Theodor W. Adorno zum Gedächtnis* (Frankfurt. Suhrkamp, 1971): 13.
250 Bloch, *Heritage*, 85.
251 Max Horkheimer, "The Jews and Europe," Trans. Mark Ritter. In Stephen Eric Bronner and Douglas Kellner (eds.), *Critical Theory and Society: A Reader* (New York and London: Routledge, 1989): 78.
252 The Editors, "Introduction," 3.
253 Knödler-Bunte, "Fascism as a Depoliticized Mass Movement," 39.

254 Ibid., 39.
255 Ibid.
256 Ibid., 40.
257 Ibid.
258 Bloch, *Heritage*, 58.
259 Ibid., 62.
260 Ibid., 46.
261 Rabinbach, "Unclaimed Heritage," 3.
262 Quoted in ibid., 3.
263 Ibid., 6.
264 Steven Poole, "Is Our Love of Nature Writing Bourgeois Escapism?" *The Guardian* July 6, 2013. https://www.theguardian.com/books/2013/jul/06/nature-writing-revival.
265 Emphasis original.
266 Bloch, "Nonsynchronism and the Obligation to Its Dialectics," 7.
267 James Dickey, *Deliverance* (New York: Delta, 1994): 50.
268 Ibid.
269 Ibid., 43.
270 Ibid., 44.
271 Ibid., 36.
272 Jameson Fredric, *The Seeds of Time* (New York: Columbia University Press, 1996): 29.
273 Fredric Jameson, *Archaeologies of the Future: The Desire Called Utopia and Other Science Fictions* (London and New York: Verso, 2005), 161.
274 Ibid., 9.
275 Ibid., 56.
276 Mark C. Taylor, *Speed Limits: Where Time Went and Why We Have So Little Left* (New Haven: Yale University Press): 236.
277 Comaroff and Comaroff, *Millennial Capitalism*, 10.
278 Ibid.
279 Franco Berardi, *The Uprising: On Poetry and Finance* (Cambridge: MIT Press, 2012): 17–18.
280 Comaroff and Comaroff, *Millennial Capitalism*, 12.
281 Darren Fleet, "The Narcotic Abstractions of Finance," *Adbusters* 109 (2013). https://adbusters.org/tag/109/.
282 The relationship between the abstraction of finance capitalism and the cultural and epistemological struggles to come to terms with it has recently received sustained attention in an impressive special edition of *Textual Practice* titled

"How Abstract Is It? Thinking Capital Now" (28.7, November 2014). In particular Rebecca Colesworthy's introduction, "Capital's Abstractions," and the first three articles in the issue by Nicky Marsh, Timothy Bewes, and Alberto Toscano offer brilliant analyses of this topic and offer important contributions to this general debate.

283 See Howard Kunstler, *World Made by Hand* (New York: Atlantic Monthly Press, 2008).
284 Rabinbach, "Unclaimed Heritage," 14.
285 Ben Beaumont-Thomas, "Fight Club Author Chuck Palahniuk on His Book Becoming a Bible for the Incel Movement," *The Guardian*, July 20, 2018. https://www.theguardian.com/books/2018/jul/20/chuck-palahniuk-interview-adjustment-day-black-ethno-state-gay-parenting-incel-movement.
286 Chuck Palahniuk, *Fight Club* (New York: W.W. Norton, 2005): 114–115.
287 Ibid., 117.
288 Ibid., 116.
289 Ibid., 41.
290 Jordy Rosenberg, "The Daddy Dialectic," *LA Review of Books*, March 11, 2018. https://lareviewofbooks.org/article/the-daddy-dialectic/#!.
291 Palahniuk, *Fight Club*, 164.
292 Bloch, *Heritage*, 49.
293 Ibid., 51–52.
294 Ibid., 53.
295 Sartre, "Time in Faulkner," 229.
296 Bloch, *Literary Essays*, 296.
297 Ibid.
298 Ibid., 297.
299 Ibid., 303. Emphasis Original.
300 Ibid., 303.
301 Ibid.
302 Rich, *Odds Against Tomorrow*, 3.
303 Ibid., 4.
304 Ibid., 19.
305 Ibid.
306 Ibid., 20.
307 Ibid.
308 Ibid., 31.
309 Ibid.
310 Ibid.

311 Ibid., 97.
312 Ibid., 108.
313 Ibid., 195.
314 Ibid., 236.
315 Ibid., 237.
316 Ibid., 280.
317 Ibid., 283.
318 Ibid., 286.
319 Ibid.
320 Ibid., 302.
321 Wajcman, *Pressed for Time*, 27.
322 Bloch, "Dialectics and Hope" (the English translation of the relevant chapter of *Subjekt-Objekt*), 4.
323 Bloch, *Heritage*, 54.
324 Ibid.
325 Ibid., 55.
326 Thompson, "Bloch, Badiou, Saint Paul, and the Ontology of Not Yet," 35.

Chapter 5

327 Peter Thompson, "Ernst Bloch, *Ungleichzeitigkeit* and the Philosophy of Being and Time," *New German Critique* 42, no. 2 (2015): 56.
328 Oskar Negt, "Ernst Bloch, the German Philosopher of the October Revolution," Trans. Jack Zipes. *New German Critique* 4 (1975): 12.
329 Ibid.
330 Ibid.
331 Rabinbach, "Unclaimed Heritage."
332 Ibid.
333 Ibid., 7.
334 Bloch, *Heritage*, 19.
335 Rabinbach, "Unclaimed Heritage," 19.
336 Ibid.
337 Ibid.
338 Ibid.
339 Douglas Kellner, "Ernst Bloch, Utopia and Ideology Critique," *Vlaams Marxistisch Tijdschrift* 44.2 (2010): 41–42.
340 Ibid., 41.

341 Ibid.
342 Ibid.
343 Rabinbach, "Unclaimed Heritage," 12.
344 Jean François Lyotard, *The Postmodern Condition: A Report on Knowledge* (Minneapolis: University of Minnesota Press, 1979): 13.
345 Ibid.
346 Terry Eagleton, *Hope without Optimism* (Charlottesville: University of Virginia Press, 2015).
347 Ibid.
348 Ibid.
349 Ibid.
350 Ibid.
351 Ibid.
352 Ibid.
353 Tomba, *Marx's Temporalities*, xi.
354 Ibid.
355 Bloch, *Literary Essays*, 340.
356 Ibid.
357 Ibid.
358 Ibid.
359 Thompson, "Introduction," 3.
360 Ernst Bloch, *A Philosophy of the Future*. Trans. John Cumming (New York: Herder and Herder, 1970): 2.
361 Bloch, "Dialectics and Hope," 3.
362 Ibid.
363 Ibid., 5.
364 Thompson, "Introduction," 8.
365 Ibid., 11.
366 Bloch, "Dialectics and Hope," 6.
367 Ibid.
368 Ibid., 7.
369 Thompson, "Introduction," 13.
370 Ibid.
371 Ibid.
372 Beat Dietschy, "Ungleichzeitigkeit, Gleichzeitigkeit, Übergleichzeitigkeit," in Beat Dietschy et al. (eds.), *Bloch-Wörterbuch: Leitbegriffe der Philosophie Ernst Blochs* (Berlin and Boston: De Gruyter, 2012): 626.
373 Ibid.

374 Ibid.
375 Kellner, "Ernst Bloch, Utopia, and Ideology Critique," 45.
376 Ibid., 42.
377 Theodor W. Adorno, "On Lyric Poetry and Society," in *Notes to Literature Vol. 1*. Trans. Shierry Weber Nicholsen (New York: Columbia University Press, 1991): 40.
378 Ibid., 39.
379 Theodor W. Adorno, "The Position of the Narrator in the Contemporary Novel," in *Notes on Literature Vol. 1*. Trans. Shierry Weber (New York: Columbia University Press, 1991): 32.
380 Timothy Bewes, "Temporalizing the Present," *Novel: A Forum on Fiction* 45.2 (2012): 160.
381 Carlos Fuentes, "In Praise of the Novel," *Critical Inquiry* 31.4 (2006): 614.
382 Ibid., 616.
383 Ibid.
384 Ibid.
385 Ibid.
386 Ibid.
387 Ibid., 617.
388 Milan Kundera, *The Art of the Novel*. Trans. Linda Asher (New York: Harper Perennial, 2003): 15.
389 Ibid., 14.
390 Ibid.
391 Ibid.
392 Alain Badiou, *The Age of the Poets and Other Writings on Twentieth-Century Poetry and Prose*. Trans. Bruno Bosteels (New York and London: Verso, 2014): 136.
393 Ibid., 137.
394 Jameson, *Seeds of Time*, 56.
395 Bloch, *The Utopian Function of Art and Literature*, 155.
396 Ibid.
397 Ibid., 223.
398 Ibid.
399 J.M. Bernstein, *The Philosophy of the Novel: Lukács, Marxism and the Dialectics of Form* (Minneapolis: University of Minnesota Press, 1985): 145.
400 Peter Boxall, *The Value of the Novel* (Cambridge: Cambridge University Press, 2015): 96.
401 Ibid., 97.

402 Ibid.
403 Ibid.
404 Ibid., 108.
405 Ibid.
406 Ibid., 112.
407 Bloch, *A Philosophy of the Future*, 140.
408 Ibid., 140–141.
409 Ibid., 141.
410 Ibid.
411 Ibid., 143.
412 Ibid.
413 Ibid.
414 Ibid., 144.
415 Higgins, "Salvaging the Future."
416 See Sesshu Foster, *Atomik Aztex* (San Francisco: City Lights Publishers, 2005).
417 Carleigh Baker, "'Review" Tracey Lindberg's Debut Novel Birdie Introduces an Important New Voice in Canadian Fiction," *The Globe and Mail*, June 12, 2015. https://www.theglobeandmail.com/arts/books-and-media/book-reviews/review-tracey-lindbergs-debut-novel-birdie-introduces-an-important-new-voice-in-canadian-fiction/article24940197/.
418 Ernst Bloch, *The Spirit of Utopia*. Trans. Anthony A. Nassar (Palo Alto: Stanford University Press, 2000): 188.
419 Cherie Dimaline, *The Marrow Thieves* (Toronto: Cormorant Books, 2017): 87.
420 Ibid.
421 Ibid., 24.
422 Ibid., 87.
423 Ibid., 26.
424 Ibid., 88.
425 Ibid.
426 Ibid., 89.
427 Ibid.
428 Ibid.
429 Ibid., 90.
430 Ibid., 32.
431 Ibid., 25.
432 Ibid.
433 Ibid., 107.
434 Ibid., 172–173.

435 Ibid., 173.
436 Ibid., 152.
437 Ibid., 226.
438 Chrostowska, "Thought Woken by Memory," 94.
439 Ibid.
440 Ibid., 95.
441 Ibid.
442 Chrostowska quoting Boym's phrase. Ibid., 93.
443 Jack Zipes, "Traces of Hope: The Non-synchronicity of Ernst Bloch," in Jamie Owen Daniel and Tom Moylan (eds.), *Not Yet: Reconsidering Ernst Bloch* (London and New York: Verso, 1997): 4.
444 Ibid.
445 Vincent Geoghegan, "Remembering the Future," in Jamie Owen Daniel and Tom Moylan (eds.), *Not Yet: Reconsidering Ernst Bloch* (London and New York: Verso, 1997), 22.
446 David Kaufmann, "Thanks for the Memory: Bloch, Benjamin, and the Philosophy of History," in Jamie Owen Daniel and Tom Moylan (eds.), *Not Yet: Reconsidering Ernst Bloch* (London and New York: Verso, 1997): 41.
447 Zipes, "Traces of Hope," 5.
448 Quoted in Tomba, *Marx's Temporalities*, x.
449 Ibid.
450 Ibid., xi.
451 Marc Augé, *The Future*. Trans. John Howe (New York and London: Verso, 2015): 7.
452 Ibid.
453 This is the editor's account of Samuel Delany's contribution to their volume, his essay "Historifying Marginal Practices" that contains a forceful critique of the relation between time, futurity, and African-American literature. See Karen Newman, Jay Clayton, and Marianne Hirsch (eds.), *Time and the Literary* (New York and London: Routledge, 2022): 5.

Index

10,000 Year Clock 1–4, 7
9/11. *See* September 11 attacks

Adam, Barbara 26, 28
Adbusters 128
Adorno, Theodor W. 13, 26, 56–8, 118,
   158–9, 164, 174–6
   Dialectic of Enlightenment 56
   Minima Moralia 57
aesthetic form 35, 36
affective capitalism 31
Afro-Futurism 167
alienation 26, 33, 34, 40, 47, 75, 78, 81,
   110, 115, 123, 128, 149, 150, 158
Amazon 2
America First 111
anagnorosis 175
anamnesis 175
Andersen, Hans Christian 133
anticipatory consciousness 35–6, 145–6
anti-Oedipalism 68
anti-paternalism 67, 69, 81–2
a-temporality 9
Augé, Marc 177
authenticity 121
authoritarianism 39, 129
automation 44–5, 75

Badiou, Alain 160–1
Baker, Carleigh 167
Balzac, Honoré de 54
Barekat, Houman 69, 71, 92
Barthelme, Donald 67–8, 75
   The Dead Father 67–8, 75
Baudrillard, Jean 26
Beaumont-Thomas, Ben 129
Benjamin, Walter 13, 58, 59, 111, 158
Berardi, Franco "Bifo" 29, 31, 81, 127
Berlant, Lauren 80–1
   Cruel Optimism 80–1
Bernstein, J. M. 162

Bewes, Timothy 159
Bezos, Jeff 2–3, 35
Black Lives Matter 110
Black Panther Party 110
Blechman, Max 56
Bloch, Ernst 12–16, 22, 36–7, 41–52, 54,
   55–9, 62–3, 70–1, 76–7, 81–2, 86–8,
   95, 101, 110–13, 115–23, 125, 129,
   131–3, 140–58, 161–2, 164–6, 168,
   174–7
   Heritage of Our Times 49, 58, 62, 101,
   148
   Literary Essays 51
   Principle of Hope 58, 153
   The Spirit of Utopia 56, 158
   Subjekt-Objekt 140
   Tendez-Latenz-Utopie 55
Bould, Mark 20
Bowie, David 67
Bowles, Nellie 61, 91
Boxall, Peter 163–4
Boym, Svetlana 174
Brand, Stewart 2, 9–10
Branson, Richard 35
Brogan, Jacob 19
Brooks, Geraldine 80
   March 80
Buck-Morss, Susan
   The Origin of Negative Dialectics 56
Buffet, Warren 8
Butler, Octavia E.
   Parable of the Talents 76–8, 167

Canadian residential school system 169,
   171
capitalist modernity 39, 163
Carver, Raymond 38
Chabon, Michael 4–5
Cheever, John
   Oh What a Paradise it Seems 74–5
Chrostowska, S. D. 56–7, 174, 175

Clark, T. J. 101–2
class consciousness 111
classic British liberal 71
The Clock of the Long Now. *See* 10,000 Year Clock
clock time 26–7
cognitive capitalism 31
colonialism 141, 145, 164–7
Comaroff, Jean and John L. 80, 86, 127
  Millenial Capitalism and the Culture of Neoliberalism 80
Communism 23, 52, 58, 92
conservation 57, 106
Conservatism 87, 93–4, 104–5, 113, 175
Cosslett, Rhiannon Lucy 103
Coupland, Douglas 19
  Generation X 19
creative capitalism 31
crisis of futurity 9–10, 14, 19, 21, 27, 40, 82, 91, 150, 165
critical fatalism 167
Cua Lim, Bliss 26
cultural Marxism 15, 61, 93
cultural surplus 36, 158

Deconstruction 97
Dee, Johnathan 80
  The Locals 80
Deleuze, Gilles 96–7
DeLillo, Don 80
  Falling Man 80
deregulation 76, 88
Derrida, Jacques 92, 96–7
dialectic 35, 156
Dickey, James 124–5, 127, 130
  Deliverance 124–5, 127, 130
Dietschy, Beat 157
Dimaline, Cherie 145, 169–77
  The Marrow Thieves 145, 169–77
disenfranchisement 40, 110, 150
diversity 66, 76, 98, 107, 112
Durant, Cédric 27

Eagleton, Terry 152–4
  Hope Without Optimism 152–4
École Normale Supérieure 92
Elias, Amy 25
Engels, Friedrich 133
Eno, Brian 2

environmental destruction 125, 169
Erdrich, Louise 174
  Future Home of the Living God 174
excess synchronism 144, 157, 158
exploitation 15, 16, 23, 33–4, 40–1, 43, 67, 78, 102, 106, 110, 115, 129, 149, 169–70

Fascism 12, 15–17, 42, 44–5, 47, 48, 51–4, 59, 63, 70–2, 85–6, 91, 96–8, 101, 111, 113–15, 117–21, 123, 129, 131–3, 141, 145, 147–51, 156
fatherhood 15
Faulkner, William 56
  The Sound and the Fury 56
Felski, Rita 40
Ferrante, Elena 69, 86, 91
finance capitalism 127, 136, 140
Fincher, David 129, 131
First Nations 106, 145
Fleet, Darren 128, 136
Foer, Johnathan Safran 80
  Extremely Loud and Incredibly Close 80
Ford, Henry 89
Fordism 88–90
  The Forever Now: Contemporary Painting in an Atemporal World 9
Foster, Sesshu 167
Foucault, Michel 92, 96–7
Frankfurt School 12–14, 37
Franzen, Johnathan 80, 83–7
  The Corrections 80, 83–7
free speech 92, 98, 117
Fuentes, Carlos 159–60
Fukuyama, Francis 23, 103–10, 112
Fuller, R. Buckminster 6
futurity 3–4, 8, 10, 15, 21–2, 25, 35, 41, 49, 51, 54–6, 59, 63, 80, 83, 103, 118, 125, 133–4, 139–40, 142, 144, 146, 150–1, 157, 165–6, 168, 170–2, 174–7

Gardner, Jared 29
gender 47, 70, 72–5, 87, 93–4, 96, 101–2, 105–7, 109, 115
Geoghegan, Vincent 175
Gibney, Bruce 20–1
  What Happened to the Future? 20

Gibson, William 9, 80
  Pattern Recognition 80
Globalism 111, 114
Grabar, Henry 19
Guattari 97

Haider, Asad 109–10, 116
  Mistaken Identity 109
Haider, Shuja 65–6, 92–3
Harootunian, Harry 22–3, 41–2, 48
Harvey, David 25, 86
  The Condition of Postmodernism 92
Hawking, Stephen 30
Hegel, G. W. F. 57, 156, 158
Hicks, Stephen
  Explaining Postmodernism 92–3
Higgins, David M. 19, 20, 166
Hills, Danny 2
Hitler, Adolph 45, 97
Hopkinson, Nalo 167
Horkheimer, Max 56, 58, 118
  Dialectic of Enlightenment 56
Husserl, Edmund 41

identitarian movement 105
identity politics 98, 103–10, 112
Illing, Sean 12
Immanence 56
Indigenous art 177
Indigenous culture 168, 170
Indigenous Literature 17
Indigenous speculative fiction 167
individualism 35, 37–8, 84, 86
inequality 15, 23, 101–2
Institute Without Boundaries 5
Irving, John
  Until I Find You 80

Jameson, Fredric
  Postmodernism or, the Cultural Logic of Late Capitalism 64, 92, 125, 161
Janus 51, 148
Jemisin, N. K. 167

Kalfus, Ken 80
  A Disorder Peculiar to the Country 80
Kaufmann, David 176
Kavanaugh, Brett 72
Kellner, Douglas 148–9, 158

Knödler-Bunte, Eberhard 111, 114, 118–19
knowledge economy 31
Koselleck, Reinhart 25
Kracauer, Siegfried 59
Kühnl, Reinhard 118
Kundera, Milan 160–1
Kunstler, Howard 128

labor 26, 31, 33, 46, 127, 129
latency 54
Lefèbvre, Henri 117
Leonard, Jennifer 6
Levine, Caroline 40
Leys, Ruth 36
Lindberg, Tracey 167, 174
  Birdie 167, 174
Long Bets 8
long now 3–5, 7–11, 16–17, 22–3, 28, 29, 35, 37, 39–41, 44, 51, 55–6, 62–3, 102–3, 121, 138–9, 142–6, 150, 156, 159, 162, 164, 166, 168, 175–7
The Long Now Foundation 2, 7–10
Lukács, Georg 13
Lyotard, Jean-François
  The Postmodern Condition 92, 151–2
lyric poetry 158

Marazzi, Christian 31
Marcuse, Herbert 58
Marx, Karl 26, 125, 152–3, 176
Marxism 55, 90–2, 97, 115, 147–8, 152
masculinity 15, 62, 70–4, 87, 88, 101, 103, 106–7, 121–2, 124–5, 130–2, 139, 141
Massive Change 5–7, 42
Mau, Bruce 5–6
Mazzoni, Guido 37–8
McCarthy, Cormac 89–90, 143–4
  The Road 89–90, 143–4
McGurl, Mark 28
Menand, Louis 103
mindfulness 34
Mishra, Pankaj 73
misogyny 11, 73–4, 87–8, 98, 132
Moir, Cat 36, 54, 57
Mozart, Wolfgang Amadeus 50
  Fidelio 50
  The Magic Flute 50
multiculturalism 105

Multiethnic art 177
Multiethnic literatures 166–7
multiverse 166
Müntzer, Thomas 49
Musk, Elon 35
Mussolini, Benito 97
mustiness 101–2

Nagle, Angela 113
   Kill all the Normies: Online Culture Wars from 4Chan and Tumblr to Trump and the Alt-Right 113
National Socialism 59, 111–12
natural time 24
nature writing 122
negation 9, 54, 158
Negt, Oskar 146
neofascism 53
neoliberalism 76, 81, 85–6
New Deal 88
New German Critique 113, 118
new paternalism 88
nonsynchronism 14, 15, 22, 41–9, 54, 62, 70–1, 82, 85–6, 88, 95, 101–2, 121–3, 126, 129, 140, 142, 144–5, 147, 150, 155, 156–8, 165, 168
Noonan, Peggy 73
nostalgia 10, 39, 44, 48, 70, 74, 79, 82, 85–6, 102, 121, 123, 128–9, 139, 175
not yet 50, 54–5, 144–5, 160, 173
Novelistic realism 161–2
Novum 175

old paternalism 67
omnipresent instant 28
optimism 2, 4–5, 80, 86, 154, 156

Palahniuk, Chuck 129, 131
   Fight Club 129, 131–2
paternalism 14, 39, 62–3, 66–73, 75–7, 79–90, 97, 101, 121, 130
Peterson, Jordan 61–2, 65, 82, 90–7, 105, 115
   12 Rules for Life 66, 69–71, 105, 115
Pfeil, Fred 90, 94
Plato 104
pluralism 66, 76, 81, 96–7
Poole, Steven 122
populism 15, 41, 65, 70, 103–5, 108–9, 113, 114

postcolonial literature 166
postcolonial subject 43
postmodernism 15, 61, 64–6, 67, 68, 69, 80, 90–8
post-structuralism 83
poverty 78, 108–9, 146
Proulx, Annie 80
   The Shipping News 80

Rabinbach, Anson 59, 111, 121, 122, 129, 147–8, 150–1
racism 11, 15, 98, 103, 109, 113, 117–18, 146, 167
Rancière, Jacques 52
Rannard, Georgina 72
real-time capitalism 28, 35, 41, 150, 164
rebellious lack 157, 160, 163, 176
Reed, Adolph Jr. 110
reflective nostalgia 174
restorative nostalgia 174
retrofuturism 167
rhythms 40
Rich, Nathaniel 8, 133, 136–7, 139, 140
   Odds Against Tomorrow 8, 133, 136
right-wing anti-capitalism 11, 85, 113
right-wing extremism 17, 22, 39, 51, 85, 87, 89, 98, 116, 120, 145, 149, 177
right-wing identitarianism 109
Robin, Corey 90–1, 93, 113
   The Reactionary Mind 90
Romantic anti-capitalism 120
Rosenberg, Jordy 131
Ross, Mark 12
Roufos, Pavlov 113
Rovelli, Carlo 30–1
Ruge, Karl 153, 176
Russo, Richard 80

Sartre, Jean-Paul 56, 132
Scholz, Roswitha 83
Schwartz, Fredric J. 44, 58, 59
science fiction 19, 20, 53, 166
Sennett, Richard 81–4, 88–9
   The Culture of New Capitalism 81
sentimentalism 74, 121
September 11 attacks 23, 73, 79–80, 95
Sex Pistols 4
Shore, Marci 96–7
simulacra 10
simulacrum 126

Sinclair, Peter 118
socialism 23, 44, 58, 92
space Nazis 53
speculative fiction 166–8
Stalinism 58
Stanley, Clarke "Rattlesnake King" 11
Stiegler, Bernard 28–9

Taylor, Mark C. 126, 128
Taylorism 88–9
temporal imagination 3, 23, 24–7, 29, 36, 41, 43, 124, 146, 163–5, 167
temporality 1–2, 5–6, 9, 11, 15, 17, 21–2, 25–8, 37, 39–40, 43, 52, 55, 88, 128, 144–5, 150, 153, 156–7, 159, 163, 165–8
temporal standardization 27
Thiel, Peter 20
Thompson, E. P. 26
Thompson, Peter 9, 22–3, 36, 49, 54–5, 59, 77, 87, 101, 142, 144, 154, 156–7
timelessness 9, 137–8, 168
Tomba, Massimiliano 27, 153–4, 176
totalitarian 97, 160, 166
totalitarianism. *See* totalitarian
toxic masculinity 62
Trenkle, Norbert 26–7
Trudeau, Justin 106–7
Trump, Donald 12, 72, 91, 94, 105, 108, 111–14, 120, 177

value 26–7, 31, 45, 84
venture capitalism 20

Vint, Sherryl 20, 166
Virilio, Paul 27–8
 The Futurism of the Instant 27–8
Virno, Paulo 33
Vlautin, Willy 80
völkisch 122–3
Von, Julie 33–4
Vonnegut, Kurt 67
 Breakfast of Champions 67
Vorschein 54
Vuorensola, Timo 53
 Iron Sky 53
 Iron Sky: The Coming Race 53

Wagner, Whilhelm Richard 50
Wajcman, Judy 40, 140
Watson, Paul Joseph 94
Weimar Germany 149
wellness 33–6, 41
Wells, H. G. 163
 The Time Machine 163
Western modernity 37–8
white nationalism 141, 145
white supremacy 141
Williams, Raymond 125
Williams, Rhys 20
Wong, Kristin 32

xenophobia 11, 15, 73, 98, 103, 109, 118

Zeitgeist 38
Zipes, Jack 58–9, 175–6
Žižek, Slavoj 59

www.ingramcontent.com/pod-product-compliance
Lightning Source LLC
Chambersburg PA
CBHW052043300426
44117CB00012B/1947